TEXT & PRESENTATION, 2006

TEXT &
PRESENTATION,
2006

Edited by Stratos E. Constantinidis

The Comparative Drama Conference Series, 3

McFarland & Company, Inc., Publishers
Jefferson, North Carolina, and London

ALSO BY STRATOS E. CONSTANTINIDIS

Text & Presentation, 2005 (McFarland, 2006)

Text & Presentation, 2004 (McFarland, 2005)

Modern Greek Theatre: A Quest for Hellenism (McFarland, 2001)

*Greece in Modern Times: An Annotated Bibliography of
Works Published in English in Twenty-Two Academic
Disciplines during the Twentieth Century* (vol. 1, 2000)

Theatre under Deconstruction? A Question of Approach (1993)

ISSN 1054-724X • ISBN 978-0-7864-3077-2
(softcover : 50# alkaline paper) ∞

Cover photograph ©2007 Clipart.com

Manufactured in the United States of America

*McFarland & Company, Inc., Publishers
Box 611, Jefferson, North Carolina 28640
www.mcfarlandpub.com*

Acknowledgments

This issue of *Text & Presentation* and the 30th Comparative Drama Conference were funded, in part, by the Department of Theatre and Dance, the College of Communication and Fine Arts, and the Bellarmine College of Liberal Arts at Loyola Marymount University, Los Angeles; the Department of Greek and Latin, the Department of East Asian Languages and Literatures, the Department of English, the Department of Spanish and Portuguese, and the Department of African American and African Studies at the Ohio State University.

This publication would not have been possible without the commitment and expertise of our editorial board: Marvin Carlson (*City University of New York, Graduate Center*), William Gruber (*Emory University*), Harry Elam (*Stanford University*), William Elwood (*Southern Connecticut State University*), Les Essif (*University of Tennessee, Knoxville*), Carol Fisher Sorgenfrei *(University of California, Los Angeles)* Jan-Lüder Hagens (*University of Notre Dame*), Karelisa Hartigan (*University of Florida*), Graley Herren (*Xavier University, Cincinnati*), William Hutchings (*University of Alabama, Birmingham*), David Krasner (*Yale University*), Jeffrey Loomis (*Northwest Missouri State University*), Helen Moritz (*Santa Clara University*), Jon Rossini (*University of California, Davis*), Elizabeth Scharffenberger (*Columbia University*), Tony Stafford (*University of Texas, El Paso*), Ron Vince (*McMaster University*), Kevin Wetmore (Loyola Marymount University, Los Angeles), and Katerina Zacharia (*Loyola Marymount University, Los Angeles*). I am also grateful to a significant number of additional specialists who participated in the anonymous review of the many manuscripts submitted to me for publication consideration. I would like to thank our associate editor, Kiki Gounaridou (*Smith College*), who assisted with the proofreading of this volume, and our book review editor, Verna Foster (*Loyola University Chicago*) who solicited, edited, and proofread the book reviews.

The past editors of *Text & Presentation* deserve recognition for their contribution in establishing the reputation and standards for this annual publication: Karelisa Hartigan (1980–1993), Bill Free (1993–1998), and Hanna Roisman (1998–1999).

The inclusion of photos in some of the articles of this volume was made possible with the permission of the following copyright owners: Stratos E. Constantinidis for the two photos on page 1 in his Preface; Jason Groves for the photo on page 78 in his article; Laurie M. Shanda for one photo on page 96, and Jeff Kaplan for the nine figures on pages 97, 103, 104, 105, 106 in his article; and Claudio Etges for the photo on page 146 in Carla Melo's article.

Last but not least, I want to thank the Executive Board of the Comparative Drama Conference and the hundreds and hundreds of scholars who presented the results of their research — both creative and analytical — at the Comparative Drama Conference, an annual three-day event which is devoted to all aspects of theatre scholarship — *S.E.C.*

Contents

Review of Literature: Selected Books

Preface

Text & Presentation is an annual publication devoted to all aspects of theatre scholarship and represents a selection of the best papers presented at the Comparative Drama Conference. For the past 29 years, participants to the Comparative Drama Conference have come from 35 countries: Australia, Austria, Belgium, Brazil, Bulgaria, Canada, China, Cyprus, Denmark, Egypt, England, Finland, France, Germany, Greece, Iceland, India, Iraq, Ireland, Israel, Italy, Japan, Jordan, Korea, Malaysia, New Zealand, the Philippines, Russia, Saudi Arabia, Slovenia, South Africa, Taiwan, Tanzania, Turkey, and the United States of America.

This volume of *Text & Presentation* features sixteen research papers, one review essay, and eight book reviews. The papers included here were among a total of 138 research papers which were presented and discussed at the 30th Comparative Drama Conference. The presentations, which were divided into 53 sessions of 75 minutes each, were discussed by 152 program participants at the Marina del Rey Hotel in Los Angeles, California, during a three-day period, March 30–April 1, 2006.

The four concurrent sessions per day were complemented by three plenary sessions and a show. The keynote address, "Staging Beckett for a New Century," was given by Professor Stanley E. Gontarski (Florida State University) on March 31. Professor William Hutchings (University of Alabama at Birmingham) and Professor Jaime Morrison (California State University, Northridge) responded to the keynote address. The session was moderated by Professor Graley Herren (Xavier University).

The second plenary session — Translation in the Theatre — was a round-table panel. It was moderated by Professor Kevin J. Wetmore Jr. (Loyola Marymount University) on March 31. The panelists were Jose I. Badenes S. J. (Loyola Marymount University), Michael Ewans (University of Newcastle), Katherine B. Free (Loyola Marymount University), Mary Kay Gamel (University of California, Santa Cruz), M. Cody Poulton (University of Victoria), Gregory Reid (Universite de Sherbrooke), and J. Michael Walton (University of Hull).

The final plenary session, Author-Meets-Critic, on April 1 was devoted

to the discussion of one of the books (*Past as Present in the Drama of August Wilson*) that was reviewed in *Text & Presentation, 2005* (pp. 241–244). Its author, Harry J. Elam, Jr. (Stanford University), discussed his book with the following critics: Professor Kathryn M. Ervin (California State University, San Bernardino) and Professor N. Graham Nesmith (Columbia University). The session was moderated by Professor Verna Foster (Loyola University, Chicago).

The show, George Orwell's *1984*, adapted and directed by Tim Robbins was performed at the Actor's Gang Theatre in Culver City on March 30. In addition, staged readings of six new plays were presented by their authors with a cast drawn from conference attendees. One of the plays, If the *Whole Body Dies*, by Robert Skloot, was subsequently published by Parallel Press in Madison, Wisconsin.

The Executive Board welcomes research papers presenting original investigation on, and critical analysis of, research and developments in the field of drama and theatre. Papers may be comparative across disciplines, periods, or nationalities, may deal with any issue in dramatic theory and criticism, or any method of historiography, translation, or production. *Text & Presentation* is edited by scholars appointed by the Executive Board of the Comparative Drama Conference, of which it is the official publication. *Text & Presentation* is indexed in the MLA International Bibliography.

Stratos E. Constantinidis
February 2007

Opposite: Professor S. E. Gontarski (top) is delivering his keynote speech, "Stagging Beckett for a New Century," and Professor William Hutchings (bottom) is giving his response, "Saving Your *Breath* —And Beckett's Too," during Session No. 37 (plenary) at the 30th Comparative Drama Conference in Los Angeles, California, on March 1, 2006.

1

Post-Beckett Theatre

S. E. Gontarski

Abstract

It may not be too early to suggest the possible obsolescence of Samuel Beckett and his art. I am not merely suggesting that a year of overexposure of Beckett's work in the centenary year of 2006 may saturate the market, intellectual and commercial. Who might dare to launch a Beckett season or publish a major Beckett book in 2007, 8, 9? I am not necessarily arguing that Beckett's work is increasingly falling victim to the cultural, political rejection of dead, white, straight, European, male writers, or of single author research in general, although that is not beyond my point. Nor am I necessarily arguing that Beckett too will fall victim to a pervasive devaluation of literature, from both the political right and left, the former because it appears somehow still dangerous and needs to be restricted, the latter because it is increasingly preoccupied with forms of discourse other than fictions, as theory has taken a more ethical turn, something like a re-turn to the metanarrative of the great march of human progress and equity. What I am arguing is simply that everything has an end and so posing the possibility that Beckett's work, like the avant-garde itself, or more broadly art as a whole, may be approaching its cultural limits, may in fact have died in the smothering embrace of late capitalism. In this essay I explore the issue of literary or artistic obsolescence as a cultural critique, in particular as the justification (if any) of Beckett's survival, particularly in performance, into the 21st century. Need Godot, say, to focus on Beckett's most performed play, reflect the 50 years of cultural change since its creation? That is to say does Beckett's theater need periodic freshening, and how can that be accomplished amid the current legal restrictions on performance imposed by the Beckett Estate. How much new can be introduced? Should the focus not rather be on sharpening the presentation of what has already been done, values at least implicit in the Estate's stance, or is that a death sentence to Beckett's art? In this essay I examine the specifics of what such survival, if survival is indeed in the offing, might look like, in print, on stage, and in the critical discourse.

Let me begin with heresy, with the suggestion that in the hundredth year since his birth and the fiftieth (plus) year since *Waiting for Godot* exploded on to the Paris and international stages, in the seventeenth year of the post–Beckett, Samuel Beckett may have become irrelevant to the theater of a new century, celebratory productions emitting more the sweet scent of nostalgia than the piquancy of radical change. In a year that will have seen all 19 of his stage plays performed as a group in the theatrical capitals of the world, his native Dublin, London, New York, his adopted Paris, the gestures billed as celebrations, the events take the form of a desperation, like baby boomers restoring Mustang convertibles. It may not be too early to suggest the possible obsolescence of Samuel Beckett. If part of the anti–Enlightenment project of the second half of the twentieth century, in theory as well as literature, of which Samuel Beckett was very much a part, was to assault universal, eternal values, especially those once deemed foundational to art, as little more than the hegemonic extension of a ruling class, literature becomes entangled in relativistic social constructionism; thus one can no longer rely on the old bromides that the work of art is somehow eternal or universal, beyond the reach of time and culture, as it were. It has, instead, to support itself, constantly, amid the marketplace of ideas, subject to the viruses of change, in this age of late capitalism; just ask any publisher or theatrical producer. In one of Beckett's favorite jokes, everything has an end — except, goes the punch line, the sausage. It has two. One of Beckett's ends was surely his corporeal demise on 22 December 1989, but might we be in the midst of the second? I am suggesting here that the mass of attention generated by celebrations in the centenary year of his birth may be as destructive as constructive, the signal of a second end, the monument under construction in 2006 become an artistic gravestone. I am not merely suggesting that a year of overexposure may saturate the market, intellectual and commercial, although that point is also not beyond my argument. Who might dare to launch a Beckett season or publish a major Beckett book in 2007, 8, 9? Nor am I necessarily arguing that Beckett's work is increasingly falling victim to the cultural, political rejection of dead, white, straight, European, male writers, or of single author research in general, although that is also not beyond my point. Nor am I *necessarily* arguing that Beckett too will fall victim to a pervasive devaluation of literature, from both the political right and left, the former because it appears somehow still dangerous and needs to be restricted, the latter because it is increasingly preoccupied with forms of discourse other than fictions, as theory has taken a more ethical turn, something like a return to the metanarrative of the great march of human progress and equity. What I am arguing is simply that everything has an end and posing the possibility that Beckett's work, like the avant-garde itself, or more broadly art as a whole, may be approaching its cultural limits, may in fact have died in the smothering embrace of late capitalism. I would like to explore this issue of literary or artistic obsolescence as a cultural critique, in particular as the justification (if any) of Beckett's survival, particularly in performance, into the 21st century. More important we might need to examine the specifics of what such survival, if survival is indeed in the offing, might look like, in print, on stage, and in the critical discourse.

One grand problem is the law, or rather legal ownership. Samuel Beckett's art is owned, and its owners exercise almost unrestricted property rights. Amid the restrictions on performance imposed by the Beckett Estate is its insistence on faithful and accurate performances, which amounts to, *de facto*, a repetition of the already done. Its ideology is decidedly Enlightenment, as Edward Beckett has argued in a letter to *The Guardian;* his mission is to protect "the image and universality that the author sought," never mind that the author himself would wince (has indeed winced) at such cavalier use of the word "universality" (Beckett, Edward 25). Does Beckett's theater need freshening and amid the current legal restrictions, how much new can be introduced? Should the focus not rather be on sharpening the presentation of what has already been done, values at least implicit in the Estate's stance? Need *Godot*, say, to focus on Beckett's most performed play, reflect the 50 years of cultural change since its creation? Beckett himself seems to have accepted a more or else exigent approach to his theater during his lifetime, modulating the antinomies of his vision and that of performance, his or that by another director. He was far from consistent in this respect, of course. For all that he believed in authorial control, in practice, when it came to "alternative" productions, "it made a tremendous difference if he liked and respected the persons involved," as biographer James Knowlson has observed (608). On certain matters he remained steadfast, especially on the issue of gender change. Writing his American publisher and theatrical agent, Barney Rosset on 11 July 1973 he noted: "I am against women playing *Godot* and wrote Miss [Estelle] Parsons to that effect. Theatre sex in not interchangeable and *Godot* by women would sound as spurious as *Happy Days* or *Not I* played by men. It was performed once in Israel, without our authorization, by an all-female cast, with disastrous effect."[1]

The position that Beckett himself took with regard to Joanne Akalaitis's December 1984 ART production of *Endgame* is the one that currently holds sway internationally. Hours before the opening lawyers were still negotiating the Akalaitis's textual alterations. Her "crimes" were that she had set her production in a subway station with an abandoned subway car as backdrop, adding music by her ex-husband, Philip Glass. Beckett was convinced, with much encouragement, if not prodding, from Alan Schneider, that the production was an unacceptable alteration of the text, particularly of the stage directions. He further objected to the increasingly common American theatrical practice of color-blind casting, black actors here in two of the play's four roles. A final compromise allowed the production to open but only with Beckett's disclaimer printed in the playbill: "A complete parody of the play. Anybody who cares for the work couldn't fail to be disgusted." The principle that Beckett tried legally to enforce in Cambridge, Massachussetts was that the author would be the sole authority on and arbiter of what is permissible with regard to his theatrical works, the sole judge of how much latitude was acceptable and permissible in performance. That position is now accepted and extended by his Estate and buttressed by international law.[2] In other words, the process of reinvention that had been the very hallmark of Beckett's creative life has apparently come to an end, Beckett's theater rapidly becoming part of the quid pro quo of bourgeois commerce, a system he struggled so hard to unmask. One consequence of such a re-positioning is that the climate in which scholars and theatre practitioners investigate the complexities of Beckett's theatrical oeuvre and his theatrical career has been chilled.

In addition to their most publicized interventions into performance, for example, the executors have much more silently, out of the glare of the media, all but kept from the public the principal work of the final two decades of Beckett's creative life, his continuation of the creative process after publication, his full revisions of his dramatic texts. These revisions are available in a *limited* capacity, in the very expensive editions of *The Theatrical Notebooks of Samuel Beckett*, which Beckett himself had not only authorized but (astonishingly) financed as well, but their expense restricts their availability. Even major research libraries have resisted such expenditure under current budgets, and the Estate has refused permission to lower the cost and so increase availability, to publish the revised or acting texts separately or to re-issue the *Notebooks* in affordable, paperback editions, for example. That is, much of Beckett's theatrical legacy, the major theatrical labor of the final two decades of his life, is virtually inaccessible to the theatrical community for legal reasons.

Part of the reason for the Estate's position is practical, the admitted difficulty of determining authorial intent off the page. Which of the revisions in Beckett's productions are meant for the local contingencies of particular actors or a particular stage? As Beckett wrote to Polish director Marek Kędzierski on 15 November 1981, "Herewith *corrected* copy of *Fin de partie*. The cuts and simplifications are the result of my work on the play as director and function of the players at my disposal. To another director they may not seem desirable" (emphasis added). What Beckett sent Kędzierski, however, is simply not readily available to other directors, except in the *Theatrical Notebooks*.[3] Moreover, Beckett did not systematically direct and revise each of his plays, and so not every text has been systematically reinvented.

That is, Beckett's productions did not always result in permanent changes to a printed text. Occasionally, local revisions were made by Beckett to respond to the process of collaboration and to the nature of a particular theatrical space, or changes were contemplated that were never formally incorporated into any text or production. In his notebook for *Damals*, the German translation of *That Time*, which he directed along with *Tritte* (*Footfalls*) at the Schiller-Theater in 1976, for instance, Beckett offered an alternate staging of the play, one that substantially increased its verisimilitude. If Listener's hand were *seen* at full light, he noted, it should be clutching a sheet around his neck. The tension of that grip should then increase during the silences. That detail added to the play's limited frame suggests that *That Time* is something of an experiment in perspective. We perceive the figure as if we were watching him from above as he lay in a bed.

Furthermore, in the annotated text for his second German production of *He Joe* at the Süddeutscher Rundfunk studios in Stuttgart in 1979, Beckett altered the closing fade of the German text by cutting "*Image fades, voice as before*" just after "In the *stones*," and in the margin he wrote "Hold image to end of voice +5' before fade." This is a change that he had been working with for well over a decade and suggesting to every director interested in the teleplay. As he elaborated to his American director Alan Schneider on 7 April 1966, to that hold he added a smile thus changing not only the closing visual image of the play, but its import as well: "I asked in London and Stuttgart for a smile at the end (oh not a real smile). He 'wins' again. So ignore the direction 'Image fades, voice as before.' Face fully present till last 'Eh Joe.' Then smile and slow fade" (Harmon 202). As a result of his stagings, Beckett simplified the presentation of the ending voice over as well: "I decided that the underlining of certain words at the end was very difficult for the speaker and *not good*. So I simplified second last paragraph [...]" (emphasis added, Harmon 202). He also outlined a change that could only grow out of the practicalities of staging: "In London the only sound apart from the voice was that of curtains and opening and closing at window, door and cupboard. But in Stuttgart we added sound of steps as he moves around and made it interesting by his having one sock half off and one sock and slipper. Sock half off because at opening he was taking it off to go to bed when interrupted by sudden idea or sudden feeling that he hears a sound and had better make a last round to make sure all is well" (Harmon 202). The German text also ends with three additional entreaties by Voice to "Imagine," and a renewed emphasis on "The breasts," now repeated a second time in Beckett's revision. These alterations were admittedly not made to the facing English text of the tri-lingual German edition that Beckett used, but, of course, Beckett was directing the *German text* at the time. Moreover, the almost exact repetition of those revisions to Schneider, all clearly charted on paper and part of the two versions Beckett directed, have never been incorporated into any English language text and so have been seen in no other productions than those of Beckett and Schneider. Currently most directors are not only faced with the texts as published, texts that Beckett considered "not good," but are contractually, legally bound to follow what Beckett rejected. The director may put his or her career in jeopardy by daring to "ignore the [stage] direction."

Admittedly, few directors have re-filmed *Eh Joe*, but it is not infrequently staged. Beckett himself consented, albeit reluctantly, to Jean-Claude Fall's staging of *Dis Joe* at the Théâtre de la Bastille in 1984, which was both televised and live, the stage split in two, half for Joe's cubicle in which Fall sat on a bed, and half a darkened wall with television set inserted. Robert Scanlan staged it as well, with music, no less, at the American Repertory Theatre, Cambridge, MA in 1996, with Alvin Epstein as Joe, this also with the permission of at least the Beckett Estate through its American agent Georges Borchardt. Here again the performance presented both Joe live and a simultaneous televised image, this time on a huge, commanding, oversized screen, which dominated and dwarfed Joe. Most recently Canadian director Atom Egoyan directed a stage version with Michael Gambon and Penelope Wilton as part of the Beckett centenary celebrations at Dublin's Gate Theater in April of 2006. Here Joe was separated from the audience by a nearly invisible scrim that then bore his projected image as voice began to speak. The production subsequently moved to London for 30 performances, from 27 June to 15 July 2006. In none of those productions was any of Beckett's revisions apparent; that is, each was staged as if Beckett never directed the work, with a text that Beckett found wanting.

Beckett never got around to committing his final revisions to an English text for a number of other productions as well, revisions which were clearly part of his developing conception of the play and as such testimony to the vitality of his theater and his willingness to accept change. In his three productions of *Footfalls* in three languages (with Billie Whitelaw at the Royal Court Theatre in London in 1976, shortly thereafter with Hildegard Schmahl on the bill with *That Time* above, likewise in 1976, and finally with Delphine Seyrig at the Théâtre d'Orsay in 1978), Beckett revised the English and French scripts substantially, changing, for example, the number of May's pacing steps from seven to nine. Many, but not all, of these revisions were incorporated into Faber and Faber and Grove Press reissues of the text. But Beckett also made some fundamental changes to the lighting that he never incorporated directly into English language texts, changes that were central to and consistent in all three of his productions. For each of his productions

Beckett introduced a "Dim spot on face during halts at R [right] and L [left]" so that May could be fully seen during her monologues. In addition, Beckett introduced into his stagings a vertical ray of light as if it were coming through a partially opened door, this to balance the horizontal beam on the floor. These lighting changes were incorporated into the French translation but appear in no English text other than that in *The Theatrical Notebooks*, which the market keeps from most directors and which the Estate refuses to publish separately. Directors conforming to the dictates of the Estate's contracts must have May recite most of *Footfalls* in the dark, an image that Beckett himself quickly and repeatedly rejected as soon as he saw it on stage. The one exception is that in the "Beckett on Film" production of *Footfalls* directed by Walter Asmus, who was Beckett's directorial assistant on his staging of the play in Berlin.

In addition, for his television adaptation of his stage play *What Where* as *Was Wo*, Beckett revised the German text extensively, but again he never fully revised the stage directions of the original. This was due in part to the fact that Beckett continued to work on the visual imagery of the play all through rehearsals. By this stage of his directing career he had developed more confidence in or grown more trusting of the creative collaborations that theatre entails, and he was creating his theater work in rehearsals, directly on the stage (or in this case on the set), and not working everything out to the most minute detail on paper in his study before rehearsals, although he did make a pre-production notebook for the *Was Wo* filming as well. As his technical assistant, Jim Lewis, who also worked with Beckett on *He Joe* in 1966, recalls:

> If you want to compare this production [of *Was Wo*] with the others for television, there's one major difference. And that is his concept was not set. He changed and changed and changed [...]. I've never experienced that with him before. You know how concrete he is, how precise he is. Other times we could usually follow through on that with minor, minor changes; but this time there were several basic changes and he still wasn't sure. Many things, different things [Fehsenfeld 236].

Lewis's observation suggests the single most salient element in Beckett's evolution into a theatre artist: his commitment to the idea of performance and his willingness to accept a variety of possible outcomes. In practical and literary terms such a commitment meant that nothing like a final text of his work could be established before he worked with it on stage. Writing to Alan Schneider in response to his American director's queries about staging *Play*, Beckett expressed what had become axiomatic to him: "I realize that no final script is possible until I work on rehearsals." Almost simultaneously, after he has just seen a cut of *Film* in 1964, Beckett argued quite clearly against the idea of slavish fidelity: "that the work's value does not depend on the extent to which [his] own intentions have been realized." Beckett continued to Schneider:

> Generally speaking, from having been troubled by a certain failure to communicate fully by purely visual means the basic intention, I now begin to feel that this is unimportant and that the images obtained [the compromise images that he could not control] probably gain in force what they lose as ideograms. It does I suppose in a sense fail with reference to a purely intellectual schema but in doing so has acquired a dimension and a validity of its own that are worth far more than any merely efficient translation of intention [Harmon 166].

The issue of textual fidelity is further complicated by the inconsistency of texts currently available to the public. Textual variants among the commercially published texts testify to the fact that Beckett's plays do not exist in a uniform, static state. Legally, a director can follow any of these various published texts thereby conforming to current contracts and still conflict with Beckett's recorded intentions. Most English editions of *Krapp's Last Tape*, for instance, still depict Krapp with a red, clown's nose and wearing white boots, and the play is still performed thus even as Beckett himself rejected this image in his first production of the play. Arguments about staging a *Godot* respectful of Beckett's wishes are frequently based on the assumption of the existence of a single authoritative script. In the general editor's preface to the *Theatrical Notebooks* (vii), James Knowlson makes clear that "whole sections of the text have *never* been played as printed in the original editions," and even after innumerable corrections major differences exist between British and American editions. Even the usually impeccable Germans had managed to use the wrong text as the basis of their sumptuous trilingual edition that Beckett thought generally fine — except for the *Godot* text. Writing his American publisher on 4 November 1963, Beckett noted "Have received another copy of 1st volume of the Suhrkamp trilingual edition (plays written in French). A fine job, though rather a lot of mistakes in French texts. And to my dismay they have used Faber's mutilated (Lord Chamberlain) version of *Godot* [of 1956] instead of yours." Beckett went on to revise the "mutilated" British text in 1965, but Fabers still managed to reproduce the censored 1956 text in its 1986 tribute volume, *Samuel Beckett: The Complete Dramatic Works*, the error corrected only in the paperback edition of 1990.

The problems with Beckett's texts are thus not inconsequential. As I myself have noted in the *Endgame* volume of *The Theatrical Notebooks*: "critics and directors [are] forced into a position of building interpretations and mounting productions of Samuel Beckett's work not so much on corrupt texts such as almost all English versions of *Waiting for Godot*, but on those the author himself found unsatisfactory, unfinished" (xxv). The response of the Estate has its own compelling logic. Edward Beckett has argued that "There are more than fifteen recordings of Beethoven's late string quartets in the catalogue, every interpretation different, one from the next, but they are all based on the same notes, tonalities, dynamic, and tempo markings. We feel justified in asking the same measure of respect for Samuel Beckett's plays" (*Guardian*, 24 March 1994, 25). He suggests that since musicians, however freely they may "interpret" a piece of music, do not deviate from the composer's notes, why should a director depart from Beckett's dialogue or directions? The analogy is, of course, imperfect. Theatre, as Beckett spent much of his career demonstrating, is as much a visual as an aural art form, at least as much gesture and plastic imagery as poetry. Theatre is not a music CD. The more apposite analogy may be with opera, and there the analogy breaks down. Most traditional operas have been staged in a myriad of what strict interpretationists might deem outlandish, disrespectful versions, and the music has survived, as would Beckett's unique music. But the Estate seems adamant, and so Beckettian performance in the 21st century may be at an impasse.

And yet art shows remarkable resilience, an uncanny ability to outlive predictions of its demise. Theatre, like the novel, has been pronounced dead, through most of the twentieth century. Among his earliest manifestos (1913), F. T. Marinetti issued his death kneel thus: "We have a deep distaste for the contemporary theater (verse, prose, musical) because it oscillates stupidly between historical reconstruction (pastiche or plagiarism) and the photographic reproduction of everyday life; petty, slow, analytic, and diluted theater that is worthy, at its best, of the age of the oil lamp." Despite Marinetti's diatribe, theater has remained central to at least the Modernist enterprise, and predictions of its obsolescence, my own included, may be premature. Despite the restrictions currently in place, the insistence of the Estate to demand that what is performed is only that which has essentially already been performed, the same might be said for Beckett's theatre as a resilient and imaginative set of theatrical directors continues to re-invent Beckett and thereby, more broadly, revitalize theater for the 21st century. The Egyptian film director Atom Egoyan, is a case in point. Egoyan directed a traditional production of *Krapp's Last Tape*, starring John Hurt, for the Beckett on Film series, but he then used the film to build his own artwork, an installation in London's Museum of Mankind, which folded showings of the film in altered perspectives into a larger, environmental exhibit of recorded memory called

"Steenbeckett." Egoyan's installation focused on memory and its preservation. Participants walked passed stacks of obsessional 19th century diaries that documented the diarist's every meal, every journey, every bed slept in, or every partner slept with. It was the obsessive completeness, the exhaustiveness of such documentation that appealed to Egoyan, as it did to Krapp, and perhaps Beckett. Spectators walked through a darkened warren of passages, up stairs, through tunnels, past discarded typewriters, phonographs, disks, "spoooools," photographs, to a projection room where the traditional, commercial film of *Krapp's Last Tape* was screened for small audiences of 10–12 at a time. Audience members who could fit into the room sat on a makeshift bench no more than six feet from the projected images on the opposite wall, images which were a massive 12 to 18 feet high and so dwarfed the spectators. From there spectators walked, groped, or found their way to another room through which masses of film ran continuously and noisily along rollers, up and down, back and forth, in and around the room, over and over again, and finally through an antique Steenbeck editing table at the far end of the room, where the film was screened in miniature and seen through the maze of noisy, rolling film. Obsolete, the Steenbeck editing machine was, however, the equipment that Egoyan deemed apt for editing his film of *Krapp's Last Tape*. As important as the film itself, both its materiality and the miniaturized images it provided, was the machine, central to Egoyan's reinvention of *Krapp's Last Tape*.

For the centenary year, Egoyan turned his attention to Beckett again, staging the television play *Eh Joe*, and effectively adding a new work to the Beckettian theatrical canon. The tour de force performance of Michael Gambon and the hybrid technology of stagecraft, television, and film allowed for the seamless translation of the television work to the stage. In both of Beckett's own productions the nine camera moves towards Joe, the physical image of the increasing intensity of Voice's assault and the confirmation of the interiority of the conflict, were conspicuous, almost clumsy, but Egoyan's use of zoom added another dimension to the play; camera movement was imperceptible but at some point audience members realize that they were suddenly watching a more intense close-up; what was a full body shot of Joe on his bed, face in ¾ profile, had become just face. All was poised for that perfect, ending smile, through which, as Beckett tells us, Joe has done it again, stopped the assaulting voice again. Egoyan's production ends with the agony of the assault, however, Voice with "plenty of venom. Face just listening hard and brain agonizing" (Harmon 198). All pain. For Beckett, however, the ending, discovered and shaped in production, was Joe's successful throttling of Voice: "Smile at very end when voice stops (having done it again)" (Harmon 198). Egoyan's production was stunning, but it suggests as well that much is left to discover in this new stage work, *Eh Joe*, and with Beckett's guidance, by paying attention to his late, developing theatrical aesthetics, and by the Estate's understanding of the necessary artistic collaboration in the theatrical process, Beckett's work may indeed be powerfully reinvented for a new century.

FLORIDA STATE UNIVERSITY

Notes

1. Letters to and from Rosset throughout are part of the Rosset Archive at Boston College (copies in Rosset's personal archive) and are used with the permission of the publisher and the Beckett Estate.

2. The Estate's "iron grip" on the plays shows occasional signs of weakening. In February 2006 an Italian court overruled an injunction prohibiting The Compagnia Laboratorio di Pontedera, Tuscany, from using two women in the central roles for its *Aspettando Godot* (*Waiting for Godot*), directed by Roberto Bacci. See *http://www.pontederateatro.it/news_contenuto.php?ID_news=673* for production images and details.

3. Most of these changes are outlined in Beckett's letter to Blin of 3 April 1968 as Beckett notes, "I strongly recommend to you the following simplifications." The letter is printed in Lois Oppenheim, *Directing Beckett* (Ann Arbor: University of Michigan Press, 1994), 299. English translation is Oppenheim's.

References Cited

Fehsenfeld, Martha. "Beckett's Reshaping of *What Where* for Television." *Modern Drama* 29:2 (June 1986): 236.

Gontarski, S. E, ed. *The Theatrical Notebooks of Samuel Beckett*, Vol. II, *Endgame*. New York: Grove Press, 1993.

Harmon, Maurice, ed. *No Author Better Served: The Correspondence of Samuel Beckett and Alan Schneider*. Cambridge, MA: Harvard University Press, 1998.

Saving Your *Breath*— And Beckett's Too

William Hutchings

Abstract

From among many intriguing subjects raised in S. E. Gontarski's keynote address—a succinct version of which appears in this volume—I limit my response to relatively few: issues of "ownership" of the play (i.e., the estate versus various interpreters), the lessons of production history (focusing on Waiting for Godot*), and the definition of what "a Beckett play" actually is (focusing on* Breath*). The long-familiar text-versus-presentation binary may need to be replaced with what is, in effect, a form of triangulation, since the rights and expectations of the audience have been for too long under-assessed, under-theorized—and often, indeed, ignored. The study of production history—that most neglected aspect not only of Beckett studies but of theatre studies in general—reveals that, even during Beckett's lifetime, issues surrounding interpolated sounds, textual alterations, and "creative" adaptations frequently arose. Specific reasons behind Beckett's objections to certain productions deserve more careful consideration—and show an abiding concern with audience reaction rather than proprietary rights over a text being developed into a performance. The long-contested binary opposition between the rights of the author (and/or his estate) on the one hand and stage (re)interpreters on the other is thus inadequate; it oversimplifies the nature of the theatrical "transaction" by ignoring the interests and rights of the audience, the vital third corner of what is, in effect, the triangulation of any theatrical event. However such audience rights are ultimately to be defined, they must exclude BOTH the myth of an endlessly replicable ideal production based on an eternally fixed text with no admissible variations AND a work that is more readily characterizable as a parody or a travesty—or something, however innovative and worthwhile on its own merits, that is no longer even remotely a "reasonable facsimile" of what the author wrote. Twenty-first-century productions of Beckett's plays are likely to continue to be the focal point of the debate over exactly these issues.*

Playwrights living in what Stan Gontarski has termed "the afterBeckett" face a particular problem that echoes the famous last line of his novel *The Unnamable*: they must go on after Beckett; they can't go on after Beckett; they go on after Beckett. As the respondent to tonight's keynote address, I know with particular clarity how they feel: I must go on after Gontarski, I can't go on after Gontarski, I'll go on after Gontarski. He is, after all, phenomenally accomplished as both a scholar/editor and as a director of Beckett's works; he has furthered our understanding of Beckett's works like no one else. From among the many intriguing subjects raised in his address, I must necessarily limit myself to a few: issues of "ownership" of the play (i.e., the estate versus various interpreters), the lessons of production history (focusing on *Waiting for Godot*), and the definition of what "a Beckett play" actually *is* (focusing on *Breath*). I propose that the text-versus-presentation binary may need to be replaced with what is, in effect, a form of triangulation instead, since the rights and expectations of the audience have been for too long under-assessed, under-theorized — and often, indeed, ignored.

The problems arising from the proprietary "ownership" of the plays by the Beckett estate, which can withhold permission before *or after* a production has been mounted, is by no means limited to Beckett's works, nor to works of drama, nor to estates of late authors. As scholars of James Joyce's writings or T. S. Eliot's poetry know well, or as those who have sought to produce Rogers and Hammerstein musicals have found out, permissions to quote and to perform may be denied for any reason or nearly none. Permission to produce Joyce's play *Exiles* was abruptly denied during 2004 as part of the year-long city-wide "100th Anniversary of Bloomsday" in Dublin, for example, and recent productions of *Waiting for Godot* were cancelled in quite different venues and for quite different reasons. In Nashville Tennessee the problem was that women dressed as men played Didi and Gogo and Lucky perched, ape-like, in the tree; in Sydney Australia, the production that premiered fifty years to the day after the original French premiere of Godot was threatened with closure by Edward Beckett himself unless and until an amount of unauthorized music, both live and recorded, was removed. Living authors can be aggressive in prohibiting alterations as well: Peter Shaffer's attorneys reportedly will close productions of *Equus* that do not include its nude scene, for example. Given the fact that international copyright law currently extends such "ownership" for the life of the author plus seventy years, *Waiting for Godot* remains under such "protection" until the year 2059. For better or worse (mostly worse), like it or not, scholars and producers will be coping with this problem for several generations yet to come.

Yet the study of production history — the most neglected aspect not only of Beckett studies but of theatre studies in general — reveals that, even during Beckett's lifetime, the issues surrounding interpolated sounds and textual alterations and adaptations frequently arose. Even the earliest commercial recording of *Waiting for Godot*, the 1956 two-record Caedmon set that features the original Broadway cast, was "enhanced" by a number of added "invented sounds of a more or less abstract nature, created by [producer Goddard Lieberson] with the assistance of [his] ... engineer Mr. Paul Plant." They were the first of many who have been unwilling, if not compulsively unable, to leave the play's all-important silences alone. That even Beckett's *own* changes to the text have been suppressed through the estate's unwillingness to allow wider dissemination of the texts established in *The Theatrical Notebooks of Samuel Beckett*— which are, in effect, a variorum edition of the play — is simply outrageous. In addition to the two notebooks that Beckett kept, the text presented in this volume is based on no less than three published editions of the play and six copies annotated by Beckett himself. Even the play's opening, before a word is ever spoken, gets changed: in later versions, Vladimir and Estragon are onstage from the outset, emphasizing their inseparability; in earlier versions, Estragon is alone before Vladimir makes his entrance. Beckettian textual study is no less complicated than that of Shakespeare, though obviously for different reasons, but the best results of it are, unfortunately, not widely available.

The study of production history also reveals how much the play has been enhanced by, for example, the creative uses of venue and untraditional casting that have occurred in its fifty years of stage life. San Quentin Prison, famously, was the first such non-theatrical venue to have hosted a landmark production, in 1957; an all-African-American production ran (for only five performances) on Broadway the same year. In the mid–1970's, with Beckett's explicit approval, an all-black production and a subsequent mixed-race production were performed in South Africa; in the latter, the play became overtly and topically political, with Lucky depicted as a shantytown resident and Pozzo as his Afrikaaner landlord. An Israeli production in 1984 relied on a bilingual translation into Arabic and Hebrew, with Vladimir and Estragon transformed into Palestinian laborers, speaking Arabic; the tree was replaced with iron scaffolding atop a concrete pole, and construction blocks replaced the set's usual stones. Andrew Sofer's production in 1988 set the play outdoors at dusk along a naturally occurring country road; he also cast two remarkably similar-looking brothers as the boy, the one in the second act noticeably taller than the other, thus complicating issues of how much time had passed. The 1996 premiere of the play's Polish translation had the audience sit on on-stage risers, their backs to an empty but cavernous theatre that provided an explicitly "theatrical" void, emphasizing the play's metatheatricality. Accordingly, it seems highly unlikely that the estate could stop such creative explorations of venue and casting even if it so desired.

Similar enhancement is apparent in Stan Gontarski's own recent "art museum installation" of *Breath*. The television set frame, "clownish" (his term) or not, is in many ways the postmodern counterpart of a proscenium arch, and (as always in his productions) the staging closely follows Beckett's precise specifications. Full disclosure here would be appropriate: I am the author of what was and as far as I know still is the longest article devoted to Beckett's *Breath*, apparently the most ever said about the least (apart from, of course, *The Congressional Record*). The longest word in the original edition of the *Oxford English Dictionary*—floccinaucinihilipilification — describes the dismissive attitude of surprisingly many of even Beckett's admirers in regard to this play: the act of underestimating the value of a thing because it is small, slight, or seems insignificant. My own view, opposed to theirs, is therefore antifloccinaucinihilipilificationistical. *Breath* is, in fact, the culmination of Beckett's radical excisions of theatrical form itself, the ultimate minimalist edulcoration of theatrical expression — a play with no plot, no movement, no characters, no dialogue, no *agon*, no language, and no actor in the theater at the time of the performance. Yet within those austere limitations, within a mere thirty-five seconds, it provides a uniquely theatrical metaphor for the life cycle and the state of the world (scattered detritus, nothing vertical), using only a setting (an almost-empty space that *remains* almost-empty throughout), plus a recorded soundtrack and an effect of light. Whether or not one accepts the notorious alteration of the text when it was used for the preamble to *Oh! Calcutta!* ("devised" by Kenneth Tynan and directed by Jacques Levy), its addition of nude bodies to the detritus on stage enraged Beckett by altering its presentation of time as well as (perhaps) the nature of the breath itself. Clearly it became, for Beckett at least, for better or worse and in more ways than one, "Kenneth Tynan's *Breath*" *rather than* Samuel Beckett's — even though it was, like all of the playlets in *Oh! Calcutta!*, presented without individual authorial attribution. Contributors, who also included Joe Orton and Sam Shepard, were listed alphabetically in the program but not identified with their individual skits — though in most cases it was not difficult for audience members who were at all familiar with the playwrights in question to figure out who had written what. This then is an issue fundamentally *apart from* issues of venue and casting, which Beckett sometimes objected to and sometimes did not, as Gontarski's address this evening has shown. Specifically, the questions that Beckett's reaction to "Tynan's *Breath*" raises are:

- When is a Beckett play no longer a Beckett play?
- What and where are its boundaries, and how does one know when they have been crossed? Specifically, how do we differentiate among reinvention, redaction, parody, and travesty? and finally,
- What, exactly, does a theatregoer have a right to expect when going to see "a Beckett play"?

The most interesting test case for this is not Kenneth Tynan's *Breath* but the one included among the Beckett on Film set of DVDs, presumably with the sanction and express permission of the Beckett estate. Directed by installation artist Damien Hirst, this version of *Breath* might as well be characterized as *Breath-Minus* if not, indeed, *Breath-Less*. It not only excises the theatrical elements that Beckett himself eliminated (plot, dialogue, language, action, *agon*, actor) but also the lighting effect, the timing, and the soundtrack. Its setting is a flying island in outer space, cluttered with discarded hospital equipment, which passes into and out of camera range with a sort of whoosh. So, one might well ask, minus the setting, the soundtrack, and the lighting effect that comprise it, what specifically is left of Beckett's play? Is it, in fact, the ultimate Beckettian edulcoration, Beckett minus Beckett? Indeed, it has far closer structural affinities with the opening sequence of *The Muppet Show's* "Pigs in Space" skits than it has with anything Samuel Beckett ever wrote. That being the case, in what sense is this Beckett's play at all — and why is his name even associated with it? Even more importantly, why did the estate — such aggressive defenders of adherence to the published texts — grant permission for its inclusion? Why does this blatant inconsistency by the estate not set ample precedent for similar treatment of other plays?

Within this context, then, the specific *reasons* behind Beckett's objections to certain productions deserve more careful consideration. Beckett's disclaimer in the playbill of Joanne Akalaitis's subway-set production of *Endgame* (which, by today's standards, featured only mild alterations indeed) contains two key elements and bears quoting again: the version to which he objected would be, he claimed, "a complete parody of the play" by which "anybody who cares for the work couldn't fail to be disgusted." The concerns therefore are (1) the borderline between the play itself and a parody or travesty of it, and (2) its hypothetical effect on the audience, or at least that portion of it "who cares for the work" and thus presumably comes into the theatre already having at least some knowledge of it. Though I believe that both parody and travesty are much under-appreciated as literary forms and deserve much more critical and theoretical attention than they have received, the point is that in either case Beckett's concern was that the original work has become an intertext, "expropriated" for purposes that are by definition no longer compatible or congruent with his own. That borderline, presumably, is the "vanishing point" at which a Beckett play becomes no longer a Beckett play.

Beckett's reference to the audience — and particularly his restriction of it to those "who car[e] for the work" also needs reconsideration. Apart from the premieres of wholly new works, any production has an audience that is divided into at least two groups whose interests are decidedly at odds with each other. On the one hand, there are those who come into the theatre already knowing the work, perhaps knowing it *well*—for whom a new and particularly original reworking of the long-familiar may be more than welcome (I feel this way about certain Shakespeare plays, *A Midsummer Night's Dream* in particular — approached with a sense of "yes, well, here we go yet again..."). On the other hand, there is always also a percentage of the audience that is encountering the play and/or its author for the first time. My concern, in the immediate context, is with the latter. A case in point is undoubtedly the worst production of *Waiting for Godot* that I have ever seen: a probably unauthorized production that a then-student of mine was acting in, produced by a community theatre company that, as far as I know, has ceased to exist, and performed in a small theatre on a rather distant campus not my own. (Rumors of an impending version of *Equus* involving sheep instead of horses have proved to be unfounded). Shortly before intermission, Godot — or somebody whom many in the audience *took* to be Godot — actually arrived. Clad in a hooded cowl, like the listener in *Not I*, he walked slowly and silently across the stage, scattering hundreds of tiny multicolored plastic crucifixes. It was, the director condescendingly explained to me several days later, "an interlude of performance art." Be *that* as it may, it was certainly the major topic of discussion in the lobby at intermission and after the play as well, as I indulged my bad habit of eavesdropping on audience reactions. Whatever else might or might not have happened — and whatever else Beckett happened to have written — drew virtually no attention. Many left the theatre that night convinced that *Waiting for Godot* is a play in which Godot comes and goes, a mysterious monk-like figure that scatters crucifixes across the stage. One couple, indeed, remarked that they had mistakenly thought that Godot *didn't* come in the play — and wondered how and where they had gotten *that* mistaken impression about it. So *had* they actually seen a Beckett play at all?

The long-contested binary opposition between the rights of the author (and/or his estate) on the one hand and stage (re)interpreters on the other is, from this perspective, inadequate insofar as it oversimplifies the nature of the theatrical "transaction" by ignoring the interests and rights of the audience, the vital third corner of what is, in effect, the triangulation of any theatrical event. "Bourgeois" or not, "avant-garde" or not, sophisticated or not, knowledgeable about what it is about to see or not, the audience has in effect entered into an implicit contract with all those who are involved in the production, which is itself a marketed and "branded" commodity, a "Beckett play." Yet specifically *what* the audience member has a right to expect needs far closer theoretical examination. Without such reconfiguration and re-

theorization, the seemingly endless debate between authors (or their representatives) and "creative reinterpreters" remains as futile as the argument of
the Big-Endians and Little-Endians in Swift's *Gulliver's Travels* over which
end of a boiled egg should be cracked first. However such audience rights
are ultimately to be defined, they must exclude BOTH the myth of an endlessly replicable ideal production based on an eternally fixed text with no
admissible variations AND a work that is more readily characterizable as a
parody or a travesty — or something, however innovative and worthwhile on
its own merits, that is no longer even remotely a "reasonable facsimile" of
what the author wrote. Twenty-first-century productions of Beckett's plays
are likely to continue to be the focal point of the debate over exactly these
issues.

UNIVERSITY OF ALABAMA, BIRMINGHAM

Note

1. William Hutchings. "Abated Drama: Samuel Beckett's Unbated *Breath*."
Ariel: A Review of International English Literature 17:1 (January 1986): 85–94.

New Plots and Playful Schemes

Shukô in Rakugo, Japanese Comic Storytelling

Lorie Brau

Abstract

Rakugo, a genre of traditional Japanese comic storytelling narrated primarily in dialogue and performed in small theatres called yose, developed in the early nineteenth century within a "culture of play." Many stories in the classical repertoire revolve around "shukô," a compositional device that creates its effects through the play of elements of older works with contemporary sensibilities. In rakugo, shukô also refers to schemes — performances in everyday life. This paper examines how shukô operate in both senses in the piece, "Akegarasu" (Crows at Dawn). Whether or not audiences appreciate the departure from the original melodramatic ballad that the story references, the predicament of the gullible Tokijirô, who finds himself at a bordello and not at a shrine, instructs audiences in the aesthetics of Edo play. Rakugo tales that employ shukô may also resonate with contemporary audiences because of their representations of the liberating potential of alternative role performance in everyday life.

In the nineteenth-century *rakugo* story, "Akegarasu" (Crows at Dawn), merchant Hyûgaya Hanbei enlists the help of two men about town, Tasuke and Genbei, to initiate his naïve nineteen-year-old son, Tokijirô, into the world of adult play. Since the prudish Tokijirô would never knowingly agree to visit the Yoshiwara licensed pleasure quarter, Edo's "sin city," Tasuke and Genbei con him into going by inviting him to spend a night praying at a shrine (*okomori*). They even convince the female proprietor of the teahouse to play along and pretend to be the head shrine maiden. Stifling giggles, she exclaims that all the shrine maidens will be well pleased with the polite young visitor — Tokijirô may be straight-laced, but he is very handsome. The young courtesan Urazato, "a peerless beauty," actually volunteers to take him as a client.

At the sight of the ladies of the night parading through the grand hall of the teahouse in their distinctive coiffures and rich costumes, even the innocent Tokijirô figures out that the place he is visiting is no shrine. He begins to sob uncontrollably, begging Tasuke and Genbei to let him go home. The rogues concoct a story that since they entered the quarter as a party of three, the guards at Yoshiwara's only gate will apprehend Tokijirô if he tries to leave on his own. The madam drags a kicking and screaming Tokijirô to Urazato's room. The next morning, Tasuke and Genbei find the formerly reluctant customer entwined in Urazato's arms. Pleased with his "conversion," they tell him that he is free to stay, but that they will go on ahead as to report to work. Tokijirô delivers the punch line, or *ochi* in *rakugo* terminology, a reference to the lie that they told to get him to stay: "Just try and leave without me. You'll be stopped at the gate."[1]

A number of stories in the *rakugo* repertoire revolve around such schemes, or "*shukô*," a word with varied meanings that include "plan," "plot," "device," and "novelty." Haruko Iwasaki calls *shukô* the "organizing device of Edo art," and defines it as "a way of amplifying the dimension of the contemporary elements by connecting them in some way with the old" (1993:51–52). The *shukô* that structure a number of *rakugo* stories might be described as performances in everyday life that juxtapose conventional "scenarios" or practices (e.g., a prayer vigil at a shrine) with variations (a visit to a teahouse/brothel) to generate a comic situation. These scenarios may be elaborately plotted schemes, more spontaneous practical jokes, or strategies improvised on the spot to get oneself out of a difficult situation. I focus my discussion on the story "Akegarasu" because it deploys *shukô* in two senses, as a new plot that borrows from an older work and as a comic technique in which the dissonance created by the juxtaposition of two worlds or worldviews engenders humor.

Rakugo, which means "stories with punch lines," is a form of comic monologue/storytelling that evolved in urban Japan in the Edo period (1600–1868) and began to flourish in Edo and Osaka as a commercial popular entertainment in the nineteenth century. Rakugo storytellers are called *hanashika* or *rakugoka*. Their ancestors include medieval Buddhist preachers who used comic anecdotes as exempla, sixteenth century *otogishû* (storyteller-companions) who entertained the warrior class, and seventeenth century performers who presented their humorous tales on the streets and in the salons of Edo (Tokyo), Kyoto, and Osaka. By the end of the eighteenth century, literati from a variety of classes matched their wits not only in poetry contests, but also in performing comic anecdotes of their own composition. In Edo, a few of these men began performing their material at small storytelling houses, rented rooms above shops and in larger residences in urban neighborhoods. The number of these *yose* ("gathering-in places") eventually grew to over 200 in mid-nineteenth century Edo. Their official number has decreased to five commercial *rakugo* variety theatres in Tokyo, but live *rakugo* can be heard today in all kinds of venues, from bars to concert halls.

Though *rakugo* pieces have been based on such written sources as published anecdote collections, the genre is primarily an oral form.[2] The growth of storytelling families comprised of a master and his disciples similar to those found in *nô*, *kabuki*, and other arts and crafts has fostered the codification of performance techniques and versions of stories. The repertoire has been, and continues to be (at least officially), orally transmitted from master to disciple, though fledging storytellers learn a great deal through osmosis while they work as apprentices backstage. Print versions of classical *rakugo* tales have been available for over a hundred years; however, storytellers do not use these publications as scripts. In the late nineteenth century, a few storytelling families, concerned with changes in *yose* productions that favored briefer, less substantial recitations, worked to establish new venues — concert halls for example — and higher artistic standards for the art. As part of this mission, they also established a canon of several hundred *koten*, or "classical" *rakugo*. Since then, the jokes and even the style of narration have changed to adapt to audience taste, but most of the old stories in the classical canon continue to appeal to contemporary Japanese.

While certainly not as popular as it was 150 years ago, *rakugo* still draws audiences to live venues and through the electronic media. The majority of the 300 or so professional *hanashika*[3] in Tokyo perform their versions of the classical tales, using their opening monologue, their *makura* ("pillow"), to hook the audience with contemporary material and to explain some of the more obscure, archaic details of the story. It is this introductory section of the performance that brings *rakugo* under the rubric of comic monologue. At times, storytellers forsake the classical tale entirely and present only anecdotes and jokes in a sit-down version of stand-up comedy, referred to as *mandan*, "comic chat."

In addition to its commerciality, what distinguishes *rakugo* from many other kinds of storytelling is its emphasis on mimesis. In many respects a *rakugo* session is a kind of one-man play. Tales are recited as dialogue. The storyteller assumes the roles of all of the characters he embodies through variations in diction and shifts of body and gaze to help audiences keep track of who is talking. The conventional gestures that he incorporates into his performances to represent the action in an abbreviated manner — he always remains seated *seiza* style, legs folded under him — derive in part from *kabuki*.

Rakugo developed at a time when such arts as *kabuki*, *haikai* poetry, *ukiyoe* prints and *gesaku* fiction relied heavily on *shukô*. Not only did *shukô* dominate the arts as an organizing principle, it also influenced the aesthetics of everyday life, from housing and utensils to clothes and food (Noma 1975:62). An 1801 manual for writers of *kabuki* explains the term *shukô* along with "*sekai*." *Sekai* means "worlds," traditional literary works and their characters well known to audiences that provide material for the creation of new plays. These *sekai* are transformed by *shukô* in a variety of ways, including the rewriting of plays, the joining of an unknown play to a familiar *sekai*, or the combination of two or more *sekai* to create a new work (Thornbury 1982:27–28). A *shukô* might become so popular that it is used as a *sekai* for a later work. Nakamura Yukihiko described *sekai* as the centripetal force that pulls the whole work together, and *shukô* as the centrifugal force that moves outward, seeking for something new. "The literary work is constructed through a harmony of these two forces" (1975:10).

Edo audiences took pleasure in contemplating the often witty relationship between a traditional *sekai* framework and the *shukô* that transformed it, just as an informed reader enjoys contemplating Joyce's take on Homer's *Odyssey* in *Ulysses*. To a great degree, the success of a *shukô* has been dependent on knowledgeable audiences sophisticated enough to appreciate the innovative juxtapositions as well as some of the "insider" jokes.

Shukô *as Adaptation of Earlier Material*

A sizable proportion of the *rakugo* audience today does not likely meet these criteria. Few realize, for example, that the story "Akegarasu" is a *shukô* based on an earlier "Akegarasu" *sekai*. The work that likely inaugurated this *sekai* was a *shamisen*-accompanied *Shinnai* ballad that is acknowledged as one of the masterpieces of the *Shinnai* genre, *Akegarasu yume no awayuki* (The Raven at First Light: Faint Snowfall in Dreams) (Hare 1993:118). Written in 1772, it was inspired by an actual love suicide. Because the piece was a great success, a number of treatments followed, including a *kabuki* play in 1850 (Hare 1993:117).

Evoking the mood of the pleasure quarter in its opening lines, the *Shinnai Akegarasu* tells the story of young Tokijirô, who has fallen deeply in love with the courtesan Urazato and has run out of money to pay for her services.[4] The consequences of Urazato's return of Tokijirô's affections are even more disastrous: prostitutes are never supposed to fall for their customers.

The first scene describes the lovers' surreptitious meeting in Urazato's room where Tokijrô tells Urazato of his intention to kill himself. She rebukes him for not including her in his plans. The noise of their quarrel reaches the management. Discovering Tokijirô, a customer who is deeply in debt to the house, they beat him up and throw him out. In Scene Two, the master of the brothel ties both Urazato and her young servant, Midori, to trees in the snow-covered garden as he castigates Urazato for her lack of responsibility. After apologizing to Midori, "her emotions frenzied," her tears melting the snow, Urazato "faints dead away" (Hare 1993:124). Tokijirô returns with a sword, climbing over a neighboring roof to free Urazato and Midori. The three of them then use a pine branch bent under the snow to make their way to the top of the wall. They jump off and escape, resolved to take their own lives.

How did a melodrama about the desperation of lovers embarking on a double suicide become a comic *rakugo* story? The link appears to have been a *ninjôbanashi*, or "story of human sentiment" (Tôdai rakugo kenkyûkai 1970 [1988]:44)[5] based on a *ninjôbon*, a sentimental story written by Tamenaga Shunsui in the early 1820s entitled *Akegarasu nochi no masayume* (The Raven at First Light: A Dream Come True). This tale picked up the story where the original *Shinnai* ballad left off. The lovers escape to Fukagawa in order to keep the precious sword that Tokijirô is carrying from getting into the wrong hands. There they hang themselves. Tokijirô's uncle, a priest, uses the magic power of the sword and various mantras to bring the lovers back to life. They end up living happily ever after (Hare 1993:119–120).

If this *ninjôbanashi* presented the sequel to the original *sekai*, one might say that *rakugo*'s comic *shukô* supplied the "prequel." Little remains from the *Shinnai*-based *sekai* in the comic *rakugo* version, only the setting of the pleasure quarters and the names of the main characters, the youth Tokijirô and the courtesan Urazato. Insofar as *rakugo* is an oral performance, it is impossible to determine whether nineteenth-century recitations of "Akegarasu" may have also incorporated other references to the *Shinnai* ballad, to Shunsui's sequel, or indeed to other *sekai* entirely.

The comic story inverts the tone and plot of the melodrama. *Rakugo* changes the passionate lover of the ballad, a man who chooses to die with his indentured courtesan lover, into an immature nineteen-year-old who shrieks about the dangers of venereal disease. In contrast to the Urazato of the ballad, who is tied up in the snow and beaten by her master for falling in love with a client who never pays, *rakugo*'s Urazato displays her assertiveness and independence in declaring that she will take Tokijirô as her client. Whether or not the audience is aware of the *Shinnai* ballad and *ninjôbon* on which the *rakugo* is based is immaterial: the plot of the rakugo "Akegarasu" is humorous in its own right and one need not be aware that it is a parody to enjoy it.

Shukô *as Comic Schemes*

Shukô characters' "performances in everyday life" devised for their own amusement or some other personal benefit, drive the plot in many *rakugo* stories. Such plots and schemes constitute an important compositional technique in all sorts of comedies, from Shakespeare's plays to *I Love Lucy*. To what end these contrivances are created and how they play out varies, of course, from culture to culture and author to author. I limit my discussion to the *rakugo* context.

The Edo period has been characterized as a "culture of play" (Harootunian 1989:168–177). One illustration of this playful attitude can be seen in the fondness among the leisure class for inventing and performing *shukô* (Nakamura 1966:170). For example, they put on improvisational skits (*chaban*), a kind of *shukô*, at cherry-blossom parties, occasions when transforming one's identity through "masks and masquerade was an essential feature" (Ohnuki-Tierney 1998:222).

The *rakugo* story, "Nagaya no hanami" (Cherry Blossom Viewing of the Row House Tenants) is a parody of such a cherry-blossom party skit. To improve his reputation, a landlord invites his tenants to go cherry-blossom viewing.[6] He is too cheap (or possibly too poor) to treat them to sake and a feast so he dilutes low-grade tea and pours it into a sake bottle to make it look like the real thing and slices up pickles to look like fishcake and omelet. He then orders his tenants to pretend to get drunk and have a good time, telling them to think of it as a *shukô*, in this case, a new "plot" or "twist" on the cherry-blossom viewing party *sekai*. Given the hierarchical nature of Japanese society and the relationship between landlords and tenants, the latter feel compelled to obey, but they undercut his efforts right and left, joking about the crunchiness of the "omelet," and the diuretic effects of the tea/sake. Another *rakugo* tale set in cherry-blossom viewing season, "Hanami no adauchi" (The Cherry Blossom Viewing Vendetta), features a *shukô* with potentially dangerous consequences. A few friends improvise a *chaban* about a vendetta, a practice associated in particular with the samurai class. Their scheme goes awry when their "mediator" fails to show up in time and a real samurai offers his help to slay the enemy. In both stories, the creators of the *shukô* and the other participants, officially part of the scheme or not, are not on the same page, as it were. The tenants resist the landlords' forced performance of levity and the samurai fails to see the performance as performance.

It is not only at cherry-blossom viewing parties that *rakugo* characters create such contrivances, however. In "Nishiki no kesa" (The Brocade Surplice), a few "guys from the neighborhood" hear that people are speaking ill of them in the pleasure quarters. They decide to improve their reputation with a flashy performance in which they will parade down the streets of the quarter naked, save for loincloths made of remnants of brocade fabric. Since there is not enough cloth for him to make a loincloth, Yotarô the Fool is advised by his clever wife to borrow the priest's brocade surplice, with a promise to return it by the next morning. The surplice has a white ring attached to it, which, when tied as a loincloth, hangs down right in front of Yotarô's privates. The courtesans take the group for samurai on an incognito spree and decide that Yotarô must be their lord, as his loincloth is the only one with a ring. Consequently, only the "lord" Yotarô manages to spend the night with a woman, who tells him, "By no means will I let you go (return you) home this morning" (*Anata wa dou shite mo kesa kaeshimasen*). Yotarô replies, "If I don't return (*kaesanai*) the surplice (*kesa*) (alternatively, "if you don't let me go home [*kaesanai*] this morning [*kesa*])—I'll get into trouble with the priest!" (*Kesa kaesanee* [*kaesanai* in Edo dialect], *sorya taihen da. Tera o shikujiru*) (Tôdai Kenkyû Kai 1988:340).

The object of the *shukô* in the story, "Sudôfu" (also called "Chiritotechin") is a prank. A group of friends hanging out on a summer's day are at loose ends because none of them has money to buy snacks to enjoy with their sake. There was some tofu, but Yotarô left it out overnight and it has gone bad. The ringleader decides to have a little fun with an affected young heir he sees walking toward them. He forces him to taste some of the spoiled tofu disguised under a liberal sprinkling of ground hot pepper, which he passes off as the delicacy "sour tofu." The young heir's pretensions to culinary sophistication keep him from admitting that he has been duped.

The *shukô* used in the story, "Fudôbô Kaen" (The Storyteller, Fudôbô Kaen) requires a bit more planning by the perpetrators than the sour tofu scheme. A few single men living in the same tenement row house learn to their dismay that their landlord has arranged a marriage between another single tenant and the highly desirable widow, Osaki. Osaki's departed, a storyteller of military adventures and histories named Fudôbô Kaien, left her with a mountain of debts that none of these men can afford to pay off. The frustrated bachelors decide to stage the return of Fudôbô's ghost to scare the new couple out of marrying. They hire a third-rate *rakugo* storyteller to play the ghost. He insists that they include some of *kabuki*'s special effects to enhance the atmosphere, for example, a drum beating out the ominous "*doro doro*" sound effect that usually presages the appearance of a ghost and a *shôchûbi*, an alcohol-fueled flame to represent the recently departed spirit.

Instead of the drum used in *kabuki*, however, the only instrument that they can get their hands on makes a rat-a-tat sound: one of the group shows up for the performance in his one-man band outfit, complete with advertising placard. The man in charge of procuring the alcohol mishears what was then a new "foreign" word (*arukôru*) as "*ankoro*," rice dumplings rolled in bean jam, which he has a hard time stuffing into a bottle, let alone lighting. The storyteller arrives wearing an impressively grisly ghost costume, but he forgets his lines and, even when prompted, fails to convince the new groom to cease and desist in his marriage to Osaki. He even gives away his true identity by asking for a tip! In "Fudôbô Kaen," the traditional *kabuki* ghost play "*sekai*" is used to construct the performance of an encounter with a ghost.

These and other stories demonstrate that the backfiring of characters' *shukô* creates much of the humor. To some degree this is demonstrated in "Akegarasu." Young Tokijirô, who is scandalized by the idea of sleeping with a prostitute, ends up with the star courtesan while his two "player" mentors Tasuke and Genbei are jilted by the women they've hired. On the other hand, they have succeeded in their task of loosening up the stuffy son of their rich and powerful friend, the merchant Hyûgaya Hanbei, a feat that will no doubt benefit them in the future.

Tokijirô's horror at finding himself in the Yoshiwara pleasure quarters draws listeners' attention to the question of what it meant to visit this special "village" that, along with the *kabuki* theatre, was one of the two poles of the *ukiyo*, or Floating World, an area that was geographically at the margins of Edo, but culturally at its center. The licensed quarters belonged to the realm of the *akubashô* (also called *akushô*) that Edo period bureaucrats, with their Confucian worldview, exiled from the center of the city.[7] The straight-laced Tokijirô represents this Confucian view. An older, native Shintô view would have accommodated the activities that took place in the quarter as the necessary element of *hare* (purificatory play) needed to eliminate *kegare* (pollution) in the temporal cycle of *ke* (the everyday), *hare*, and *kegare*. The moral contradiction between the native and Confucian views led to an idea of the "city apart from the city." Henry Smith explained that the "consequence was a culture of indirection and disguise, relying primarily on wit, theatre, and antiquarianism for its modes of expression" (1978:52).

Given this culture of indirection, it is no surprise that Tasuke and Genbei disguise their intentions to lead Tokijirô astray by suggesting they spend a night praying at a shrine (*okomori*). The parody implied in this pairing of sex and religion is not as shocking as it might seem. *Hare*, which can also mean "sacred," refers to purificatory *play*. The sacred, sexual and, indeed, comic have long been associated in Japan, as early as the origin myth of Japanese performance, the goddess Ame no Uzume's humorous strip tease.

In medieval Japan, some itinerant Buddhist nuns and shamanesses danced, sang, and even bedded down with customers. Thus it is not too far a stretch to imagine Yoshiwara courtesans as shrine maidens.

Genbei's comparison of the Yoshiwara to an Inari shrine resonates all the more deeply because "Akegarasu" is set on Hatsuuma (First Day of the Horse), the Inari god's festival day.[8] Originally an agricultural deity, Inari became popular in urban areas as a god of luck and prosperity. Inari also protected property, which was no doubt a concern of Tokijirô's father. The fact that Inari's messenger is the fox, one of whose associations is with sexuality, especially female sexuality (Smyers 1999:127), also strengthens the association of the Inari Shrine with the Yoshiwara. Additionally, in traditional Japanese belief, foxes are known as shape-shifters. One of their most frequent transformations is into beautiful women who trick men, as in the *rakugo*, "Yoshino kitsune." On the day of Inari's festival, a courtesan might well transform herself into a shrine maiden. In any case, "foxy" Urazato seduces Tokijirô.

In a sense, the loss of Tokijirô's virginity at the Inari shrine cum Yoshiwara brothel is as crucial to the success of the family business as an offering at a real shrine would be. One of the main arguments that Tokijirô's father makes to his wife at the beginning of the story is that being studious and proper is all well and good, but to succeed in business one must know how to entertain clients, know how to "play." The *ukiyo*, or Floating World, most often associated in the Edo period with the artificially constructed fantasies conjured up in the pleasure quarters and at the theatre, was not a place but a way of life and "as such it fostered its own code of behavior and set of values" (Jenkins 1993:15). "Akegarasu" teaches the rakugo audience the ethos and aesthetics of this way of life, of Edo play.

In the Edo period, "playing" often referred to the *sandora* (*san dôraku*), the three amusements of "drinking," "gambling," and "buying [women]," i.e., engaging prostitutes. "Akegarasu" provides a guide to at least one of these practices. It also offers a glimpse of the Yoshiwara experience to members of the *yose* audience of old who, for reasons of gender or finances, could not visit the pleasure quarters, and to all *rakugo* listeners today, for whom Yoshiwara no longer exists.

In the Floating World, style was paramount (Jenkins 1993:15). "Akegarasu" is particularly instructive about Edo style, or "*iki*." The tale even communicates how to be *iki* in an amusing fashion, in part by representing its opposite in the prim and pedantic Tokijirô. Initially associated with *kabuki* and the pleasure quarters, the aesthetic of *iki* represents Edo "cool" in the full sense of the word in that it prizes emotional detachment. Unlike his son Tokijirô, Hanbei represents the epitome of *iki*. When Tasuke and Genbei hear that Tokijirô has been given a hefty allowance to pay for the "vigil at the shrine" they are duly impressed: "*Iki na oyaji ga aru mon da* (He sure has a stylish father)," one comments.

Indeed Hanbei's instructions to Tokijirô for the trip to the "shrine" comprise a lesson in an "*iki*" visit to the pleasure quarter. Hanbei tells his son to change into a nice kimono, because the "grace of the gods" shines more brightly on someone who dresses well. He explains the custom of *naka-tsugi*, stopping at a restaurant for a drink and a bite to eat before entering the quarter, a kind of "warm-up." He knows that his son will not touch alcohol, but he tells him to take a sip when he is poured a cup so as not to dampen the mood. He advises him to discretely empty what he cannot finish into the basin used for washing out the cups. He also explains how to handle the bill. Tokijirô is to tell Tasuke and Genbei that he is going to the restroom and instead go and settle the tab. When Tokijirô asks if he should solicit his companions' contributions later, his father warns him that Tasuke and Genbei are notorious in the neighborhood and that there would be terrible consequences if he asked them for their share. The unsophisticated young heir proceeds to repeat all these instructions to Tasuke and Genbei, including the part about their unsavory reputation. It is not an *iki* thing to do, but a very funny technique commonly used in *rakugo* in which characters try out and bungle newly learned scripts. In addition to creating laughs, the repetition reinforces the lesson.

Hanbei does not anticipate his son's outburst, unfortunately. Tokijirô's lack of emotional control represents the opposite of *iki* behavior. As he weeps with indignation at having been brought to a wicked place like Yoshiwara, he destroys the party atmosphere. The *hanashika* thus teaches his audiences how to behave in the pleasure quarters, a place that may represent freedom from everyday responsibilities, but also requires knowledge of an elaborate code of behavior — in itself a kind of *sekai*— in order to be well-received.

Akanuke (urbanity) is one of the qualities associated with *iki* (Nishiyama 1997:54). Until the "morning after" in "Akegarasu," Tokijirô is both too hysterical and naïve to embody anything like the sophistication of *iki*. Only when the crows caw at dawn and he sheepishly admits to Genbei and Tasuke that his *okomori* was "just splendid" does it appear that Tokijirô will be able to take over his father's business after all.

Schemes, improvised skits, and con games are among the most common plot techniques used in *rakugo*. *Rakugo* characters often place themselves in make-believe situations to better themselves or make life easier, more fun. Their behavior reflects the storytellers' behavior: like all performance, *rakugo* is reflexive. Perhaps tales like "Akegarasu" that employ *shukô* resonate with contemporary audiences because they represent the liberating potential of alternative role performance in everyday life.

UNIVERSITY OF NEW MEXICO

Notes

1. This précis of "Akegarasu" is based on a version by Katsura Bunraku VIII (Katsura Bunraku 1989:7–31) and a recording by Kokontei Shinchô (1993[1982]).
2. Henry Smith suggests that the government's formal ban on writings about politics or other current events may have encouraged the "formal elaboration of oral culture" (1993:41). The ephemeral comic monologue/storytelling form offered an outlet for the expression of critique in an oblique, comic form.
3. As in other traditional Japanese theatres, until very recently, only men have performed *rakugo*. At present there are probably less than a dozen professional female *hanashika* in Tokyo.
4. My outline of the ballad is based on Hare's translation (1993:120–125).
5. *Ninjôbanashi* were a subgenre of *rakugo*, usually of greater length, that emphasized drama and the conflicts caused by human emotions. It is unclear whether *Rakugo Jiten* (Tôdai rakugo kenkyûkai 1988) refers to an orally performed story based on Tamenaga Shunsui's text or the published story itself, as the titles are identical.
6. I have used the term "landlord" for what might more properly be called "property superintendent." These people collected rents and supervised properties for absentee landlords. They did not own property and were not wealthy (Smith 1993:29).
7. In fact, the original Yoshiwara was located in the heart of Edo, near Nihonbashi. After a fire there in 1657, it was moved to the outskirts of the city.
8. Hatsuuma, the "first day of the horse" of the second month of the old lunar calendar, usually fell sometime in March.

References Cited

Hare, Thomas Blenham. "'The Raven at First Light': A Shinnai Ballad." In *New Leaves: Studies and Translations of Japanese Literature in Honor of Edward Seidensticker*, edited by Edward Seidensticker, Aileen Gatten and Anthony Chambers, 115–125. Ann Arbor: Center for Japanese Studies, University of Michigan, 1993.

Harootounian, H.D. "Late Tokugawa Culture and Thought." In *Cambridge History of Japan: The Nineteenth Century*, Volume 5, edited by Marius B. Jansen, 168–177. Cambridge, England and New York: Cambridge University Press, 1989.

Iwasaki Haruko. "The Literature of Wit and Humor in Late-Eighteenth-Century Edo." In *The Floating World Revisited*, edited by Donald Jenkins and Lynn Jacobsen Katsumoto, 47–61. Honolulu, HI: Portland Museum of Art and Uni-

versity of Hawaii Press, 1993, Jenkins, Donald. "Introduction." In *The Floating World Revisited*, edited by Donald Jenkins and Lynn Jacobsen Katsumoto,
3–23. Honolulu, HI: Portland Museum of Art and University of Hawaii Press,
1993.

Katsura Bunraku. "Akegarasu." In *Koten rakugo: Bunrakushû*, edited by Iijima Tomo-
haru, 7–31. Tokyo: Chikuma bunkô, 1989.

Kokontei Shinchô. "Akegarasu." On *Rakugo meijin kai I: Kokontei Shinchô*. Recorded
April 15, 1981 at Sanbyakunin gekijô. Tokyo: Sony, 1993 [1981]. Compact disk.

Nakamura Yukihiko. *Gesakuron*. Tokyo: Kadokawa, 1966.

_____. "Modes of Expression in a Historical Context." *Acta Asiatica: Bulletin of the
Institute of Eastern Culture* 28 (1975): 1–19.

Nishiyama Matsunosuke. *Edo Culture: Daily Life and Diversions in Urban Japan,
1600–1868*. Translated by Gerald Groemer. Honolulu: University of Hawaii
Press, 1997.

Noma Kôshin. "Saikaku's Adoption of *Shukô* from *Kabuki* and *Jôruri*." *Acta Asiatica: Bulletin of the Institute of Eastern Culture* 28 (1975): 62–83.

Ohnuki-Tierney, Emiko. "Cherry Blossoms and Their Viewing: A Window Onto
Japanese Culture." In *The Culture of Japan as Seen Through its Leisure*, edited
by Sepp Linhart and Sabine Frühstück, 213–236. Albany: State University of
New York Press, 1998.

Smith, Henry D. II. "The Floating World in its Edo Locale, 1750–1850. In *The
Floating World Revisited*, edited by Donald Jenkins and Lynn Jacobsen Kat-
sumoto, 25–45. Honolulu, HI: Portland Museum of Art and University of
Hawaii Press, 1993.

_____. "Tokyo as an Idea: An Exploration of Japanese Urban Thought Until 1945."
The Journal of Japanese Studies 4:1 (Winter 1978): 45–80.

Smyers, Karen A. *The Fox and the Jewel: Shared and Private Meaning in Contemporary Japanese Inari Worship*. Honolulu: University of Hawaii Press, 1999.

Thornbury, Barbara. *Sukeroku's Double Identity: The Dramatic Structure of Edo
Kabuki*. Ann Arbor, MI: Center for Japanese Studies, University of Michigan,
1982.

Tôdai rakugo kenkyûkai. *Rakugo jiten*. Tokyo: Seiabo, 1988.

Iphigenie's Power in Goethe's *Iphigenie auf Tauris*

Michael Ewans

Abstract

In the closing scenes of Iphigenie auf Tauris it is generally felt that Goethe places Iphigenie on a Romantic pedestal (cf. 2127ff.), and presents her as an image of Woman, passive Redeemer of violent, sinful men. However, Iphigenie herself explicitly rejects the subordination of women in marriage, in the opening scenes. And as the play proceeds the stern moral purity which she tries to maintain, as the priestess of a virgin goddess, comes under attack from outside. This paper therefore examines the closing scenes from a fresh viewpoint, and asks exactly how Iphigenie gains in Act 5 the strength to resolve apparently irreconcilable pressures and oppositions. It will be shown that her power in the final scene comes from the courage she has gained from intense suffering, and from transcending her family's hereditary predisposition to monstrous crime.

At the end of Euripides's *Iphigeneia among the Taurians*, even Iphigeneia's ingenious deception of the Taurian king Thoas, and the heroism of her brother Orestes and his companion Pylades, are not enough to save them from death at the hands of the barbarians. Athena has to intervene as *dea ex machina* to soothe the waves so Iphigeneia and Orestes may return home, and take with them the image of Artemis (Diana), which Apollo had commanded Orestes to remove from her temple in Tauria and bring back to Greece.

Euripides's play is concerned with questions, which were central in the late fifth century BCE: are the gods just or unjust? Do they tell the truth to human beings through dreams and oracles? And do they reward those who obey them? However, from Goethe's standpoint as an enlightened humanist, all belief in the gods' commands is simply a projection of human desires. Human beings need to recognize that they must solve their own problems.

Goethe's *Iphigenie auf Tauris* is a meditation on the unequal roles of men and women in contemporary eighteenth-century society. Near the end of his play, the situation is very similar to that at the parallel point in Euripides; Orestes and Pylades and their forces are facing military defeat by the Taurians. But Iphigenie has already revealed that one of the Greeks is her own brother, and placed their fate in the hands of the Taurian king Thoas. She now pleads for peace and reconciliation, picking up the Euripidean theme of the miserable lot of women (2064ff.). Goethe's Orestes then resolves the conflict. He realizes that Apollo simply asked him to "bring back to Greece that sister who is held/against her will within the sacred shrine at Tauria" (2112ff.). The oracle means Iphigenie, not the image of Diana. Orestes now praises his sister, whose hands healed him from the pursuit of the Furies. In a speech which seems to sum up Iphigenie's role in the play, he puts her womanhood almost literally up on a pedestal:

> For like an image
> which secret breath from heaven had imbued
> with power immutable to rule the fate
> of some great city, you have been preserved
> in silent sanctuary, to afford your brother
> salvation, to redeem your house and land [2127ff.].[1]

And he begs Thoas to let them go free because:

> Force and cunning, proudest boasts of men
> are put to shame by the truthfulness of her radiant soul [2142–2143].

Woman is here imaged as a passive redeemer and savior of violent, sinful men (Gretchen's soul will play the same role at the end of *Faust II*).[2] In the 1780s, when the play was first written, contemporary social conditions were increasingly confining middle-class women to the home, while men went out into the workplace and were there obliged to become as pragmatic as Pylades in Goethe's play; this led to a sentimental view of family life, with woman seen as the bringer of bliss to the family and the savior of men; Orestes' speech, placing his sister on a pedestal for her moral purity, fits in well with the social background.[3]

But is it right? Does Goethe's Iphigenie really gain the strength to resolve the dilemmas of the play from a "pure and childlike trust" (this is how Orestes describes her virtue at the end of his speech, 2144)? I shall show that the sources of her strength lie elsewhere; Goethe deliberately allows his Orestes to misread the situation, and this illustrates an important sub-theme — the tendency of men to misunderstand the sources of female strength, creating a passive ideal of womanhood rather than accepting that a woman can be morally strong in her own right.[4]

In the opening scenes, Iphigenie herself explicitly rejects the subordination of women in marriage (cf. Rasch 1979:92–94 and Borchmeyer 1981:58). And as the play proceeds the stern moral purity which she tries to maintain, as the priestess of a virgin goddess, comes under attack from outside — both through the pressure which Thoas brings upon her, for his own political reasons, to marry him, and through the arrival of her brother, on his quest for the statue of Diana.

In the opening scene Iphigenie laments the lot of women:

> At home and in the wars a man is master—
> even in exile he can help himself.
> Possession thrills him: victory is the crown.
> A death of honour is prepared for him.
> But how restricted is a woman's fortune!
> Even obedience to a brutish husband
> is duty, consolation. What affliction
> comes when fate compels her into exile! [25ff][5]

Iphigenie apparently accepts in this first speech that for a woman even a circumscribed life in marriage is preferable to solitary exile, and she indulges in self-pity for her wasted life (115–116). Nonetheless in the second scene Iphigenie does not accept the arguments of Arkas, king Thoas's confidante, who wants her to marry the king. Arkas clearly sees Iphigenie's role in the marriage and in Taurian society as being to provide her mate with moral goodness from "on a pedestal":

> The counsel of a woman's heart inspires
> good men to greatness [213ff].

Iphigenie rejects this, and refuses to allow herself to be trapped in the conventional female role which Arkas, like Orestes at the end of the play, assigns to her (Prandi 1983:21).

In the third scene, when the king himself pursues his suit, Iphigenie refuses him. Thoas angrily claims that because she is a woman she listens to her heart rather than to reason and good advice. Iphigenie meets this diatribe calmly, and replies:

> Do not upbraid poor womankind, my Lord.
> The weapons of a woman lack the glory
> that shines from yours, but they are not ignoble.
> Believe my intuition can foresee
> your future with an eye more clear than yours.
> You neither know yourself nor me! [481ff; cf. 2065ff]

However, as the first four Acts unfold Iphigenie is increasingly circumscribed; by Thoas' threat that if she does not marry him, the Taurians will resume their practice of sacrificing strangers to the goddess; then by Arkas's appeal to the obligations she has created during her time among the

Taurians[6]; and finally by Pylades, who demands that she should, like Euripides's Iphigeneia,[7] deceive the king to save her brother:

> Stern purity was yours within this temple,
> but life persuades us we must deal more gently
> both with ourselves and others. You will learn it.
> Humanity is fashioned with such wonder,
> so subtly interwoven, so conjoined,
> that no man lives, alone or in society,
> untainted and uncompromised [1653ff].

Iphigenie eventually finds the strength to confront Thoas, without the falsehood and deception that Pylades has urged on her, and recognizing the legitimate obligations on her both of her brother and of the Taurians who have given her a second life. But she does not gain this strength from a passively conceived female virtue.

If we compare Goethe's *Iphigenie auf Tauris* with all the ancient Greek tragedies about the house of Atreus — including Aeschylus's *Oresteia*, Sophocles's *Electra*, and Euripides's *Electra*, *Orestes* and *Iphigeneia at Aulis* as well as *Iphigeneia among the Taurians*— it is immediately striking that Goethe's version concentrates far more than any Greek source on the past crimes of the house.[8] In a remarkable innovation, Goethe's Iphigenie has kept her identity a secret from the Taurians; so when she seeks to dissuade Thoas from wanting to marry her, she tells him her name and provides a full history of every crime of her ancestors (300ff): Tantalus's expulsion from Olympus, Pelops's treachery and murder to obtain Hippodamia as his bride, Thyestes's rape of his brother's wife, Atreus's murder in ignorance of his own son, and his revenge for that, the banquet where Thyestes was made to feast on his own children's flesh. And then in Act 3 Iphigenie learns that her father is dead, murdered by Klytämnestra and Ägisth, and that her brother bears the guilt of having murdered Klytämnestra in revenge. When she hears how Agamemnon died, she curses Mycenae and exclaims:

> Thus Tantalus and all his line have sown
> Curse upon curse in barbarous profusion.
> And like a weed that shakes its noxious heads
> to strew a thousand evils around itself,
> they sow the seeds of parricide among
> their children's children to beget fresh vengeance! [968ff].

When brother and sister have recognized each other, Orestes in a speech of bitter irony bids the Furies enter the sacred grove to see "the last, most hideous show" that the self-destructive house of Atreus has to offer — a sister, filled with love, driven to murder her own brother (1223ff)!

The central theme of Goethe's *Iphigenie* is simple: can the curse be transcended? Have the gods predisposed the whole house to kindred murder? Or can Iphigenie escape?

At the crisis in Act 4, when Pylades has bitterly reproached her for her refusal to compromise, Iphigenie wonders out loud whether she may transcend the curse:

> Shall this curse rule forever? Shall our house
> be never granted respite, never find
> new favour with the gods? All things must end:
> the fairest fortunes, brightest powers of life
> grow weary at last. Why not this curse?
> Then have I hoped in vain that here preserved
> and sundered from the evil of my line
> I might still keep my hand unstained, my heart
> immaculate, and thus redeem the house
> so deeply steeped in evil? [1694ff].

In Act 5 scene 3, when she confronts Thoas for the last time, she finds the strength within her to transcend the curse. She defies Thoas and his barbaric insistence that the prisoners must be killed,[9] and she begins, as a woman normally would in eighteenth century society, with pleading and an appeal to his sense of honor. But when he rejects this, she asks herself:

> What weapons then remain for my protection?
> Must I beseech Diana work some wonder?
> And is my heart itself bereft of power? [1883ff].

Thoas sees that the "strangers" have disturbed Iphigenie; he challenges her to explain. After a silence, she begins her climactic speech (1892ff). Will only the deeds of heroic men be recorded as great actions, does man have the sole claim to courage? What options are left to women?

> Must gentle woman
> then set aside her birthright and become
> brutish to fight with brutes? Like Amazons
> must we usurp man's right to wield the sword,
> avenging this oppression with his blood? [1908ff].[10]

Iphigenie's first option was accepting that a woman is limited to submissiveness and pleading. But it has not worked. Now she briefly contemplates an alternative; for women to adopt male values, and become as combative and brutal as men. But she rejects this in favor of a third course of action — she tells him the truth. Her brother is here, and both the last remaining heirs of Tantalus are in the power of Thoas; "destroy us, if you can!" (1936).

Iphigenie is not now pleading, as she did before — nor has she adopted manly attributes and male weaponry like the Amazons. Thoas realizes that Iphigenie now poses him a new and higher challenge, and asks with heavy irony:

> You think that I,
> the uncouth Scythian, the barbarian,
> will hear the voice of truth and human-kindness
> when Atreus, the Greek, was deaf? [1936ff].[11]

And Iphigenie responds:

> All men
> within whose veins the pristine source of life
> flows unimpeded, hear that voice, whatever
> horizon rimmed the purlieus of their birth.

This is the clarion call of the Enlightenment, evident elsewhere in Schikaneder's libretto for Mozart's *The Magic Flute*[12] as in Schiller's *Ode to Joy*, set by Beethoven as the finale of his Ninth Symphony; *Alle Menschen werden Brüder...,* "all human beings shall be brothers"; and sisters too.

Thoas is not easily convinced. At the end of Scene 3, he declines to accept her challenge: "You ask much of me in so short a space" (1988). But in Scene 5 he abjures the use of force, even though his forces are winning, and agrees to an armistice — "And let there be no fighting while we speak" (2023). Thoas is only persuaded in the final scene, after Orestes has resolved the issue of the statue of Diana (2107ff). At first Thoas simply orders Iphigenie to go — but in a powerful speech (2151ff) she refuses to part from him without his blessing, and in unresolved conflict with him. The play ends when Thoas responds to her in the exact words of her heartfelt plea, "May you fare well" (2168) (cf. Borchmeyer 1981:71).

As she hoped (1885), Iphigenie has finally found the power within herself to persuade him, just as earlier in the drama her influence freed Orestes from the Furies (1341ff; cf. 2118–2125). I see four reasons why Iphigenie gains what Rasch rightly terms her "Autonomie,"[13] and succeeds: a) because she has inherited a strong will and a sense of self-worth from her ancestors (cf. Prandi 1983:24–25); b) because suffering and loneliness in exile have sharpened her sense of the value of other people; c) because during the course of the play she has discovered the strength to resist male efforts to persuade her to be untrue to her inner values[14]; and finally d) because having rejected both the passivity of the pleading woman and the aggressiveness of the Amazonian woman, she finds in Act 5 Scene 3 a third way; women can challenge men to meet them on the common ground of respect for *Wahrheit und Menschlichkeit* (1938), truth and a fellow-feeling for each other as human beings.[15]

At this point Goethe is in total opposition to his source text. Euripides's

Iphigeneia has no hesitation in using deception in the attempt to gain her escape, while Goethe's Iphigenie rejects deception and takes the road of Truth. But Goethe's conclusion is deeply Greek; more specifically, it is Aeschylean. In the *Oresteia*, Aeschylus confronts the characters, from the aftermath of the murder of Agamemnon onwards, with the question how the house of Atreus can escape the *daimon* or divine power, which appears to be driving it to destruction (*Agamemnon* 1560ff.). In the third and final drama, *Eumenides*, Orestes is eventually freed after suffering and time have given him the strength to withstand the Furies (276ff). Similarly, suffering and time have in Goethe's play given Iphigenie the strength to transcend the curse. Iphigenie finally persuades Thoas to honor his promise (1970ff) and allow her to leave by the integrity and power of her last two speeches (2146ff and 2151ff), which she delivers with the assumption of absolute equality between herself as a woman and Thoas as a man — an ideal which she declared to him at 1856ff. She presents herself at the end of the play neither as a submissive woman, nor as Orestes's lofty but passive inspirer of goodness, nor as an Amazonian aggressor. She is the perfect embodiment of Goethe's ideal of an equal and non-manipulative interaction between people of opposite sexes. In later life Goethe was to look back ruefully on this ideal as "devilishly humane,"[16] and indeed it has still not been generally attained in modern society; but Goethe's conception of the character of Iphigenie remains a compelling portrait of how a woman can become empowered.

UNIVERSITY OF NEWCASTLE, AUSTRALIA

Notes

1. Cf. Arkas at 1477ff. All translations from Goethe's *Iphigenie auf Tauris* are by Prudhoe, except the citations of 2142–3 and 2144ff, where I have supplied a more literal translation.

2. Cf. Prandi 1983:40 and Wagner 1988, *passim*.

3. Cf. Prandi 1983:13ff. For the "feminization" of classicist aesthetics in the late eighteenth century cf. Rigby 1996:133–4.

4. *Pace* e.g. Rigby 1996: 146–8, for whom (accepting Orestes' vision) it is her "feminine intuition, a kind of enlightenment grounded not in the abstract reason of the intellect, but in the intuitive reason of the heart" that gives Iphigeneia her strength. Rigby rightly notes the problems inherent in this idealizing and fetishing of women, but does not see that Goethe's play itself undermines the stance exemplified by Orestes. Cf. also Wagner 1988:234–58.

5. For her loneliness cf. Euripides *Iphigeneia among the Taurians* 220, "unmarried, childless, bereft of my native city and my relatives," and ff.

6. Note especially his argument that a young and forceful nation (Goethe is thinking of Germany rather than of ancient Tauria) needs the female quality of gentleness (*Milde*); 1476ff.

7. In Euripides, *Iphigeneia among the Taurians* 1017ff, Iphigenie displays initiative and cunning. For the Greeks, despite the mythological exemplar of Odysseus, cunning and deception were specifically female abilities, cf. 1032 "women are terrifyingly good (*deinai*) at finding means to an end." Aeschylus' Clytemnestra and Euripides' Medea are famous examples of deception used to less noble ends than Iphigeneia's.

8. Euripides hardly explores the past at all, after the prologue. But cf. 822ff; Pelops' murderous spear has somehow ended up as a souvenir in Iphigeneia's bedroom!

9. Herein lies Goethe's critique of tyranny and absolute monarchy: on 1810–1841 cf. Rasch 1979, 152–7.

10. Cf. 1677ff, where she briefly wishes for "a male heart," which once resolved is deaf to other voices.

11. Goethe obviously remembered how Euripides's Thoas, when Iphigeneia told him that one of the strangers had killed his mother, replied: 'Apollo, not even a barbarian would do that!' (Euripides *Iphigeneia among the Taurians* 1174). Borchmeyer (1981: 80) rightly compares Pasha Selim's reproach to Belmonte at the end of Mozart's *Die Entführung aus dem Serail.*

12. Borchmeyer 1981:68 draws the parallel with Pamina's answer to Papageno's "What are you going to tell Sarastro?"—"The truth! The truth! Even if it were a crime!" and Kant's description of lies as "crimes committed by a human being against his or her own self."

13. Rasch 1979, e.g., 161, 188.

14. Especially n.b. 1645ff (against Pylades); cf. Rasch 1979, 143–4.

15. Borchmeyer 1981:70 speaks of her as setting up a "Weibliches-Humanes Heldentum" to replace "des männlich-kriegerischen."

16. Goethe to Schiller, 10 January 1802.

References Cited

Borchmeyer, Dieter. "Johann Wolfgang von Goethe: Iphigenie auf Tauris." *Deutsche Dramen: Interpretationen zu Werken von der Aufklärung bis zur Gegenwart*, edited by Harro Müller-Michaels, 52–86. *Bd. 1: Von Lessing bis Grillparzer* Königstein/Ts.: Athenäum, 1981.

Goethe, Johann W. Von. *Iphigenia in Tauris.* Translated by John Prudhoe. Manchester: Manchester University Press, 1966.

Prandi, Julie D. *Spirited Women Heroes: Major Female Characters in the Dramas of Goethe, Schiller and Kleist.* Basel: Peter Lang, 1983.

Rasch, Wolfdietrich *Goethes Iphigenie auf Tauris als Drama der Autonomie.* Munich: Beck, 1979.

Rigby, Catherine E. *Transgressions of the Feminine: Tragedy, Enlightenment and the Figure of Woman in Classical German Drama.* Heidelberg, 1996.

Wagner, I. "Vom Mythos zum Fetisch: Die Frau aus Erlöserin in Goethes klassichen Dramen." *Weiblichkeit in historischer Perspektive*, edd. U.A.J. Becher and J. Rüsen, Frankfurt: Suhrkamp, 1988.

Mabou Mines
Stage Beckett, 1965–1975
The Discipline
of Word and Body

Iris Smith Fischer

Abstract

In Paris, in 1965, JoAnne Akalaitis, Lee Breuer, Philip Glass, Ruth Maleczech, and David Warrilow came together to work on Samuel Beckett's Play. *Using this and other texts as the basis for improvising a new kind of performance, in 1970 they returned to the United States and founded the theatre company Mabou Mines. While faithful to Beckett's words, the company did not adopt his view of the actor as interpreter. The Mabou actor is an artist in his or her own right, who uses the self as material for the work process. Beckett's stage directions created a discipline that allowed the actors to mine their own experience. In 1971, they took up* Play *again in lower Manhattan—then a bohemia of unsupervised, unstructured artistic experimentation. While often considered to be avant-garde in the sense of "undisciplined," Mabou Mines have fostered an artistic discipline, one that runs counter to conventional notions of authority, just as Beckett's texts do.*

Although the New York theatre company Mabou Mines has long been identified with its productions of Samuel Beckett's works, it would be a mistake to claim that these productions alone define the company. The founding members — JoAnne Akalaitis, Lee Breuer, Philip Glass, Ruth Maleczech, Fred Neumann,[1] and David Warrilow — set out to create original pieces using no fixed working method and adhering to no particular aesthetic. Mabou Mines' oeuvre is eclectic, from the performance art of *Arc Welding Piece* (1972) to the impressionistic *Dressed Like an Egg* (1977), adapted from texts by Colette; politically-oriented pieces such as *Dead End Kids* (1980, film 1986) and *Cold Harbor* (1983); the gender-reversed *Lear* (1990); the puppetry-rich *Peter & Wendy* (1996); and the darkly lyrical *Red Beads* (2005). The company's single most visible line of work has been writer-director Lee Breuer's ongoing vision of life in the United States, staged in several parts, most recently in *Summa Dramatica* (2005). Countering familiar realist notions of character and story, Breuer offers "choral narrations" that are "animated" by several actors using a variety of playful parodist, citational techniques. Between 1970 and 1978, the company produced a series of three Animations that established these techniques. They also established Mabou Mines as a distinctly American theatre whose productions emerge from an extended work process in collaboration with colleagues in dance, sculpture, painting, music, puppetry, and other performance traditions.

Set in this context, the company's productions of Beckett chronicle the development of the company's identity and working methods, as they emerged from youthful experiments in the 1960s. Mabou Mines used the discipline invoked by Beckett's spare language and setting, among other influences, to develop a performance discipline of their own. But Beckett was only one influence. His flattened, reduced characters do not resemble the extravagant personalities that populate the Animations. The company used techniques learned from the work of other writers, such as Jean Genet and Bertolt Brecht, and from productions they saw and created before the company formed in 1970. Sorting out Beckett's place and significance in Mabou Mines' initial work from these other influences is my purpose here.

In the 1970s Mabou Mines performed five Beckett texts: *Play* (1971, first performed 1967), *Come and Go* (1971), *The Lost Ones* (1975), *Cascando* (1976), and *Mercier and Camier* (1979). In more recent years, Mabou members have undertaken other Beckett pieces, many of them done outside the company, such as the controversial 1984 production of *Endgame* directed by JoAnne Akalaitis for the American Repertory Theatre. That Samuel Beckett attempted, through his representatives, to shut down that production has given the impression that he disapproved in general of Mabou Mines' productions of his plays. In fact, Beckett never explicitly opposed any production undertaken by the company and often lent them warm support. He wrote *A Piece of Monologue* for David Warrilow and provided suggestions to Fred Neumann for his productions of *Mercier and Camier, Company* (1983), and *Worstward Ho* (1986). These three, like *Cascando, The Lost Ones,* and *Imagination Dead Imagine* (1984), are prose texts Mabou Mines adapted for the stage.

Many actors find performing Beckett's plays (and adapting his prose) to be demanding, even severe; some have found a kind of discipline in his strictures on the actor's range of motion and speech. Discipline may seem a self-evident concept referencing the actor's physical and mental control and ability to reproduce words and gestures exactly. Before turning to Beckett's notion of discipline, though, it is important to point out that Mabou Mines already had acquired disciplinary habits before they formed the company or presented *Play*. In 1971 the members were largely in their thirties — young, but not blank slates. Maleczech, with Breuer, had begun doing experimental performance at UCLA in the late 1950s, where they had first read Beckett and Breuer had early success as a playwright in the style of Camus (Wetzsteon 1987:19–20). After working with the R.G. Davis Mime Troupe (later the San Francisco Mime Troupe) and the San Francisco Actor's Workshop in the first half of the 1960s, when they met Akalaitis, Breuer and Maleczech worked and traveled for five additional years in Europe, where Akalaitis introduced them to Glass, and where they saw the Living Theatre, the Berliner Ensemble, the Theatre Laboratory, and many others. By then the four of them knew they wanted the freedom to work for themselves. They hankered to be their own bosses, not forced to audition continually with directors or producers who might not recognize their credentials, but free to form a collaborative arrangement with each other, and with other artists of various backgrounds and talents. The place to do that work in 1970 was New York City. There they sought a form of artistic discipline congruent with that idea of self-determination. Although they did not embrace a single aesthetic, or seek to imitate an admired director, group, or writer (such as Beckett), they had done enough performance to understand that the work needed parameters. Thus, Mabou Mines did not seek to follow Beckett as *disciples* might follow a teacher. Their guide for performance discipline came from the downtown world of artists and performers who regularly witnessed and commented on each other's work. As Breuer noted, Mabou sought to combine the cool of downtown abstract art and music with the warm of motivational acting (Houston 1975). Indebted to the avant-garde, the downtown counterculture retained something of its militancy in rejecting middle-class values and behaviors. At the same time, the militancy of Mabou's notion of artistic discipline did not involve adopting any dogma.

The discipline invoked by Beckett's writing made sense to young artists working their way toward a new concept of performance. His work encouraged discipline without requiring dogma. Akalaitis, who had studied in the 1960s with a variety of acting teachers, found the Stanislavskian director-actor relationship manipulative and unproductive. She was ready for a different kind of discipline. Breuer and Maleczech had learned a great deal working with Herbert Blau in San Francisco. With Ronnie Davis Breuer had interesting discussions about Brecht. Maleczech took on a wide variety of roles, from commedia dell'arte to Genet's *The Balcony*. Rather than join an acting studio or enroll in a university theatre program, they sought to learn outside "the college box," as Breuer has called it (Wetzsteon 1987:19), in ways that may seem undisciplined in the current brass-hat world of degrees, head shots, and resumes. In 1970, seeking freedom and self-determination did not mean they did not engage in disciplined practices. As Beckett knew, the writer or actor must cultivate an "inner force" in each piece in order to operate on his or her own artistic terms. Speaking of his 1982 play *Catastrophe* as "an ironic portrayal of the discipline of theatrical production," Anna McMullan finds "it is also a defence of the play/writer/actor who ... has access to an inner force, which, within the moral order of the play, wins out" (McMullan 1994:205). Without adopting Beckett's view of life or his aesthetic, Mabou Mines learned much about cultivating an inner force by performing his work.

While faithful in presenting Beckett's words, the company did not adopt his view of the actor as interpreter. Then as now, Mabou treat the actor as an artist in his or her own right, one who uses the self as material for the work process. To trace the arc of Mabou Mines' early development as a company is to link the use of the self as material to the cultivating of each piece's inner force. Their first piece, *The Red Horse Animation* (1970), grew out of a lengthy collaboration. Maleczech, Akalaitis, and Warrilow performed the Red Horse working with text supplied by Breuer and music written by Glass, but the young horse's restless desire for a new sort of life came from all of them. For the company's second major piece, *The B. Beaver Animation* (1974), Breuer went back to a text he had written in 1968; he lured Neumann from Paris to join the new company and help develop the piece. Neumann played the figure of the stuttering, middle-aged B.Beaver, surrounded by a hooting, vamping chorus of his inner voices. As the company began to rehearse the third and longest piece, *The Shaggy Dog Animation* (1978) in the mid–1970s, it had become apparent that Breuer's insistence on animation as a focal technique of the young company had trumped other lines of inquiry. In each case the character was mined from the outlines of the company's lived experience, including the song lyrics and television personalities that attempted to shape popular desire. The company sought to put their own cultural experience on stage, and indeed all of Breuer's seems contained in *Shaggy Dog*, which can now be seen as the first piece of his continuing magnum opus.

Ironically, though, the company's reputation did not yet rest on this essential trilogy. While they toured *Red Horse* and *B.Beaver* to art galleries and universities around the country, they first came to the attention of the New York theatre world in 1975 after showing an evening of short pieces by Beckett. Praised by Jack Kroll of *Newsweek*, the productions of *Play, Come and Go,* and *The Lost Ones* set a series of events in motion that helped the company to stage *Shaggy Dog*, among other plays, at Joseph Papp's New York Shakespeare Festival. Mabou's reputation became linked in the public mind with Beckett. As Akalaitis, Neumann, and Maleczech began to direct, though, generating new lines of work for the company, Beckett was only one of several writers they sought to stage.

From the first, Mabou Mines were attracted to the precision and concreteness of Beckett's writing, but as many young actors and directors have found, they had to learn to let the texts lead them. As a student, Breuer was more interested in Genet and Camus, but when in 1962 Blau offered him the opportunity, he agreed to direct *Happy Days* at the San Francisco Actor's Workshop. *Happy Days* featured Beatrice Manley, one of the Workshop's repertory players, as Winnie. Breuer had assistant-directed for Manley's husband, Herbert Blau. Like Ronnie Davis, Breuer took on smaller productions at the Workshop's second space, the Encore Theatre, from 1960 to 1964. Pinter's *A Slight Ache* was followed the next year by the American premiere of *The Underpants* by Sternheim and Lorca's *The House of Bernarda Alba*. Outside the Workshop, he directed a production of Genet's *The Maids*. By Breuer's account, the earliest of these, *Happy Days*, was ultimately the least satisfying (Breuer 1993b). It took him longer to appreciate the density of signs that lay hidden in the spare language of Beckett. During rehearsals he had disagreed with Manley on the interpretation. She had wanted to create a thoroughly bourgeois figure, but the young writer-director viewed Winnie from a more literary point of view as a ghostly existential presence, and the play as a stark exploration of Man condemned to an increasingly foreshortened existence. Breuer's approach apparently met with approval (theatre critic Paine Knickerbocker described Manley's performance as an "acting triumph" [quoted in Fowler 1969:626]), but Breuer later realized that Manley had been right. He had misunderstood *Happy Days*, taking Winnie's apparent superficiality at face value (Breuer 1993b). Moreover, he had imposed a meaning on the production rather than allowing the inner force of the piece to present itself.

By the time they began work in Paris on *Play*, Breuer was beginning to appreciate the multiple levels of Beckett's irony (Breuer 1993b). The five unaffiliated artists explored the characters and then allowed psychology to fall away. The piece required three actors — a man (Warrilow as "m1") and two women (Maleczech as "w1" and Akalaitis as "w2") — to perform kneeling or standing in large urns, only their heads visible, much as Winnie is played fixed to the waist, and then the neck, in her mound. Maleczech remembers that the group approached the characters as a stereotypical Frenchman with both wife and mistress: "We worked on it exactly as you would a play, or maybe like you would a movie. We worked on it in an apartment with realistic acting and Stanislavsky-style objectives and character and emotional life and everything — all staged outside the urns" (Maleczech 2006). Maleczech sees the play dividing into two parts, the description of the characters' lives before they entered the urns and their life in them, subject to the inquisition of the light that shifts from face to face and compels their speech. At first the actors made no effort to speed up the lines, Maleczech recalls, but played the roles "exactly as though people were moving in and out of rooms, sitting at dressing tables, and doing their nails and so on" (Maleczech 2006).

Maleczech's description suggests that the group, starting from the familiar parameters of psychological realism and motivational acting, worked to remove such recognizable details from the performance, much as Beckett did in writing his texts.

> Beckett's instruction is to speak as rapidly as possible throughout, which we took to heart and did. Our version of the play was nineteen minutes long, twice through and beginning the third time. That's very, very fast.... We wanted to be sure that the underlying meanings and life and internal workings were in place so it wouldn't be empty conceptualizing.... If you've done a lot of good groundwork the residue of that work will be in the performance. And it was [Maleczech 2006].

In interviews Warrilow recalled the initial work on *Play* as a pleasurable, unpressured exploration of the script and the body.[2] Exploring a text through body and voice was a new, exhilarating experience for the literary editor. The group took their time laying bare the characters, devising the makeup to match the appearance of the urns, and learning how to convey each character's compressed passion without moving either the unseen body or the visible head.

Although it is easy for a reader to grasp the strained comedy of the love triangle, the immobility of those three touching urns belies the intimacy of the three characters' lives. To the audience their melodrama seems distant and foolish. The sense of the characters' individuality is obscured by each actor's lumpy, grayish makeup and hidden body, "the neck held fast in the urn's mouth" (Beckett 1964:9). That is not to say, however, that the words actually spoken do not have a delicate and important role to play in the spectacle. In fact, they do. Taken purely as a written text, the characters' lines, not surprisingly, are full of recriminations and one-sided recollections. Each head recounts events, producing clichéd scenes of confrontation that alternate between pairs of characters, although all voices are represented in the speaker's "narration." "'I smell her off you,' she kept saying," comments m1. The wife's words take on an ironic edge in the husband's voice; like the encapsulated bodies of the actors, the characters' melodrama is contained.

While the specifics of the dialogue never come into focus, the immediacy of the characters' suffering and the claustrophobic banality of their romantic triangle seem inescapable in the spectacle of the bodies trapped and displayed as objects before the audience. Bonnie Marranca wrote after seeing the play in 1975 at Theatre for the New City:

> Lee Breuer ... has captured the Beckettian landscape of lost souls in stunning *mise-en-scènes*. Front spotlights that first surface on the three horizontally aligned urns (designed by Jene Highstein) suggest the Byzantine icons of medieval art. The cascading flow of words that pour out of the mouths of husband, wife, and mistress in sequential monologues are interwoven and repeated endlessly, orchestrated by an inquisitory spotlight. The eternal triangle is doomed to repeat the banality of their soap-opera drama that only Beckett could give philosophical significance to by dividing it into two parts: the emptiness of the past and the now of recognition [Marranca 1975].

After they had presented *Play* in 1967 at the American Cultural Center on the rue de Dragon, they set aside the piece and went on to other interests, among them a staging of *Mother Courage*. When Akalaitis and Glass and then Breuer and Maleczech returned to the U.S., where Warrilow soon joined them, they took up *Play* again in 1971 in a very different environment. First, upon their return they had become a theatre company. As such, they became part of a community of artists who had turned Soho and the East Village into a bohemia of unsupervised, unstructured artistic experimentation. In their first production, *The Red Horse Animation*, they subversively explored the human experience — specifically, their own. Early on, they improvised on Tina Girouard's sculpture at the 112 Greene Street gallery for *The B.Beaver Animation*. They saw work done in various unstructured spaces. In this minimalist and conceptualist performance context, Beckett's insistence on the discipline of word and body began to make a different kind of sense to them. In artistic terms, Mabou were cultivating a discipline of their own. They combined motivational acting with the techniques of what was becoming known as performance art. What resulted was a unique juxtaposition of representation and abstraction that seemed (in the words of one observer) "to make the audience *concentrate*, as if its vision were framed by a lens, not on people as speakers but on objects in the space, be they people or things" (Houston 1975). In other words, they subjected the audience to a kind of discipline. It was Brechtian, in that the framing distanced the audience from the characters (as did Beckett's fast pacing). This approach fit well with the discipline required of the actors in *Play*.

As a company Mabou Mines returned to *Play* less out of an interest in rethinking the piece than in expanding their repertoire. The rehearsals for *Red Horse* had taken most of a year. Ellen Stewart, who had taken the young company under the wing of La Mama, paid them regular salaries, provided rehearsal space, and underwrote the cost of the set's acoustic floor. The experiences of the past four years, though, brought new dimensions to the Beckett work. For example, in Europe Breuer and Maleczech had seen the Berliner Ensemble at work. Akalaitis and Glass had talked with Julian Beck and Judith Malina after watching their production of *Frankenstein*. Perhaps, most importantly, Maleczech and Akalaitis had taken a two-week workshop with Jerzy Grotowski and Richard Cieslak in 1969. As a result, Beckett's bottled-up *comédie* lost its French context for Mabou, and, when they began to rehearse, the company did not repeat their Stanislavskian exercises.

Instead, psychology was replaced by Grotowskian techniques that extended Stanislavsky, mixing warm and cool in the animation of the characters. The company did not consciously employ Grotowskian techniques, but in the two years since the workshop, they had made their way into the work process, as Maleczech and Akalaitis taught what they had learned to the others. Mabou were careful to separate Grotowski's technique from his aesthetic, which they did not adopt:

> Lee and I did go to see his work in Poland and saw what the aesthetic was really — kind of angst-ridden, Second World War — no postmodernism, virtually no art-world content to it at all. It was largely Biblically based.... But the core was that you could extend Stanislavsky beyond a kind of American movie-acting level of performance — realism, or naturalism even. You could push the boundaries of that into other areas, areas that could include great extensions of motion and physicality. That was what was important about Grotowski (for us) [Maleczech 2006].

Akalaitis and Maleczech had discovered in Grotowski's discipline, rather than in his dogma, a way to explore and create through bodily movement. He had extended Stanislavsky, by allowing them to find compressed in the urns not "a version of behavior, a version of realism," with its focus on the recognizable patterns and tiny details of daily life, but the larger human story. Maleczech recalls having to restrain herself from pressing forward in the urn as she spoke, in order to re-channel the realist, Stanislavskian impulse into her voice and the impossible speed of the words. The actors projected an "affective athleticism," a concept used by Antonin Artaud and found in Grotowski's work as well. Artaud had in mind forces channeled through the actor's body and released in part through the voice, which could be used as a musical instrument or transmitter of sound images. In *Play* this athleticism communicated the actor's energy entirely through the breath channeled through the unseen torso. For this reason, I believe, Beckett's stage directions instruct the actors to kneel or stand, rather than sit, in the urns. The actor's physical discomfort contributes directly to the play's impression of anxious, fragmented subjectivity.[3]

Akalaitis, speaking to an interviewer in 1976, identified Grotowski as the teacher who had encouraged her to think of herself differently as an actor: "It is very important to me that Grotowski said that an actor is as much an artist as a writer, a painter, as the playwright — that he's not an interpreter" (Akalaitis 1976:6). Akalaitis noted that, as a result, she did not work to please the director or the audience but "for the piece." In regard to how she approached character through physical action and task, Akalaitis described a breaking down of the Enlightenment distinction between self and world that seemed to owe as much to the company's work with Beckett's texts as to Grotowski's techniques:

> I notice in rehearsal that there is an idea ... executed physically. I do not mean in terms of movement, but in terms of changing your body. And when you change your body, you change your face, ... your voice.... I go beyond myself one more level, and keep looking at myself, and try to get a picture of someone, and then try to fill in the picture *through myself*. It's like you project something, like a slide on a wall and try to fit yourself into it.... You put yourself in a physical posture, and it changes your voice — and it begins to change the way you feel [Akalaitis:1976:8–9].

A literal example of this technique occurred in Mabou's production of Beckett's "dramaticule" *Come and Go*, first developed in 1971. Once again, Breuer directed Maleczech and Akalaitis. The third character, however, was played first by Dawn Gray, whom they had met in San Francisco, and later by Ellen McElduff, who began working with the company in 1974. Maleczech describes a process by which the actor linked the words to images from the actor's past, while the audience viewed the actors literally as images framed in a mirror, Breuer's addition to the piece. The actors performed behind the audience, at a spot from which their image would be visible in the mirror. It was as though the audience was "spying through a telescope, or down Alice's rabbit hole, at a shimmering trio clustered on a park bench" (Gussow 1975:46). Just as *Play* used a spotlight (run by Breuer) to compel speech from each figure, *Come and Go* constrained and distanced the movement of the three figures by framing them in the mirror's rectangle, as though they were "birds on a branch" (Breuer 1993a). Each character harbors a secret, which she shares with one of her companions while the character about whom the secret is told is off-stage. The character rejoins her friends, and the sequence is repeated twice, the roles changing each time. Thus, physically and narratively, the piece comprises a series of interlocking circles. In the final moments, the three figures join their hands in an elaborate pattern: "I can feel the rings," says one, but as Beckett notes in his stage directions, "No rings are apparent" (Beckett 1984:194, 196). As in *Play*, any differences that might suggest individual, realist characters fade in the more formal counterpoint of the movement, colors, and voices. As McElduff comments:

> [The costumes] were long, Victorian style coats. Mine was purple, Ruth's was a kind of burnt orangy-red — these were very dull colors — and JoAnne's was kind of a yellow-green color, kind of a gold. We all had small hats [with] feathers [and] veils, just the kind that cover your eyes.... It was all very small and faded in a way.... One actress would lean towards the actress sitting immediately next to her and whisper in her ear and then go back.... When the whispering started, when one would lean over to the other, it was kind of a little quick movement, a birdlike movement.... Unless you were whispering to someone, your hands were folded in your lap, except at the very end of the play ... [when] we were all touching hands. It was, I think, a beautiful image [McElduff 1994].

Maleczech notes that, while the actors did not excavate their characters, as they had done in 1965 with *Play*, she recalls the use of secrets, a Stanislavsky exercise, to inform the "tiny responses" the characters have to one another as the tension and awkwardness grows among them. In order to project themselves into the frame of the mirror, the actors used images from their own experience to shape body and voice (Maleczech 2006). Moreover, because the actors were positioned behind the audience, they had to project their voices backwards, in a sense through the backs of their heads, so the audience did not sense their presence and break their concentration on the framed images before them. For McElduff, the visual focus in the mirror was complemented by the aural icon of the actors' voices. Breuer wanted a crying sound to emerge from the whispered lines, just "lips with a sibilant sound behind it." In the silences, he added a cooing which, in response to a cue light, the actors made in the top of their throats — a quick, delicate, almost inaudible pulsing that evoked the sound of birds or of crying and then, at the removal of the light, faded into silence once again (McElduff 1994).

Similarly, *Play* provided several frames into which the actors projected themselves and their experience. Chief among them was the inquisitorial light which compelled the characters' confessions. With the constraints imposed by the three urns and Beckett's stage directions regarding spatial relations and the actors' posture, the precise movements of the spotlight reinforced the discipline of Grotowski's techniques. Thus, while Grotowski freed

Mabou Mines from authorial intent, apparently in direct collision with Beckett's expectation of adherence to textual "author-ity," yet in the work process the two disciplines meshed well. Mabou had made no changes in Beckett's text. The New York production may have hewed more closely to Beckett's direction not to allow the characters' emotions to spill over into a growing intensity in the words and the lighting. Intonations and expressions remained even and precise, as Beckett had specified. The company also removed several musical phrases written by Glass in 1965 to appear at random moments in the piece. Breuer recalls:

> [Philip] produced four or five alto or soprano saxophone phrases that were rather abstract, ... on a tape. [Y]ou wouldn't know precisely where they would come in. They were like another voice ... a contextual voice.... So there was this variable that when an actor was speaking with this music behind him, they would have an emotional quality that would be different from another time. It was like a little air in the piece [Breuer 1993b].

For Maleczech the music had added little to her experience: "It was like an element that went through the play, like the wind or the rain. That's the way I related to it. I was never able to take it into account rhythmically, for example.... So I treated it as though it were a natural element" (Maleczech 2006). Although Maleczech regrets not being able to take advantage of the music, it appears that the randomness of the phrases tended to work against the willful rhythm set up by the light. In New York, Breuer counted out music beats for Beckett's punctuation: one count for a comma, two, a semicolon; three, a period; four, an ellipsis. Mabou recognized that the artist's acquired sense of discipline is the necessary guide. As actor Brenda Bynum — not a Mabou member — has said, "The rules give you the freedom" (quoted in McMullan 1994:202).

Mabou Mines acquired another form of discipline from the Berliner Ensemble, whom they had observed at work in the late 1960s. Mabou's rehearsals were and are more public and dialogic, indeed more raucous, than those of the Theatre Laboratory. It was crucial to develop the work under the gaze of their colleagues — each other. Projecting an image, an "other," which the actor then attempts to become, suggests the Lacanian search for wholeness described by Anna McMullan as integral to Beckett's later plays (McMullan 1993). In Mabou's work, however, the actor's anxiety about that projected image is modified by the experience of trying on its behaviors in the course of the work, done not in isolation, but in concert with the rest of the company. As Beckett found writing to be an activity both painful and essential, one with which he could not go on and yet did go on, so the work process for Mabou Mines was the essential activity, allowing the actors to take on externalized images, postures, and utterances.

The most complete expression of this form of discipline occurred in Mabou Mines' 1975 evening of Beckett, which brought together for the first time their productions of *Play* and *Come and Go* with a new production, *The Lost Ones*. In this celebrated evening, as McMullan claims for Beckett's later plays in general, "the performer's body is ... at the intersection of resistance and subjection of the will to authority and control which Beckett both parodies and enacts" (McMullan 1994:203). Now McMullan's earlier point can be quoted in full: "[Beckett's] portrayal of the discipline of theatrical production ... is also a defence of the play/writer/actor who, *due to his/her subjection to (and therefore non-exercise of) political or actantial power,* has access to an inner force, which, within the moral order of the play, wins out" (205; italics mine).

David Warrilow's performance in *The Lost Ones* sought to cultivate that inner force. Breuer and Warrilow had adapted the text in three weeks from the story Beckett published in 1970. Thom Cathcart designed a cylindrical playing space that evoked the confining dimensions in which the Lost Ones live. Warrilow performed only inches from the spectators who shared the cramped cylinder. The actor's own concentration and disciplined awareness of the body seemed to contribute directly to the spectator's engagement, as Ruby Cohn describes:

> Shoeless, the spectators enter a dark foam-rubber cylindrical space in which tiers of foam-padded steps are built from floor to ceiling. An ugly sulfurous glow emanates from the sides of the steps, but spotlights follow Warrilow around the cylindrical playing area. Electronic music by composer Philip Glass approximates the text's "faint stridulence as of insects." Cutting Beckett's text by a third, Warrilow graduates from a dry and seedy academic clinically observing a small cylinder to a naked human essence who draws an equation between the tiny celluloid dolls and ourselves, but his involvement deviates, mesmerizing us to its changes. In various dull lights ... he recites Beckett's text, his voice a resonant stringed instrument. After about half the playing time, but quite late in Beckett's text, as the temperature rises in *our* fetid cylinder, Warrilow removes his clothes to enact the several torments of the cylinder's inhabitants [Cohn 1987:176].

It appears that Warrilow focused from the first on the demands of the text, letting it inform his choices, rather than excavating the psychology of the Lost Ones. He did not engage in the "forfeiting" of character that he and his fellow actors had undertaken in their first rehearsals for *Play.* Speaking of Hildegard Schmahl, who had similarly researched the characters of May and her mother for the German production of *Footfalls,* Jonathan Kalb comments that she only "succeeded [in the role] by means of a radical self-denial" (Kalb 1989:64). Under Beckett's direction, Schmahl focused instead on the externalities of the role.

This orientation allows a clear and unsentimental image to develop, for both the actor and audience: "An artificial immovability develops; a tauter articulation takes over the soft, agreeable modulation. A concentrated creation of art does indeed emerge, a cold, stiff encapsulated being; the 'being for itself' of the figure comes across" (Asmus 1986:344). The clarity of this stage image makes it possible to see how the parts of Beckett's play relate to one another. Just as Schmahl's concentration was enhanced, the onlooker (in this case, Asmus) found himself fully engaged in the action. The actor's own concentration and disciplined awareness of the body seem to contribute directly to the spectator's interest, in spite of the fact that actor and spectator may be focusing on somewhat different aspects of the action. Kalb praises Warrilow as one such "inadvertent interpreter" of Beckett:

> Warrilow *does* think about text, but does not use those thoughts consciously to motivate his performance. He internalizes them, makes them a part of his general attitude toward the play; one might say that he translates them, in a way, into musical terms, becoming a kind of informed instrument.... It's as if actors were required to undergo a two-step process in which the second step cancels the first: analyze the text as a conventional play, and then push that knowledge to the back of your mind in order to concentrate on the verbal music. But [Warrilow does] not need to work at forfeiting character because he never consciously adopt[s] recognizable personalities to fit decided-upon ideas about text [Kalb 1989:61].

What made *The Lost Ones* so memorable that spectators still mention it thirty years later? Warrilow did not assume his character's essence before he began; rather, he stayed on the surface of the role, focusing on its external qualities and projecting himself into a moving, if unsentimental image. Beckett's narrative suggests that such a whole being does not exist within the walls of the cylinder. It is merely "the ideal preying on one and all" (Beckett 1972:21). As Warrilow shifted from ironic academic narration to the embodiment of a Lost One, the audience felt themselves Lost Ones as well. There was probably a moment in this experience, as there was in the production of *Play*, when the audience's gaze subjected Warrilow's body to an unendurable form of discipline — unendurable, in this case, not for Warrilow, but for the audience. Their complex, difficult position of surveillance undermined the authority of their position as watching subjects, and thus the distinction between themselves and the objectified actor. In this way, Mabou Mines found the inner force of *The Lost Ones*, which put the human subject, as McMullan puts it, "on trial." It is not surprising that a long silence often followed the performance, as spectators struggled to deal with the piece's powerful rearrangement of their understanding.

Mabou Mines sought to cultivate the inner force of the actor, by using artistic discipline to counter conventional notions of authority, just as Beckett's texts do. Although the company was only half a decade old in 1975, their long years of work together, in some cases since the late 1950s, had begun to bear remarkable fruit. Breuer's youthful, rather academic notion of *Happy Days*, followed by a work process on *Play* that began with French sexual comedy and ended by forfeiting character, had profited by the development of the company's own sense of artistic purpose and discipline with the Animations. In 1975, why did Mabou's evening of Beckett make such an impression? As suggested earlier, discipline, when embraced, produces readiness. Mabou Mines presented mature work, brilliantly conceived and executed, a clear example of the company's readiness to use themselves fully as material for performance.

UNIVERSITY OF KANSAS

Notes

Acknowledgments. I'd like to thank the members of Mabou Mines, both present and former, who took the time to provide essential information and answer my many interview questions; the *Text and Presentation* readers for their helpful comments; the members of the Performance & Culture Seminar, sponsored by the Hall Center for the Humanities at the University of Kansas, where I presented a related paper on Mabou's early productions of Beckett; my colleagues and friends Vicky Unruh and Janet Sharistanian, for their insights and support throughout the writing of the longer project to which this article is related; and Hans J. Fischer, for his patience and encouragement.

1. I include Fred Neumann here because, although technically he joined the company in 1971, a year after its founding, he had worked with these five in Paris in the late 1960s and was part of the company's early plans.

2. Quoted in Lassiter 1985:3. Warrilow, who had been working in Paris as a literary editor, had been considered for roles in two Beckett productions despite his lack of acting experience. First approached to join a production of *Endgame* in 1962 (at which time he met Beckett briefly), he had later joined rehearsals for an American production of *Godot* for a short time. Although he did not perform in either production, Warrilow felt himself "bitten" by the acting bug and ultimately left the literary life to join Mabou Mines in 1970.

3. Beckett inconveniences the actors apparently out of concern for the urns' appearance, which should be tall and slim. Maleczech noted in our conversation, though, that for the restaging Highstein designed the urns, without altering their appearance, so the pregnant Akalaitis could sit (Maleczech 2006).

References Cited

Ackerley, Chris, and S. E. Gontarski. *The Grove Companion to Samuel Beckett: A Reader's Guide to His Works, Life, and Thought*. New York: Grove Press, 2004.

Akalaitis, JoAnne. Interview by Sally M. Sommer. *TDR* 20, No. 3 (1976): 3–16.

Asmus, Walter. "Rehearsal Notes for the German Premiere of Beckett's 'That Time' and 'Footfalls,'" in *On Beckett: Essays and Criticism.* Edited by S. E. Gontarski. New York: Grove Press, 1986.

Beckett, Samuel. *Play and Two Shorter Pieces for Radio.* London: Faber and Faber, 1964.

_____. *The Lost Ones.* New York: Grove Weidenfeld, 1972.

_____. *Collected Shorter Plays.* New York: Grove Weidenfeld, 1984.

Breuer, Lee. Telephone interview by the author. November 20 and 22, 1993. [1993a]

_____. Telephone interview by the author. December 14, 1993. [1993b]

Cohn, Ruby. "Mabou Mines' Translations of Beckett." In *Beckett Translating/Translating Beckett,* edited by Alan Warren Friedman, et al. University Park, PA, and London: Pennsylvania State University Press, 1987.

Fowler, Keith Franklin. *A History of the San Francisco Actor's Workshop.* Ph.D. dissertation, Yale School of Drama, 1969.

Gussow, Mel. "Mabou Mines Inhabits Beckett Landscapes on Jane St.," *The New York Times,* 23 October 1975.

Houston, Gary. "They Mix Acting and Performing." *Chicago Sun-Times,* April 27, 1975.

Kalb, Jonathan. *Beckett in Performance.* Cambridge: Cambridge University Press, 1989.

Lassiter, Laurie. "David Warrilow: Creating Symbol and Cypher," *TDR* (T108) 29.4 (1985): 3–12.

Maleczech, Ruth. Telephone interview with the author. August 8, 2006.

Marranca, Bonnie. "There, There, and There." *The Soho Weekly News,* October 23, 1975.

McElduff, Ellen. Telephone interview with the author. February 11, 1994.

McMullan, Anna. "Beckett as Director: The Art of Mastering Failure." In *The Cambridge Companion to Beckett,* edited by John Pilling, 196–208. Cambridge: Cambridge University Press, 1994.

_____. *Theatre on Trial: Samuel Beckett's Later Drama.* New York and London: Routledge, 1993.

Wetzsteon, Ross. "Wild Man of the American Theater," *The Village VOICE,* May 18, 1987.

Stoppard vs. Brecht
Competing Visions of Galileo
John Fleming

Abstract

Galileo Galilei (1564–1642) stands as a pivotal historical figure in the development of Western civilization and modern scientific thought. To theatre audiences, Galileo's story is best known via Bertolt Brecht's play Life of Galileo. *Viewing Brecht's presentation as a materialist manipulation of Galileo's story, Tom Stoppard, in the early 1970s, crafted a more historically accurate play version of Galileo's life and conflict with the Catholic Church. Stoppard's previously lost (and still unpublished and unproduced) play is examined here for the ways in which his liberal humanist sensibilities offer a more positive image of Galileo that rebuts Brecht's more negative, Marxist-influenced view. By examining each author's selection of events and interpretation of Galileo's actions, their respective ideologies and biases result in Brecht's condemnation of Galileo versus Stoppard's admiration of him.*

While it is well known that Bertolt Brecht wrote three versions of *Life of Galileo*, few people are aware that in the early 1970s Tom Stoppard wrote a play about Galileo. Based on his own unproduced screenplay, Stoppard's *Galileo* was partly intended as a rebuttal to Brecht's depiction of Galileo as an anti-hero whose recantation was a betrayal of society. Stoppard believed that "Brecht's play was nonsensical in certain historical respects," and so he wanted to write a version that "would be essentially faithful to history"(Letter to Peter Bart 1971).[1] Stoppard intended his play for production at the London Planetarium, but the project was shelved, and the manuscript was removed from circulation until it was delivered to the University of Texas's Harry Ransom Humanities Research Center in the 1990s.[2] *Galileo* stands as the only unproduced, unpublished stage work of Stoppard's post–*Rosencrantz* career.

While both Brecht and Stoppard are writing "history plays," what they choose to cover and how they cover those events reveal their reflective biases and ideology. Stoppard's metaphysical position stands in stark contrast to Brecht's materialist view of life. This fundamental disparity in worldviews, liberal humanist versus Marxist, helps account for the divergent presentations of Galileo. Through his successive revisions, Brecht turned Galileo into an anti-hero, a "social criminal" whose recantation was a traitorous act against humanity. In contrast, Stoppard, likely drawing on Gerhard Szczesny's *The Case against Bertolt Brecht*, views Galileo in a more positive light and seeks to redress some of Brecht's historical distortions.

In 1970 Paramount Pictures hired Stoppard to write a screenplay loosely based on Brecht's play *Life of Galileo*.[3] Stoppard wrote two drafts, but the screenplay was ultimately rejected. Stoppard's rebuttal to Paramount's rejection indicates his approach to Galileo's story, the same approach he would take when he converted the script into a stage play. Stoppard writes:

> If growing jeopardy and personal ordeal were the keynotes of Galileo's story you would have every right to complain, and clearly your complaint springs from such an expectation, as though Galileo were a man who from the beginning put his life on the line (for Conscience, truth, and so on) and who was in constant danger from the Inquisition until, finally, they got him. But the equally interesting truth is that Galileo was a brilliant man of wide scientific interest who, living in a time of transition between the medieval and modern ages, was a gregarious irritant to disputing scholars and clerics of older persuasions, but who was widely admired and celebrated for most of his life until he took a calculated risk in publication and was brought down (rather gently for that time) because political considerations triumphed over Reason. He was a man who knew that Reason would triumph in the end but he was careful to test the wind and indeed stayed safe in Venice [for a number of years] emerging to be applauded by the Church. He did not leave himself open to serious attack until [later], and the [initial] attack failed. Certainly there was opposition, as is widely indicated throughout the script, but Galileo was a man who took some care not to put himself in jeopardy, who "played the system," was attractive, witty, irreverent and proud, but who finally miscalculated [Letter to Peter Bart 1971].

Stoppard viewed Galileo favorably and his sense that Galileo made a tactical error in judgment stands in contrast to Brecht's negative judgment of Galileo and thus his intended portrait of Galileo as an "anti-hero."

While Brecht follows his usual pattern of dividing his plays into discreet scenes, each with its own summarizing caption and *gestus*, Stoppard's script is cinematic as it flows freely among events and locations as it spans from 1600 to Galileo's recantation in 1633. A diligent researcher, Stoppard freely admits that his script "does not wear its research lightly" (Fax to Michael Eisner 1993),[4] and indeed in presenting Galileo's story, Stoppard emphasizes documentary "fact" over narrative suspense. Like a documentary filmmaker, Stoppard uses a narrator to inform the audience about the background and significance of the various historical figures. Stoppard's main use of poetic license is the creation of the character Father Colombe. The play's Narrator explains that Colombe "is a fictitious person" who is based on "a real-life pursuer of Galileo" and that this character will "represent the various clerics and teachers who opposed the new astronomy" (1.19).[5] Throughout the play, Stoppard's narrator notes when and how the play deviates from the historical record. In other plays Stoppard problematizes history and historical accounts, but here the Narrator speaks with a sense of omniscience. Likewise, instead of creating Brechtian alienation, this breaking of the fourth wall asserts the authority of the author. It is the confident voice of the historian, stating: "I have done the research, and this is how things were." It might also be a subtle critique of Brecht in that Brecht presents his play as history, while never acknowledging deviations from the historical record.

Any history play inevitably involves selection and interpretation, and how each playwright handles Galileo's "invention" of the telescope highlights their different approaches. In Brecht's play, Galileo steals the invention outright, and the focus is on Galileo as opportunist who financially profits by claiming the telescope as his own invention. In Stoppard's play, Galileo's source does not know all the details, and so Galileo must deduce the scientific principles necessary to create a device that makes distant objects appear closer. Stoppard proceeds to ignore the ways Galileo profited from his deception, but instead emphasizes the fact that Galileo created a telescope of much greater power; in fact, he created the first telescope capable of astronomical observations.[6] Each writer includes aspects of the historical event, but Brecht's emphasis is on the economic/material issues of the incident while Stoppard's is on the qualities that made Galileo a scientific genius. These patterns of selection and emphases are repeated throughout their respective plays.

While the focus of each play is Galileo, Brecht continually uses Galileo's work as a means of exposing the material conditions that lead to specific choices and actions. In Scene 12, Brecht aptly shows the hypocrisy of the church when economic benefits are at stake:

> INQUISITOR: The north Italian ship owners keep clamoring for Mr. Galilei's
> star charts. We shall have to yield to them, since material interests are involved.
> POPE: But these star charts are based on his heretical statements, on
> the movements of certain heavenly bodies which become impossible if his doctrine is rejected. You can't reject the doctrine and accept the star charts.
> INQUISITOR: Why not? It's the only solution [80].

The Church's pragmatic solution richly characterizes Brecht's materialist view of human behavior and the power structures that govern society.

In addition to wanting to focus on events that offer the opportunity for reflection on social and economic issues, Brecht's revisions continually strove to make Galileo a less sympathetic character. Commenting on the first draft of his play, Brecht stated: "It was my purpose to depict the heroic struggle of Galileo in support of his modern scientific conviction that the earth moves" (quoted in Szczesny 1969:9). Via his collaboration with the actor Charles Laughton this initial characterization of Galileo as a "fighter for progress" gradually gave way to a portrayal that was to show him as "a vain and cowardly sensualist and opportunist" (Szczesny 1969:10–11).

While neither playwright delves much into Galileo's personal life, Brecht's desire to cast Galileo in a less favorable light includes a wholly invented courtship between his daughter Virginia and a wealthy merchant. Notably, in Brecht's first version, Virginia recognizes her fiancé's narrow-mindedness, and so she herself breaks off her engagement. In the revision, Galileo is the force that ends the engagement and in the words of another character Galileo is "trampling on his daughter's happiness" (*Life of Galileo* 1956:67).[7] Virginia's subsequent reproach of her father and his indifference to her fainting add to the depiction of a selfish, unfeeling father.

Brecht's assertion that Galileo "neglected to instruct" his daughter ("Building up a Part" 1956:255) is aptly countered by Stoppard's more accurate depiction of Galileo taking an active part in his daughter's education. Stoppard also accurately notes that Virginia entered a convent at a young age, and that father and daughter remained close throughout their lives. Near the end of his life Galileo wrote: "I loved my daughters dearly, particularly [Virginia] who had outstanding talents of the intellect associated with a rare goodness of the heart. She was deeply attached to me.... [and her premature death has left] me behind in profound sorrow" (quoted in Szczesny 1969:106). The trauma of her father's trial and recantation undermined Virginia's health, and she died less than a year after Galileo was placed under house arrest.

Since Brecht uses Virginia as a vehicle to portray Galileo in a negative light, it is not surprising that Virginia is pivotal to another revision equally unfavorable to Galileo. In the original version of Scene 14 (where Galileo is under house arrest), Virginia is seen recording a passage from the *Discorsi*, Galileo's groundbreaking physics book that covers the laws of movement and the behavior of solids. Written while under house arrest, the completion and dissemination of the *Discorsi* is seen as a positive result of Galileo's recantation. However, while working with Brecht on a second version of the play the actor Charles Laughton insisted on "a scene in which Galileo collaborates before the eyes of the audience with the powers that be" ("Building up a Part" 1956:256), and so the content of the dictation between father and daughter was changed. Instead of hearing a passage from the *Discorsi*, Galileo now dictates a submissive letter to the Archbishop in which he advises him on how the Bible can be used to oppress workers upset with low wages.

At the same time that Brecht added this depiction of Galileo as actively cooperating with the suppression of the poor, he removed the historically accurate account of Galileo's frequently getting his writings smuggled out of the house. Indeed, in real life, only a month after his recantation Galileo successfully sent a copy of *Dialogues*, his banned book, to a scholar "in Strasbourg with the request to have a Latin translation of it prepared and published" (Szczesny 1969:106). Within two years of his arrest *Dialogues* was published in both Latin and English editions, and he corresponded with scholars throughout Europe. In Brecht's first version, an ordinary craftsman was Galileo's co-conspirator in the dangerous practice of smuggling out his manuscripts. Thus, Brecht's initial impulse of Galileo and the average citizen joined in opposition to the power of the church gave way to an image of Galileo as enemy of the common man.

This alteration is in keeping with Brecht's other major revision. In all versions, Galileo's disciple Andrea is the one who smuggles out the *Discorsi*. In the first version, Brecht agreed with Andrea's view that "[Galileo's] recantation had given him the chance to create a seminal work. He had been wise" ("Notes" 1956:230). However, in his revisions, Brecht added Galileo's self-condemnation, the belief that he is a treasonous criminal who has betrayed society. In Brecht's own words, "Galileo's crime can be regarded as the 'original sin' of modern natural sciences" ("Praise or Condemnation" 1947:225).

While Brecht focuses on Galileo's "social crimes" and the material implications of his choices and actions, Stoppard emphasizes metaphysical issues and Galileo's restless inquisitiveness. Stoppard's play begins with a Narrator who establishes the scene in 1600 on the day that the Copernican, and thus heretic, Giordano Bruno was executed. Throughout the play, Bruno is used as the touch point for whenever someone wants to warn Galileo of the danger he faces in contradicting Church teaching. The debate between the Copernican and Aristotelian view of the universe is not just a scientific debate, it is political, philosophical, and religious. Believing that scientific proof will change the Church's mind, Galileo asserts: "Bruno burned because he could not prove what he asserted. But when the senses apprehend what the reason demands, then no man need fear for the truth" (1.15). Embodying the traits of the modern scientific era, Galileo is convinced that truth and reason will prevail.

The teenage Prince Cosimo presses the issue of whether Galileo is willing to die for his beliefs, but Galileo responds: "I believe in reason. And it is not reasonable to die for that. That would be a defeat. It proves nothing. The reasonable act is to live for the victory of reason, for if God's hopes in us are to be justified it will be in the ultimate triumph of reason over prejudice" (1.16). Whereas Brecht positioned Galileo's eventual recantation as a betrayal of truth, science, and humankind, Stoppard's Galileo views events through a more pragmatic lens, arguing that there would be nothing to be gained from martyrdom. His death would not change anything, and he can better serve humanity by engaging in what scientific research he can. Thus, as a man of reason, it is more reasonable to go on living.

In Brecht's version, Galileo's self-condemnation includes the lines: "I have betrayed my calling. A man who does what I have done, cannot be tolerated in the ranks of science" (94). In contrast Szczesny argues: "Scholars throughout Europe accepted Galileo's submission. They knew the power of the church and had no desire to have the great man fall silent as a hero and martyr at the stake or in prison. They were more interested in having him complete his work. Their resentment, their indignation, and their contempt were leveled at Rome, not at Galileo" (107).

In line with Szczesny's research, Stoppard's Galileo is a practical man with great survival skills. He is also a champion of reason and observation. Stoppard shows the delicate balancing act Galileo engaged in throughout his life via a speech he gave in 1605 in which he declared: "[T]he laws of nature are not written in the language of philosophy, they are written in mathematics!" (1.18). This statement that mathematics is the language of the Creator and the key to humanity's understanding of the universe causes an uproar. The Narrator explains: "It was an idea which he did not dare publish for another twenty years: to churchmen it seemed to say that God was a mere mathematician, but to Galileo it said that mathematics was divine" (1.19). Indeed, later in Act One a character remarks: "Science and theology will always find a way to dance together to the music of the universe, because time, which will reveal all truth, is infinite. But politics are matters of the moment" (1.28).[8] Here, as elsewhere in Stoppard's canon, science and religion are presented not as adversaries, but as corollaries, arguing that God has a scientific mind. Thus, where Brecht selects events for their viability of commenting on social class issues, Stoppard seeks out the aspects of Galileo's story that offer the possibility of joining science and theology.

Dramatically, as well as historically, Galileo remains a devout member of the Church who continually believes that his scientific findings reaffirm the glory of God and his creation. However, Galileo errs when he tries too forcefully to articulate the validity of a metaphorical, as opposed to literal, reading of the Bible. The Narrator notes that "Galileo's letters on the subject of Biblical authority [were] in the perspective of history, ... the moment when Galileo made his first, and ultimately crucial, tactical error" (2.9). Stoppard weaves Galileo's views into a banquet scene where there is the following exchange:

> BACCINI: Yet it is written in the Bible, "The World also shall be stable, that it be not moved."
> GALILEO: But who wrote it?
>   (It is as though he had slapped them across the face....)
> BARBERINI: That was not prudent, Signor. Do not play the theologian.
> GALILEO: And let not the theologians play the scientist.
> CHRISTINA: Signor Galileo, can the scriptures be in error?
> GALILEO: The scriptures cannot be in error, your Serene Highness, but its expounders and interpreters can err in many ways, and the most frequent is to invest in the words of scripture a literal meaning which they may not always bear.... We cannot be certain that all previous interpreters have been divinely inspired — Lactantius, a most religious scholar, expounded that the Earth was flat. (Defiantly) It would be prudent if men were forbidden to employ passages of scripture for the purpose of sustaining what demonstrable proof contradicts [2.13–14].

Dramatically, as well as historically, Galileo believes that the Copernican system can be reconciled with belief in the Bible. Those who fear the ramifications of a Copernican view rely on a strict, literal interpretation, whereas Galileo believes that the demonstrable proofs of science simply showed the grandeur and beauty of God's creation.

Stoppard proceeds to show the delicate balancing act that both Galileo and the Church engaged in over a number of years. Galileo's comments at the banquet make it back to Church officials, but they decide that directly confronting Galileo carries unnecessary risks. Instead, in 1616, the Church rules on Copernicus, officially censuring and prohibiting the expression of the Copernican worldview. Pope Paul V considers making the resolution official dogma, but Cardinal Barberini (the future Pope Urban) counsels against such action: "St. Augustine guards us against making propositions of natural science a matter of faith, for demonstrable truths will demonstrate themselves.... One must not put the authority of the Church into a position from which there is no escape but retreat" (2.17). Barberini, the man of science, recognizes the validity of Galileo's claims, yet also knows the theological and political danger of accepting them. The Pope opts for a less public means of dealing with Galileo. He orders Galileo be given a private admonition to abandon the Copernican propositions. In 1616, the orders are carried out, but their exact execution remains a source of contention when Galileo is put on trial in 1633.

Galileo's recantation is the climax to his story, but each writer handles the moment very differently. In Brecht, the Pope and the Grand Inquisitor discuss the situation and then Galileo's friends discuss the implications should he recant. The pivotal decision to recant occurs off-stage. The fact that Galileo is absent during the crucial scenes might be read as an embodiment of Brecht's belief in the dialectical force of history, with the aftermath of the clashing sides being the ramifications of Galileo's recantation; i.e., in Brecht's play the thematic climax is the scene 14 debate between Galileo and Andrea regarding the value of the production of the *Discorsi* versus his belief that he "turned his back on the people" squandering the opportunity to create a scientists' Hippocratic oath to "use knowledge only for the good of mankind" (94).

In contrast, Stoppard, the liberal humanist, stresses the idea of humans in actions, and so he shows the recantation. Whereas Brecht's Galileo is a sensualist and opportunist who recants due to fear of physical pain, Stoppard's Galileo is a staunch believer in reason who deftly negotiates the political terrain of Rome until he makes a fatal error. Determined to publish his views and proofs of the Copernican system, Galileo devises a strategy that will prove to be his undoing: "I have written two books in one, giving equal voice first to the truth of Aristotle and second to the hypotheses of Copernicus and I shall have a third character Simplicio, a common man to speak for common men" (2.25). By acceding to two papal requests — to create a "Preface re-affirming the wisdom of the decree of 1616" (2.26) and to include Pope Urban's own argument that definitively asserting the truth of either system would limit God's omnipotence — Galileo convinces the Papal Censor that the book falls within acceptable boundaries of being a hypothetical discussion of the issues. Six months after its publication, the Papal Censor altered his view and banned the book. Galileo's nemesis, Colombe, points out Galileo's strategic error. The Pope's argument is placed in the mouth of Simplicio, the Simpleton. Feeling that he has been mocked, the Pope turns against Galileo and seeks his prosecution.

In the midst of Galileo's trial by the Inquisition, Stoppard concocts a private meeting between the frail, elderly Galileo and his former supporter Pope Urban. Galileo sticks to his belief that the world was created by a reasonable God, and he stresses that he can provide proof for his scientific claims. Their conversation concludes:

> GALILEO: My lord, I can prove what I assert, so if it is truth they want, they will affirm it!
> URBAN: Oh Galileo ... you know something of the Earth but you know nothing of the world. This is not a trial of your science, nor even of your

> faith unless you choose to make it so. It is a trial of your strength, and you are not strong enough. For it is written that God made the Heaven and the Earth, and he made the sun to rise and set — and in the service of God the Church will crack your thumbs like walnuts, it will have you stretched till your joints crack, and branded till your fat bubbles through your skin and your veins split like flower-stems, and if the Earth still moves the Church will tie you to the stake in Campo di Fiori and make a torch of you.
>
> GALILEO: (pause) Then it does not move [2.33–34].

Realizing that he would eventually recant under the pain of torture, Galileo rationalizes his confession as the reasonable course of action. Galileo's steadfast belief that truth and reason will triumph is forced to concede defeat to the harsh realities of political and religious power.[9]

The play's denouement involves an excerpt of Galileo's official recantation as well as his pupil's reassurance that capitulation was the right and reasonable course of action. In contrast to Brecht's play, where Galileo's disciple Andrea initially castigates him for recanting, in Stoppard's play Galileo's disciple says: "To persist would have been irrational ... useless ... unscientific" (2.35). In Brecht's play, Galileo is ultimately portrayed as an anti-hero who offers a stinging self-condemnation of his recantation. In contrast, Stoppard's Galileo realizes that he has taken the pragmatic course of action, but rather than assess his own actions, he reflects on the humanistic implications of the play's events. Whereas Galileo has been the champion of reason, in his closing monologue, he asserts the value of the irrational aspects of life:

> Thirty years ago in this piazza they burned Giordano Bruno, that unreasonable man, and I think now that his irrational stubbornness and useless agony spoke more for our divinity than the divine order of mathematics. Why is that? The truth is that saints are not reasonable men. We do not love with reason, or pray with reason. We do not even pursue knowledge because reason drives us. There is something else that makes one man unreasonably stubborn and another unreasonably true to his word, and another.... No, the only triumph is that I am alive, and I may fall off my mule before I get to Florence. If so, reason will have prevailed for nothing. If not, I shall continue with my studies of how things float, or fall, or break; or bend [2.36].

While Stoppard spends the majority of the play celebrating reason and scientific advances, the closing moment gives voice to the rest of the equation — the irrational and metaphysical dimensions of human existence. While science can offer many answers to the mysteries of life, in Stoppard's eyes there will always be an indefinable element that makes humanity what it is.

In this regard Stoppard's metaphysical position stands in stark contrast to Brecht's materialist view of life. In each play, one sees how the hand of ideology writes history, how the same historical figure is interpreted in divergent ways based upon the perspective of the author. Brecht's interest in the material conditions of social systems helps him aptly show the hypocrisy of those in power when they pragmatically accept Galileo's star charts for their aid in commerce while simultaneously rejecting the doctrine that makes those same star charts possible. Brecht is less persuasive when he condemns Galileo.

In his commentary Brecht argues that Galileo's recantation robbed "these sciences of a greater part of their social importance," and that never again would the sciences "come into such close contact with the people" ("Praise or Condemnation" 1947:225). Brecht's re-reading of Galileo's story in light of the atomic age raises the important question of where the scientist's duty lies and how scientific knowledge is used, but his suggestion that a steadfast Galileo would have inspired the masses to revolt bears little resemblance to the social reality of 17th-century Italy. Even Brecht scholar Ernest Schumacher concludes that "Galileo did not commit the social treason that Brecht imputed to him"(quoted in Szczesny 1969:27).[10] Perhaps what is most ironic about Brecht's condemnation of Galileo is that between Laughton's Los Angeles production and its move to New York, Brecht himself committed the same "social crime" as Galileo. Called in front of the Committee on Un-American Activities, Brecht denied any affinity for communism and deftly convinced his American Inquisitors that "he was a harmless citizen who had nothing to do with communism in particular or with politics in general"(Szczesny 1969:24). If Galileo had not recanted, we may never have had the *Discorsi*; likewise, if Brecht had admitted to his political beliefs, we may never have had the decisive work that he did with the Berliner Ensemble. Indeed, Brecht's depiction of Galileo as a sensualist and opportunist, as a thinker who enjoys the material comforts of the world and who ultimately saves his own skin is in many ways a reflection of Brecht himself.

In contrast to Brecht's condemnation, Stoppard celebrates Galileo, presenting an image of a man who is to be respected. It is Galileo's humanness — his great intellect, his passionate search for the truth, his wit and love of wine, as well as his understandable recantation — that Stoppard presents for the audience's admiration and reflection. These traits that Stoppard admires in Galileo also reflect Stoppard's own personality and demeanor. Just as each depiction of Galileo in part mirrors the author, each play's shortcomings are indicative of artistic temperament. Brecht distorts history to argue a socio-political point (and often fails to convince audiences of his view) while Stoppard displays the extent of his research, sometimes at the expense of dramatic momentum. While it would be nice to see Stoppard return to this work and revise it for production, that prospect is unlikely.

Overall, both plays have their merits and offer an intriguing look at a pivotal historical figure. Each is a major playwright, and each play sheds a light on the individual author as well as inherent biases that go into creating both art and history.

TEXAS STATE UNIVERSITY

Notes

1. The nature of Stoppard's Galileo research is unclear. However, a work he may have consulted, and which directly bears on the historical inaccuracies of Brecht's *Galileo* is Gerhard Szczesny's 1969 book *The Case against Bertolt Brecht with Arguments Drawn from His "Life of Galileo."* The work also offers an excellent condensed biography of Galileo, particularly concerning the events germane to both Brecht and Stoppard's plays.

2. Eschewing any attempt at physically representing 17th-century Italy on stage, Stoppard deliberately crafted his script for the Planetarium because it had a projector that could create various sky effects appropriate to Galileo's story. However, it soon became clear that from the Planetarium's perspective there were too many technical difficulties to make the project feasible. The Young Vic, the forthcoming National Theatre building, and the RSC were all proposed as possible venues, but for reasons unknown, none of them produced *Galileo*. Stoppard then removed the script from circulation.

3. In a letter to Anthony Smith, Stoppard indicates that he will start writing the script in January 1970, but the contract preserved at the HRHRC lists the start date as January 1971.

4. The quotation is from a 1993 fax from Stoppard to Disney's Michael Eisner. While it is a reference to the screenplay, it also applies to the play.

5. The quotation is from Tom Stoppard's unpublished typescript *Galileo*. All subsequent citations are from this manuscript and noted (by act and page number) parenthetically in the text.

For a more detailed account of the contents of Stoppard's *Galileo* and how it fits into his canon, see chapter 3 of Stoppard's *Theatre: Finding Order amid Chaos*.

6. Szczesny provides an account (69–71) of this episode and the controversy it created.

7. This is a paraphrase of Mrs. Sarti's Scene 9 line: "You have no right to trample your daughter's happiness with your big feet!" (67). All quotations are taken from Brecht's third version of *Life of Galileo* as translated in *Brecht Collected Plays (Volume 5)*. To create the portrait of an unfeeling father, Brecht first makes Virginia ten years older than she was, and then he adds an implausible eight-year engagement (during peak childbearing years for Virginia). The engagement covers the entire eight-year period when Galileo was obedient to the Church, avoided controversy, and refrained from further research into the issue of the earth revolving around the sun. In other words, for eight years he behaved in a manner that would have pleased her fiancé's family.

8. Speaking in his own voice, this line about science and theology dancing

together as well as time revealing all truths appear in Stoppard's interview with Joseph McCulloch (41–42). Another major sentiment that Stoppard expresses as being symptomatic of his own view is that all of these scientific discoveries simply show that God has been gravely underestimated.

9. In 1992, after having a commission study the matter for thirteen years, the Catholic Church finally confirmed Galileo's findings and admitted their error in condemning him.

10. See Szczesny (24–31) for a broader discussion of the issue of Galileo as "social traitor" amid the context of seventeenth-century Italy.

References Cited

Brecht, Bertolt. *Life of Galileo.* Tr. Wolfgang Sauerlander and Ralph Mannheim. In *Brecht Collected Plays.* Volume 5. Edited by Ralph Mannheim and John Willett, 3–98. New York: Vintage Books, 1972.

_____. "Building Up a Part: Laughton's Galileo"[1956]. In *Brecht Collected Plays.* Volume 5. Edited by Ralph Mannheim and John Willett, 230–263. New York: Vintage Books, 1972.

_____. "Notes on Individual Scenes." [1956] In *Brecht Collected Plays.* Volume 5. Edited by Ralph Mannheim and John Willett, 227–230. New York: Vintage Books, 1972.

_____. "Praise or Condemnation of Galileo?" [1947]. In *Brecht Collected Plays.* Volume 5. Edited by Ralph Mannheim and John Willett, 224–225. New York: Vintage Books, 1972.

Fleming, John. Stoppard's *Theatre: Finding Order amid Chaos.* Austin: University of Texas Press, 2001.

McCulloch, Joseph. "Dialogue with Tom Stoppard" [20 March 1973]. In *Under Bow Bells: Dialogues with Joseph McCulloch.* London: Sheldon Press, 1974. Reprinted in *Tom Stoppard in Conversation,* edited by Paul Delaney. Ann Arbor: University of Michigan Press, 1993:38–45.

Stoppard, Tom. Letter to Peter Bart, 28 May 1971. Tom Stoppard Collection, Box 36, Folder 1. Harry Ransom Humanities Research Center, University of Texas at Austin.

_____. *Galileo.* Unpublished play. [1972 or 1973]. Tom Stoppard Collection, Box 43, Folder 4. Harry Ransom Humanities Research Center, University of Texas at Austin.

_____. Fax to Michael Eisner, 13 June 1993. Tom Stoppard Collection, Box 59, Folder 8. Harry Ransom Humanities Research Center, University of Texas at Austin.

Szczesny, Gerhard. *The Case against Bertolt Brecht with Arguments Drawn from His "Life of Galileo."* Tr. Alexander Gode. New York: Frederick Ungar Publishing, 1969.

New Stage Directions in *Waiting for Godot*

Jason Groves

Abstract.

The stage of Waiting for Godot *presents a scene of dramatic mastery perhaps unparalleled in the twentieth century. An exhaustive set of stage directions secures with radically limited variation the possibility of highly accurate reproductions. Accordingly, the stage of this masterpiece is the site of constraint, confinement, and manipulation. The strict direction of the stage by the authoritative text poses difficulties for understanding the dramatic characters in terms of human beings exemplifying the human condition. Moreover, an anti-humanistic dramatic language challenges metaphysical and psychological interpretations of the play. I therefore argue that a significant aspect of the predicament of Vladimir and Estragon is their confinement in, and to, a text. The constrained situation of the human in modern drama is reassessed as the constrained situation of the modern drama in modern drama. Finally, the paper considers dramaturgic strategies capable of exploiting these constraints onstage.*

A criminal on death row made to walk to the guillotine is already a dead person even as he clings, to the very end, to life. The fierce antagonism between life and death is pushed to the extreme and cohesively expressed in this lone miserable being who, in the name of the law, is forced into an unjust condition. A person not walking but made to walk; a person not living but made to live; a person not dead but made to be dead must, in spite of such total passivity, paradoxically expose the radical vitality of human nature. [...] This very condition is the original form of dance and it is my task to create just such a condition on the stage [Hijikata, 43].

In the very year and month (January 1961) that the Japanese writer and butoh dancer Tatsumi Hijikata was writing his homage to incarceration, Samuel Beckett's play *Waiting for Godot* was being performed by the San Quentin Federal Penitentiary Drama Workshop in the San Quentin Federal Penitentiary. This production, directed by San Quentin inmate and later Beckett protégé Rick Cluchey, resulted from an earlier visit to San Quentin by the San Francisco Actor's Workshop where they performed *Waiting for Godot* under the direction of Herbert Blau in 1957. That these prison performances act as two of the play's principal productions raises the question of a correspondence between the institutions of theater and prison. In the figure of incarceration — encountered throughout Beckett's work and exemplified in *Waiting for Godot*—the radical vitality of the human coincides with the passivity of the physically restrained body. Whereas for Hijikata the apparent incompatibility of passivity and vitality is overcome through the rigorous choreography of the body in dance — a "corpse, desperately standing" as Hijikata says of the body in butoh — for Samuel Beckett drama provides the arena where artistic vitality and the constraint of form coincide. The figure of the choreographer is common to both, the director and dancer who, in scripting the body and voice, submit the body and the voice to a script. Exemplified in the trajectory described by the figures of Lucky (*Waiting for Godot*), Winnie (*Happy Days*), the entire dramatis personae of *Endgame*, the Protagonist of *Catastrophe* (dedicated to then imprisoned Czech playwright and reformer Václav Havel), and Bom, Bim, and Bem of *What Where*, the stage in Beckett's drama increasingly is the site of constraint, embedment, incarceration, and total manipulation, culminating in the final play whose atmosphere has been described as unrelentingly totalitarian.

The initial gesture of a rigorous choreography is present already in Beckett's first published play. There are strict consequences for the depiction of the human that become apparent in the conclusion of both acts.

> ESTRAGON: Well shall we go?
> VLADIMIR: Yes, let's go.
> *They do not move* [36].

This scene of immobility with which both acts of the play close is a scene, in Hijikata's formula, where the characters are not immobile but made to be immobile. It is a *scripted* immobility, the immobility of persons whose actions are dictated by a script. The inability to go cannot be "their" inability to go, because this immobility does not entirely belong to them. Psychological explanations of their stasis are never entirely sufficient. The lack of resolve and volition that plagues many of Beckett's characters is for Didi and Gogo no more a crisis of willpower than a function of their operating as representations of a text wherein their immobility is prescribed. Their immobility is announced in a stage direction that precedes and indeed governs every performance. What follows in this paper is a reading of the scripted stage directions as an instrument of strict discipline that, in its more radical instances, establishes the sense of confinement that pervades the stage.

VLADIMIR: Well shall we go?
ESTRAGON: Yes, let's go.
They do not move [61].

Their passivity is not their own. Didi and Gogo do not move because they are restrained from moving. They are tied: tied to their textual doubles Vladimir and Estragon whose names occur in the script but never in the performance, for they are never once spoken. Neither will that which dictates the movements and restricts the actions of Didi and Gogo appear on the stage, for it is no more visible or intelligible than Godot. The source of their immobility is a mysterious, typographically privileged voice that everywhere prescribes and dictates both the actions and non-actions on the stage: the "voice" of the stage direction. It is a voice from outside and beyond the stage, a voice that is neither the representation nor the transcription of speech, but surrounds speech and conditions that speech. It is a voice that does not speak, a voice that has no voice, a voice that, in a text representing speech, becomes audible in those very moments and pauses where the speech on the stage ceases. Fifty-four silences occur in the first act alone, which is to say fifty-four instances of the stage direction "silence," and in the space of this enforced silence of characters not silent but made to be silent the agency that enforces the passivity of the stage begins to become apparent.[1]

This external agency is registered onstage in the dim awareness by Didi and Gogo of being "tied" (14) and it is registered in the strict sense of confinement that pervades the play in which the principal characters do not, and can not, leave the stage. The less this confinement of Didi and Gogo to the stage is presented as the result of dramatic events that transpire on the stage, the more this confinement is the very condition of the dramatic stage — a stage that is at every moment preceded by a text. The play does not need the "faint shadow of bars on the stage floor" (Knowlson, 1994:xxii) that Beckett once considered casting. Although his better judgment decided against such a degree of "explication," the implicit association between the stage of the modern drama and the prison as spaces of captivity and confinement is intelligible especially when the enforcer of that confinement is invisible.

Incarceration is not merely figurative in Beckett, although it is that too. On at least once occasion Beckett made this relation explicit to Rick Cluchey, when instructed by Beckett in a performance of *Krapp's Last Tape* to "make the thing his own in terms of incarceration, for example; incarceration in self" (Knowlson 1994:xxii). While Krapp's incarceration in the figurative space of the self is itself figurative, *Waiting for Godot* provides a more literal instance of incarceration — in the sense of a strict institutional confinement —

in the figure of Lucky.[2] Deprived of all autonomy, and for whom the stage is the site of subjugation and dictation, Lucky is perhaps the most typical character in the modern drama whose products are the very condemned identified by Hijikata: the miserable beings[3] not walking but made to walk, not dancing but made to dance, not thinking but made to think. Lucky makes visible and explicit the condition of physical and vocal constraint that pervades the stage. Unlike Didi and Gogo, who are invisibly tied to Godot (and to Vladimir and Estragon, their textual predecessors), Lucky is visibly tied to Pozzo. Pozzo, a paronomastic equivalent of Godot, whose interaction with Lucky typically consists of stage directions, is the incarnate figure of the stage director. But even Pozzo stands in relation to another — a character in a text — as Lucky stands onstage in relation to him.

Be this as it may, the conglomerate character of Pozzo and Lucky is too "explicative" of the essential form of confinement in the drama. Even Lucky's subjugation to Pozzo is a false front for his subjugation to the text whose stage directions he must reproduce faithfully. Didi and Gogo, who are invisibly tied, are far more interesting in this regard. The restriction of their movement on, and to, the stage reflects their condition as dramatic personae whose every word and movement is directed and dictated by an absent overlord. The rigorous dictation of the stage by the absent author and the absent text is reproduced in the playwright and director Beckett fiercely guarding against unauthorized deviations[4] in performance from the authoritative text. He is the exemplary master/creator identified by Derrida in his essay in *Writing and Difference* on Antonin Artaud, another institutionalized playwright, who revolted against the director of the modern drama, a director that sometimes bears a striking resemblance to Beckett, who "absent and from afar, is armed with a text, and keeps watch over, assembles, regulates the time or the meaning of representation, letting this latter represent him as concerns what is called the contents of his thoughts, his intentions, his ideas" (1978:235). What is at stake for Artaud is the production of a stage and a body that is not the representation of a text. Such a theater would be inconceivable for Beckett; his is a theater of limits, above all the limit of representation. Beckett's strict regulation of his plays on and off the stage is well documented in his correspondences with directors. Armed with a script Beckett kept watch over and strictly regulated productions of his plays, a role eagerly taken over by the Beckett estate. Armed with a text, however, and armed by the authorized and definitive text, particularly in the definitive dictation of the body and voice in the stage direction, Beckett is in a position of permanent vigilance. The text in which both the voice and the body are inscribed looms like Godot invisibly and omnisciently over every production.

It is this radical vigilance that makes *Waiting for Godot* a masterpiece, perhaps one of the last masterpieces for the theater. The vitality of the play is a direct result of the masterful regulation of the stage by the text, ensuring with radically limited variation the endless reproduction of the play. Though certainly possible, variation is far less interesting than the principle of repetition in this project of mastery. It now seems that incarceration is no longer an adequate designation for what is happening onstage; its use in this paper has been exhausted. A residue of incarceration remains to be analyzed in the sense of repetition pervading the play and a sense that repetition — the repetition of the incarcerated — is both the guiding principle of the play and at the same time a radical critique of the modern drama.

Waiting for Godot is indeed one of the crucial plays of the 20th century, but it is at once the meridian of the modern drama and its total exhaustion. The most vital play of one of the most vital modern playwrights takes place on a stage grown old and tired. The characters that stumble across it, exhausted and despairing, perpetually repeat for some fifty years now,[5] the same tired actions, always wanting and always unable to depart.[6] Such is life, perhaps, and such is the modern drama at the end of its time. *Waiting* is a tired play, but it was so already at its inception, for it is the allegory of a form of theater that is played-out. Its exhaustion is the exhaustion of an inexhaustible[7] form of theatre, and the boredom of the audience when faced with this boring play is symptomatic of an exhaustion with a form of theater, the modern drama to be more precise, that is at the verge of becoming historically and aesthetically obsolete.[8] "Nothing to be done," says an aging and exhausted man, giving up in despair *again* already in the opening scene. His despair is not only the despair of a poor itinerant tramp, though it is that too. It is the despair of a theatre that perceives its form as oppressing rather than liberating. *Waiting* will reoccur indefinitely: not only within itself, in the near identical ending of both first and second act, but in Beckett's very oeuvre. "You must realize," Beckett informs Roger Blin and Jean Martin, "that Hamm and Clov are Didi and Gogo at a later date, at the end of their lives" (Gontarski 1985:42). The resignation of Vladimir and Estragon to their tedious repetition is the resignation of a stage on which, as Vladimir says toward the end of the play, "Everything's dead but the tree" (60). The tree, of course, was never living. What was living was a certain conception of the human that lent itself to being expressed dramatically, in the intersubjective space of dialogue. Unable to enact anything in this gutted theatrical space, the play continues on, repeating the worn-out fragments of speech and repeating the conventions of modern drama though with a decreasing conviction in the viability of the form that these proceedings take.

The possibility of dialogue, which Peter Szondi argues in *The Theory of the Modern Drama* is tied to the very possibility of the drama, is suspended in the play.[9] Beckett's comment, that his "people seem to be falling to bits" (Shenker 1956:3), is best observed in the disintegration of dialogue and the increasing impossibility of communication in his plays. The dialogue is no longer the site where these dramatic subjects constitute themselves; their "blather" cannot serve as the dramatic form of their self-exteriorization. Nor, as Lucky's think demonstrates, is the monologue a viable form of self-presentation. It is much more the case that dramatic language, in *Waiting for Godot,* opens up another scene of language — far from the scene of inter-subjective understanding that dominates the stage in the classic theatre. The human condition so profoundly explored in *Waiting for Godot* is in fact achieved through a use of dramatic language that is deeply anti-humanistic. Rather than the human, it is the dramatic condition that is presented and explored onstage.

The modern drama, where the human announced itself in the interpersonal space of the dialogue, is at an endgame in Beckett's theatre. His theatre approaches another stage where the human and the individual cease to exist, that is, cease to be dramatically viable concepts. Not only his characters but with them the concept of the human disintegrates onstage. The deterioration of meaningful communication — above all dramatic dialogue — is made explicit by *Waiting for Godot* in the difficulty of finding anything to say at all.

> *Long silence.*
> VLADIMIR: Say something!
> ESTRAGON: I'm trying.
> *Long silence.*
> VLADIMIR: (*in anguish*) Say anything at all! [40–41]

The more the dialogue is merely an unsuccessful attempt to stage a conversation, the more the impossibility of dialogue becomes apparent, and the more the dramatic form is becomes incarcerating rather than liberating. What is needed and at times even demanded in the play is a way out of this constrained situation. The play does not furnish an exit for its characters; their last gesture at freedom, "Yes, let's go," is effectively devastated by the stage direction, *They do not move.* What is needed is what is impossible: a new stage direction. Nevertheless in the following section I will locate a new direction for this stage in the very textual sites, the stage directions, that otherwise would negate the possibility of anything new occurring onstage.

For a play in which words and people are perpetually disintegrating it is curious that the convention of the stage direction would be so impervious to this linguistic malaise. Particularly in the concluding scenes when

Vladimir and Estragon announce their decision to go but do not go, a scene is staged where the correspondence between language and intention is suspended. The speech act becomes a contradiction in terms. The suspension of an intention expressed in language is contradicted by an opposing intention cast in the italicized script of the stage direction. At this stage a problem arises. The very failure of Didi and Gogo to perform their expressed intention is a result of the successful performance of the stage direction forbearing their movement. Yet it also signals both the failure of an intention cast in dramatic language to be enacted and the failure of an act of dramatic self-determination. This is a primary contradiction around which this paper and the play it proposes to analyze revolve. It can be put in these words: dramatic language in *Waiting for Godot* is the scene of a radical undoing of intention in language even while it conservatively preserves in language the authorial intention of this undoing. It undermines the dramatic form even while invoking it. The show cannot go on, because Vladimir and Estragon say they will move on, and yet the show does go on, by their not moving on.

S. E. Gontarski's study, *The Intent of Undoing in Samuel Beckett's Dramatic Texts* (1985), seems to me to begin to perform, while remaining within the confinement of Beckett's texts, such an exercise of undoing. By displacing the reader's focus from the final and authoritative text and onto the manuscripts, drafts, and in general the textual genesis, the very definition of the definitive text is undermined. In his procedure of reading the work becomes a development rather than a fixed and final product. Yet, in calling attention to the intention of undoing, his study defers the ultimate undoing of intention that Beckett's theater approaches. Gontarski writes,

> While Beckett labors to undo that traditional structure and realistic content, he does not wholly do so. The final work retains those originary tracings and is virtually a palimpsest. What remains is the trace of an author struggling against his text, repenting his originary disclosure, effacing himself from the text and thereby creating himself [2].

This dialectic of erasure and disclosure is rightfully described by Gontarski as "a struggle to undo the realistic sources of the text, to undo the coherence of character and to undo the author's presence" (4). Gontarski's strategy of reading nevertheless reveals Beckett's presence to be most visible in his unsuccessful attempts at self-effacement, concluding, "The erasure of authorial presence creates an authorial presence erasing" (17). The very intent of undoing undoes the undoing of intention. The *intent* of undoing preserves and even fulfills the authorial intention, whereas a serious and thorough undoing would dismantle even the author who initiated the undoing.

Both Beckett's and Gontarski's undoing is incomplete. So long as these remain *Beckett's* dramatic texts, as the title of Gontarski's study attests, so long as they remain the property of an author, this undoing will be the scene of yet another doing rather than the ultimate undoing that Beckett's work approaches.

A reading that would take into account the destabilizing language of the text might reveal the possibility of completing this failed undoing. The detachment of the speakers from their speech, not to mention their estrangement from their names,[10] and the abyss that opens between intention expressed in language and action performed could be opened up in those exemplary instances of dramatic language — the stage directions — that would claim, by their very potency and intactness, to be impervious to the critique of dramatic language rigorously probed onstage. Considering the other scene of language that occurs onstage, the unification of language and action in the stage directions is extremely problematic. If the critique of dramatic language inherent in *Waiting for Godot* is an effective critique then the same critique could be opened up in the language of the stage direction too.

This new staging of an upstaging, the necessary upstaging signalling the undoing of intention, can occur by diverting attention toward the condition of the stage as the product of a text and the situation of its speakers as figures manipulated by language and zealous directors. Among those who engage this staging, Derrida gestures excitedly with Artaud to what this new staging will *not* entail: "Speech and *its* writing will be erased on the stage of cruelty only in the extent to which they were allegedly dictation" (1978: 239). We have seen how erasure can call attention to and thereby perpetuate what was supposed to have been erased. The erasure of dictation can occur only at the hands of a new dictator. This must be, if it can be, avoided. Therefore, in what could be called a cruel staging of this play, stage directions will be not be erased but demoted from the privileged status they enjoyed as manifestations of a project of mastery, for this is a text that, in opening up another scene where language undermines rather than constitutes dramatic subjects, sets in motion the destruction of intentionality in language. A new staging of *Waiting for Godot* could rigorously call into question the freedom and self-expression conventionally associated with the dramatic form. The scene that arises whenever the dramatic persons are discussed in terms of humans and beings could be reassessed as a scene of repetition, manipulation and confinement. This is the next stage of *Waiting for Godot*, a stage that the play anticipates and prepares but could not realize.

The modern drama, on death row already in Beckett's first play, is a dead form even as it clings to life. In staging the imminent end of a dramatic form Beckett nevertheless preserves the very feature of that drama that

The remains of the play: a post-production image from *Operation: Waiting*, a new staging of *Waiting for Godot*, directed by Jason Groves, Baltmore, May 24–25, 2006.

prevents a new dramatic form from arising: namely, the direction of the stage by the text. The gesture toward a form of freedom (not to be confused with the freedom from form) can be understood in the terms of the dramatic subjects only as death, *as the total negation of the dramatic stage*. The unsuccessful attempts of Vladimir and Estragon to hang themselves (even then it would be only Didi and Gogo who would die) underscores the ghostliness of a stage that has outlived itself. A staging that would adequately present this work would proceed, not by realizing an inexistent intention, but rather by recognizing and presenting the collapse of a scene of dramatic language capable of representing life.

THE JOHNS HOPKINS UNIVERSITY

Notes

1. While this voice will become audible in the later plays, especially *Catastrophe* and *What Where*, those voices dictating the action on the stage still are but representations of the silent stage directions dictating the dictating voices.

2. It may be said that all of Beckett's characters are Lucky.

3. The designation of "being" can be applied to Lucky only with great imprecision.

4. Although Beckett, in a more liberal mood, is known to have told Alan Schnei-

der (26 November 1963), "What matters is that you feel the spirit of the thing and the intention as you do. Give them that as best you can, even if it involves certain deviations from what I have written and said," it also is known that these deviations-and these are certain deviations-when more than minor were rarely tolerated. "I am naturally disturbed," writes Beckett to his American Publisher Barney Rosset (2 February 1956) "at the menace hinted at in one of your letters, of unauthorized deviations from the script. This we cannot have at any price." The letter, quoted in Gontarski, "Revising Himself: Performance as Text in Samuel Beckett's Theatre," (1998:133), continues, "This we cannot have at any price and I am asking [London producer Donald] Albery to write [American producer Michael] Myerberg to that effect. I am not intransigent, as the [bowdlerized] Criterion production [in London] shows, about minor changes, if I feel they are necessary, but I refuse to be improved by a professional rewriter [in this case American playwright Thorton Wilder had been proposed, and Wilder had begun a draft translation of Godot]."

5. ESTRAGON: Yes, now I remember, yesterday evening we spent blathering about nothing in particular. That's been going on now for half a century [43].

6. POZZO: I don't seem to be able ... (long hesitation) ... to depart.
ESTRAGON: Such is life [31].

And later:

ESTRAGON: In the meantime let us converse calmly, since we are incapable of keeping silent.
VLADIMIR: You're right, we're inexhaustible [40].

7. The play, of course, in inexhaustible. This is its very tediousness.

8. POZZO: You find it tedious?
ESTRAGON: Somewhat.
POZZO: (to Vladimir) And to you sir?
VLADIMIR: I've been better entertained [26].

9. "The possibility of the modern drama hangs on the possibility of dialogue" (1965:19). It was very nearly the case, were the tree slightly stronger, that the possibility of dialogue in *Waiting for Godot*— and thus the possibility of the modern drama for Beckett — would have been hanged on stage with the hanging of Didi and Gogo.

10. Naming is not a scene of identifying in the play but a scene of estrangement from identification. Vladimir and Estragon, the names given in the text, never refer to themselves as such but rather as Didi and Gogo. Pozzo is confused with Godot, Godot's existence is questionable at best, Estragon is "Adam," and the Boy does not have a name other than his gender.

References Cited

Beckett, Samuel. *Waiting for Godot.* New York: Grove Press, 1954.

Derrida, Jacques. *Writing and Difference.* Translated by Alan Bass. Chicago: University of Chicago Press, 1978.

Gontarski, Stanley E. *The Intent of Undoing in Samuel Beckett's Dramatic Texts.* Bloomington: Indiana University Press, 1985.

_____. "Revising Himself: Performance as Text in Samuel Beckett's Theatre." *Journal of Modern Literature* XXII, 1 (Fall 1998): 131–155.

Knowlson, James and McMillan, Dougald, ed. *Theatrical Notebooks of Samuel Beckett, Volume I: Waiting for Godot,* New York: Grove Press, 1994.

Shenker, Israel. "A portrait of Samuel Beckett, author of the puzzling Waiting for Godot." *The New York Times* (6 May 1956).

Szondi, Peter. *Theorie des modernen Dramas (1880–1950).* Frankfurt a/M: Surhrkamp, 1965.

Tatsumi, Hijikata. "To Prison." Translated by Nanako Kurihara. *The Drama Review* 44 (Spring 2000): 43–48.

8

Tom Stoppard, *Night and Day*, and the "Theatre in Crisis" Playwrights

Publicly Funded Arts and Freedom of Expression

Daniel Jernigan

Abstract

In 1988 Clive Barker chaired a conference titled "Theatre in Crisis" which criticized poor government funding of the arts. Notable players within the theatrical community, including Harold Pinter and Caryl Churchill, signed the accompanying petition. This essay explores why Stoppard refrained from voicing his opinion on the matter, finding the roots of his restraint in his 1978 play, Night and Day, *and its concern with how unionization in the press might curtail free speech. Briefly, just as Stoppard's sympathies in* Night and Day *explicitly favor the idea that the exchange of information (news) enjoyed the most liberty in a free market economy unencumbered by the potential abuses which might arise when a powerful union of news-reporters have their way, consistency would have required that Stoppard again favor the idea that the exchange of information (plays) would continue to enjoy the most liberty unencumbered by the abuse which might arise if a powerful "union" of playwrights was to have its way.*

In December 1988, Clive Barker chaired a conference titled "Theatre in Crisis" at London Goldsmith's College. One result of the conference was a declaration criticizing reductions in government support for the theatre signed by notable players within the theatrical community, including Harold Pinter, David Edgar, and Caryl Churchill, among others. Numbered among the declaration's resolutions was a collection of distinct appeals for a return to pre–Thatcherite attitudes about the worth of the arts (that they are essential to "the full and free development of every individual"), the necessity for an apportionment of funds which would make the arts more "accessible to that diversity of needs and interests whether they be national, regional, local, community-based, gender-based, ethnic" etc., and a proclamation that "a free market economy and private sponsorship cannot guarantee the necessary conditions for the theatre to fulfill its many functions" (Lavender 1989:211–213).

However, even while a number of playwrights (notably, Caryl Churchill in *Serious Money* [1987]) took it upon themselves to explore the impact that corporate power was having on the theatre in the late 1980's (under Conservative Party Prime Minister Margaret Thatcher), Stoppard refrained entirely from voicing his opinion on the matter (at least there is no public record of him having done so). This might easily enough be overlooked as irrelevant vis-à-vis Stoppard's own commitment to the arts except for the fact that some ten years later Stoppard did join a second group of artists (The Shadow Arts Council — headed up in this instance by Peter Hall) which also advocated for greater funding for the arts. And while this seeming discrepancy could perhaps be rationalized in any number of ways (e.g., as a simple oversight, or as in-fighting with his dramatist peers), upon closer inspection it becomes apparent that the aesthetic, economic, and ideological differences between the two movements not only provides poignant insight into Stoppard's own attitudes towards public funding for the arts, but are also consistent with his long held attitude towards organized lobbying campaigns in general, and of their potential impact on freedom of expression.

The two movements were most different from each other in the fact that it wasn't so much the amount of funding[1] which concerned The Shadow Arts Council, but, rather, how current funding levels were being spent. For what truly worried the Shadow Art's Council was that Labor was much more committed to the more popular arts of mainstream music, radio, and television than the more "elite" arts of theatre and opera (not completely surprising given that the audience for the more popular arts largely comprised Labor's electoral base). Furthermore, while we do find Stoppard in an interview at this time explaining that he supported full funding for the arts,[2] you really have to read between the lines here. As Ivan Hewitt puts it:

> The fact that everyone at the launch seemed to be nudging 60 gave a clue to the Shadow Arts Council's real aim. This is not to launch a debate, it is to return to the past.... To read these principles is to be taken back to a land far away and long ago, a land where the eternal verities of art and the personal taste of the ruling elite happily coincided. Art and culture were simply "the best that has been thought and said," in Arnold's phrase. The

Council's resources were devoted "to the fine arts exclusively"; amateur and what later came to be known as "community arts" had to fend for themselves [1999].

It would seem, then, that what The Shadow Arts Council (and, by implication, Stoppard) actually supports is greater funding for the more established "elite arts" (e.g., those arts such as Stoppard himself was involved in), not the more community based ("philistine"[3]) arts such as the "Theatre in Crisis" playwrights were fighting for. From this perspective, one reasonably persuasive explanation for Stoppard's apparent inconsistency is that it is simply indicative of his well-noted politically moderate-conservatism. For while the "theatre in crisis" conference involved "discussions held by a number of theatre people on the left ... [of] the problems posed by 'Thatcher's Theatre' and the national priorities it reflects" (Lavender 210:1989), Peter Hall's "Shadow Arts Council" was comprised of figures of a much more moderate persuasion (albeit, with the notable exception of Caryl Churchill, who also signed on).[4]

However, while remembering that this seeming inconsistency on Stoppard's part might well have been a consequence of several factors, this essay, rather, examines the discrepancy in light of the uncompromisingly free-market attitudes towards freedom of expression that Stoppard began to nurture as early as the mid to late-seventies, at which time increasing unionization activity among journalists inspired Stoppard to critically examine the implications of such unionizing activities for a free press in his 1978 play, *Night and Day*.[5] Consequently, one particularly poignant reading of Stoppard's failure to sign on to the "Theatre in Crisis" manifesto is that just as Stoppard's sympathies in *Night and Day* explicitly favored the idea that the free exchange of information (in this case, news) enjoyed the most liberty in a free market economy unencumbered by the abuse which might arise if a powerful union of news-reporters has its way, consistency alone allowed that Stoppard might once again simply be favoring the idea that the free exchange of information (in this case, theatre) would continue to enjoy the most liberty were it to remain unencumbered by the abuse which might arise were a powerful "union" of playwrights (i.e., the "theatre in crisis playwrights") were to have its way.

Indeed, one of the more explicit themes of *Night and Day* is that the unionization of the press gives far too much power over media content to the union itself, a detail which suggests that Stoppard is far less concerned with the control that multinational corporations have in deciding media content than he is by the potential abuse of organized labor within the ranks of press employees. One passage more than any other from *Night and Day* stands out as relevant in helping us to gauge Stoppard's attitude about the undue influence of corporate interests generally, and that is Ruth's rebuttal of Wagner's suggestion that the corporate press inhibits the proliferation of small newspapers:

> WAGNER: I'm talking about national papers. It's absurd to compare the free-dom of the big battalions with the freedom of a basement pam-phleteer to challenge him.
>
> RUTH: You are confusing freedom with ability. The *Flat Earth News* is *free* to sell a million copies. What it lacks is the ability to find a million people with four pence and a conviction that the earth is flat [83].

Apparently Stoppard just isn't all that convinced that small institu-tions — be they community theatres or the local press — might have their voices marginalized according to the dictates of some more powerful insti-tution. What's more, *Night and Day* very nearly stresses the opposite con-cern; i.e., that social protest movements are a much greater potential threat to freedom of expression than is corporate power. The correlation is clear. We can almost hear Stoppard lecturing the Theatre in Crisis movement sim-ilarly to how Ruth lectures Wagner in *Night and Day*: "[Even in the Thatcher era] the Flat Earth [community theatre] is free to sell a million [tickets]. What it lacks is the ability to find a million people with four pence and a convic-tion that the earth is flat."

Night and Day is set on the large estate of George and Ruth Carson in the fictional African country of Kimbawe. In addition to George and Ruth Carson, the play also focuses on three journalists, Dick Wagner, George Guthrie (who each work for the *Globe*), and Jacob Milne (an independent journalist), who are on assignment covering the events surrounding a social-ist rebellion led by Colonel Shimu against the established government and its president, Mageeba. The dramatic tension of the play is further intensified by the fact that Wagner has recently spent a single night with Ruth in a Lon-don hotel room, and, moreover, by the additional complication that upon meeting Milne she is immediately smitten with him. Thus, while Ruth wor-ries that Wagner's arrival might either lead to her husband finding out about her indiscretion — or (perhaps even worse) to Wagner's continued pursuit of her — Wagner, it seems, is more interested in acquiring a major scoop of his own than in re-acquiring Ruth.

Meanwhile Milne, a "special correspondent," has just scooped every-body else by landing an interview with Colonel Shimu that was published in *The Globe*. When Wagner discovers that Milne has had confrontations with the National Union of Journalists (NUJ) that resulted in his release from *The Grimsby Messenger* under dubious (at least to Wagner's way of thinking) circumstances, Wagner dubs him "The Grimsby Scab" (39) and takes it upon himself to inform his union brothers back in Britain about just who this "special correspondent" is. When Wagner gets his own scoop upon hearing that President Mageeba will visit the Carson compound for a secret meeting with Colonel Shimu and proceeds to crash the party, Ruth takes this opportunity to join in the resulting debate over freedom of expression. However, just on the heels of Wagner's interview with Mageeba, Guthrie returns from a trip designed to extend an invitation by Mageeba to Shimu with word that Milne has been shot and killed. It then becomes evident that Shimu will not make an appearance, and that war is imminent.

Night and Day is typical of the early Stoppard in that it employs its characters to debate disparate viewpoints (in this case Wagner argues the necessity of press unionization while Milne decries the way that unions inhibit freedom of the press). In an interview with David Gollob and David Roper, Stoppard admits that Milne best represents his own views: "Milne has my prejudice if you like. Somehow, unconsciously, I wanted him to be known to be speaking the truth" (1981:8). The play's concluding moments clearly reflect Stoppard's attitude, as one of Wagner's own stories is suppressed because of the labor activities he himself put in motion when he informed his union partners about Milne's identity.

No doubt Stoppard was aware that one year prior to *Night and Day* the 1977 *Royal Commission on the Press* had issued a study concerning the various dangers that threatened the free exchange of information. The resulting publication opened with a chapter that explained the importance of the free press to democracy:

> Newspapers and periodicals serve society in diverse ways. They inform their readers about the world and interpret it to them. They act both as watchdog for citizens, by scrutinizing concentrations of power, and as a means of communication among groups within the community, thus promoting social cohesion and social change [McGregor 1977:8].

Notably, this parallels Milne's own idealization of the press; i.e., that it is to be "the last line of defense for all the other freedoms." That Stoppard himself values the free press for just this reason is clear from an interview with Melvyn Bragg: "I always felt like that no matter how dangerously closed a society looked like it was getting, as long as any newspaper was free to employ anybody it liked to say what it wished within the law, then any situation was correctable; and that without that any situation was concealable" (1984:123).

For its part, *The Royal Commission on the Press* looked primarily at two different threats that the free press faced — corporate ownership and unionization. The Commission's evaluation of the way in which the closed shop of unionization might interrupt freedom of the press opens with a suggestion that the issue has "been the subject of intense controversy during most of the lifetime of the Commission." The report continues by noting that "Many have feared the consequences of an increase in the potential capacity of the Union of Journalists to influence or control editorial policies" (McGregor 1977:157). The Royal Commission recognized that the central dilemma resides in the fact that even while the Industrial Relations Act of 1971 had opened the door in favor of collective bargaining by unions throughout industry, this same act suddenly granted the NUJ more power than it once had:

> For the NUJ, the first priority is the freedom to improve the earnings and conditions of work of its members and to deploy its maximum strength for collective bargaining to this end. For those on the other side, what matters most is to secure the freedom of the press because they cannot "conceive of a civilised society that does not regard as its first priority the right of a man to express what he believes in whatever form he thinks appropriate..." [McGregor 1977:160].

Even while the Royal Commission understood the nature of the dilemma (admitting that "to determine what is right must involve a balancing of valid but competing claims"), The Royal Commission finally decided that there is "an important distinction between production workers and journalists in relation to closed shops" (McGregor 1977:160), explaining that "if a journalist is precluded from working in the press he is effectively silenced, and the public is deprived of the opportunity of reading what he writes" (McGregor 162). For this reason the Commission suggested a number of legislative safeguards intended to protect editors and journalists from the power of the union.

Written in the years immediately after the commission's report, it is clear that Stoppard's view was that the commission had done too much to appease the NUJ. However, even while Stoppard sides against the concerns of the NUJ, *Night and Day* isn't entirely oblivious to the counter concern of the Commission (i.e., that multinational control can also inhibit the free expression and exchange of ideas); indeed, this possibility is broached by President Mageeba himself, who expresses concern that multinational companies have too much control over press content: "So there we were, an independent country, and the only English newspaper was still part of a British Empire — a family empire — a chain of newspapers — a fleet of newspapers, shall I say" (80). Mageeba goes on to explain just how such a corporate press controls the product it presents to its readers when he responds to a question from

Wagner concerning whether he will lobby the British and the Americans to "get what you need to win the war" (80): "I know the British press is very attached to the lobby system. It lets the journalists and the politicians feel proud of their traditional freedoms while giving the reader as much of the truth as they think is good for him" (80). However, the fact that Mageeba uses this critique to defend his take-over of the press indicates just how fundamentally opposed Stoppard himself is to the possibility that the NUJ might serve as a meaningful check against abuse on the part of the corporate owners of the press (in essence, the NUJ's authoritarian control of the press is characterized as no better than Mageeba's control of the press). Moreover, this discussion with Mageeba speaks to an earlier point in the play, when Wagner related a story to Guthrie about a run-in that he had with a local government official concerning Milne's interview with Colonel Shimu in the *Globe*: "He wants to know which side the *Globe* thinks it's on. So I tell him, it's not on any side, stupid, it's an objective fact-gathering organization. And he says, yes. But is it objective-for or objective-against? (*Pause*) He may be stupid but he's not stupid" (28).

Wagner, then, even more than Mageeba, is most clearly sympathetic with the view that even a so-called "objective" press might be slanted one way or another. Indeed, Wagner defends the union from just this perspective, noting that it works as a counterbalance to corporate bias:

> MAGEEBA: I realize of course that you are only an able-seaman on the flagship.
> WAGNER: Well, sir, we've come a long way since we were galley slaves. Northcliffe could sack a man for wearing the wrong hat. Literally. There was a thing called the Daily Mail hat and he expected his reporters to wear it. Until he got interested in something else. Aeroplanes or wholemeal bread.... Those days are gone.
> MAGEEBA: Indeed, Mr. Wagner, now the hat is metaphorical only.
> WAGNER: With respect, sir, you underestimate the strength of the organized workers — the journalists. I admit that even when I started in newspapers a proprietor could sack any reporter, who, as it were, insisted on wearing the wrong hat, but things are very different now [81].

This conversation, and Wagner's response, plays up this tension over which entity is more inhibitive of a free press, corporate control or union capitulation, a tension most explicitly evidenced in Ruth's interjection that "Now the union can sack him instead" (82). Ruth's statement only elicits further discussion about which is the greater abuse to freedom of the press, during which time Wagner extols the virtues of Union power ("I'm not talking about protecting my job but my freedom to report facts that may not be congenial to, let us say, an English millionaire" [82]), while Ruth defends the millionaire owners ("You don't have to be a millionaire to contradict one. It isn't the millionaires who are going to stop you, it's the Wagners who don't trust the public to choose the marked card" [83]).

While Stoppard's attempt to present both sides of a debate equally is true to form,[6] the case against the censorship potential of the owners is so poorly argued (and to be fair, it is meant more as parody than argument) by Mageeba and Wagner that the audience never hears how the potential for corporate abuse becomes even more problematic with monopolization (not to mention multinational-monopolization). To be sure, the potential threat from corporatization is far more clearly evidenced in the Commission's report[7], which devotes an entire chapter to explaining how monopolization was influencing the industry. Monopolization's full effect on the demise of privately owned newspapers can be seen in some very telling statistics included within the report (see the graph on page 21 of the report). We get a good picture of the sheer scale of the change by considering the following passage:

> At one end of the scale, Reed International has an annual turnover of over £1,000 million and its main activity is paper manufacture and paper prod-ucts.... At the other end of the scale are family controlled companies which publish only a handful of weekly newspapers, perhaps with modest interests in contract and general printing and in newsagents shops [McGregor 1977:20].

It is evident, then, that increasing monopolization results in the loss of the local press: "In 1961 there were about 460 publishers of weekly newspa-pers only; there are now some 180" (McGregor 1977:22). The commission explains the potential consequences as follows:

> The fewer the companies owning papers in the provinces, the less the diver-sity of voices in the press as a whole, even though each is concerned mainly with local and regional issues. The ultimate danger is that if a company should fall into the hands of an irresponsible owner, the effects of his irre-sponsibility would be more dangerously widespread, the more newspapers he controlled [McGregor 1977:130].

The Commission comes closest to making the point that multinational control might develop into a new and more dangerous form of censorship with their additional statement that "the credibility of the press will dwin-dle the more it comes to be owned by large corporations whose interests are inevitably remote from those of the localities which their provincial papers serve" (McGregor 1977:130). This, then, raises the inevitable question of how someone is supposed to stand up to the millionaire owners of the multinational press when there is no remaining public forum of any size from which to confront it. Needless to say, the effect of a company that kept a firm grip on what it thought to be newsworthy would indeed be magnified in such a way that even though the press was nominally free, the effect would be such that (to use Stoppard's own words) "any situation was concealable."

From this perspective, perhaps Mageeba's concerns about the corporate press are justifiable, especially since the corporate press's interests are even more remote from Kambawe than they are from Grimsby. Indeed, that Mageeba fails to establish this point indicates just how unconcerned Stoppard is with the efficacy of representability in the era of multinational business. In responding to *Night and Day* David Edgar explains the unfairness of the implicit bias as follows: "Tom Stoppard stacked the cards so grossly against his left–wing villains ... that if any of us had tried the gambit the other way around, we would have been howled off stage" (quoted in John Bull's *Stage Right* 1994:195). That time and again Stoppard simply equates a free press with democratic social justice, without once expressing concern that even a free press might yet marginalize certain stories which run counter to its interests — and, moreover, that such marginalization might be compounded when the press is monopolized at the multinational level — only reinforces his difference with the left-wing sentiment of the "Theatre in Crisis" playwrights, concerned as they were with how too much corporate control of the theatre might marginalize certain playwrights whose ideas run counter to corporate Britain's various business endeavors.

Stoppard's uncritical attitude towards a multinational corporately controlled press becomes clearest in the final exchange of words that occurs between Ruth and Wagner before the conversation switches tracks to involve Mageeba and Wagner. Here, in response to Ruth's statement that freedom of the press is evidenced by the fact that "the country [Britain] is littered with papers pushing every political line from Mao to Mosley and back again," Wagner explains how little impact small time newspapers have when competing with national papers, explaining that "It's absurd to equate the freedom of the big battalions to the freedom of the pamphleteer to challenge them" (83). Ruth's unchallenged remark to this point (cited in brief above) is most telling:

> You are confusing freedom with ability. The *Flat Earth News* is *free* to sell a million copies. What it lacks is the ability to find a million people with four pence and a conviction that the earth is flat. Freedom is neutral. Free expression includes a state of affairs where any millionaire can have a national newspaper, if that's what it costs. A state of affairs where only a particular, approved, licensed and supervised non-millionaire can have a newspaper is called, for example, Russia [83].

Wagner isn't allowed an opportunity to respond because Mageeba interrupts to admit that the situation described by Ruth might, "of course, [refer to] Kambawe" (83). That Wagner doesn't respond indicates that Stoppard himself sees no possible response to Ruth's argument that the national press retains a large readership simply because it gives the public what it wants, while those forms of media which do not have a following fail simply because they don't provide that for the public.

That Ruth's sentiments correspond with Stoppard's own becomes clearer when we compare the first edition published in 1978 (from which I have been quoting) with the second edition published a year later. In the later edition we find that the entire debate has been replaced by parody, with Ruth simply parroting a conversation that she claims to have had with her son wherein she plays the part that had been Wagner's in the previous version, while she gives to her son the role that she had played. That once again Ruth's ideas (now Alastair's) win the argument hands down only serves to further undercut Wagner's position, now so easily refuted by a mere schoolboy (New York Edition, 83–85). Putting his own position into the "mouths of babes" is a rhetorical ploy that Stoppard has employed elsewhere, including both *Professional Foul* (1977) and *Every Good Boy Deserves Favour* (*1978*). John Fleming explicates the implication of this change similarly, explaining that it "only further skewers Wagner's views as now the suggestion is that even a child can see the "fallacy" of Wagner's leftist, union line" (2001:147), or, as Stoppard himself put it in an interview with Gollob and Roper about *Every Good Boy Deserves Favour*, even while you might be able to convince a "sophisticated person" that "life inside this wall [inside East Berlin] was admirable ... if you tried to do this to a child, he'd blow you to smithereens" (1981:164).

The play's negative attitude towards unionization is, finally, most explicit in the conclusion, at which time Wagner himself is unable to publish the scoop he has received by interviewing Mageeba. For finally (and ironically), the *Globe* has been shut down for the week due to the labor dispute instigated by Wagner's own earlier message concerning the Grimsby scab (i.e., Milne). Certainly the implication of this final irony is that Wagner "had to learn the hard way" the dangers of collective bargaining. And while Wagner had planned on leaving Kimbawe with his scoop, after hearing of the strike he decides to stay on, which begs the rhetorical question from Ruth, "Aren't you supposed to be withdrawing your labour?" Apparently Wagner has given up his labor principles, as he snaps back "Don't you get clever with me!" (92). Presumably by this point in the play the audience is also expected to have given up its labor principles as well.

At this juncture it is worth considering, by contrast, the full ramifications of Thatcher's new legislation regarding how the arts should be funded.

Following on the heels of the above research into the fate of the regional press, the following description of the fate of the regional theatre should come as no surprise:

> So in the first half of the 1990's the signs of a collapsing system appeared everywhere, ranging from the Royal Shakespeare Company closing the Barbican Theatre for six months in a desperate attempt to reduce its growing deficit to the Liverpool Playhouse appearing in court under the threat of receivership. Yet the economic misery was not evenly spread, as an acute contrast in financial performance between London's commercial theatres and the regional subsidized theatres demonstrates. There was a drastic 25% drop in total attendances at regional theatre (12 to 9 million) between 1992 and 1995, while those for London's West end rose only slightly, but produced a 6% growth in box-office revenue. In this sector, government policies that "freed" the market seemed to be working. But despite efforts by the Arts Council to prevent it, the deterioration of regional theatre continued throughout the decade, prompting even the ultra-conservative Whittaker's Almanac to pronounce in 1997 that "The days of a repertory rooted in its community and producing work which reflects that community appear to be numbered," and leading Peter Hall to claim in 1999 that "We're going to end up with almost no regional theatre except for one or two centres, say Leeds and Birmingham" [Kershaw 280].

What we find then is that the consequence of the free market arts support system encouraged and supported by Thatcher's government so benefited the large production company at the expense of the small one that the theatre, like the press before it, became dominated by fewer and fewer production companies, many of which had multinational connections. Consequently, Stoppard's refusal to comment on this situation — when considered against his implicit acceptance of press corporatization two decades earlier — comes across as at least tacit approval of the Thatcherite agenda and its consequences.

By contrast, the exploration of the corporatization of the theatre that playwrights such as Caryl Churchill undertook (in plays such as *Serious Money*) couldn't be more different from what we find in Stoppard, not only politically — as Churchill does support a social structure which would redistribute funds in such a way as to serve as a counterbalance to monopoly control of the theatre — but also in Churchill's perception of the role that she herself plays in determining the future of theatre in Britain. For while in *Night and Day* Stoppard situates himself as an outsider capable of standing back from the goings-on between the NUJ and the corporate press and, consequently, able to objectively judge the situation for what it is, Churchill uses *Serious Money* to analyze her own role in the power/knowledge theatrical hierarchy. And, moreover, while Stoppard conveniently ignores the fact that as a public figure his theatre projects at least in part succeed or fail based on how they are reviewed in the press, Churchill's *Serious Money* is framed in a way that leaves no doubt that Churchill understand the relationship between the theatrical power structure and the success and/or failure of her own work[8].

Presumably, then, Stoppard believes that cutting-edge theatre is supposed to compete with corporate sponsored theatre in the same way that the alternative press is supposed to compete with the multi-national press. And yet one can't help but wonder what would have become of Stoppard's own *Rosencrantz and Guildenstern Are Dead* had it not entered the marketplace in the comparatively hospitable environment of the late 60's, at a time when public funding for the arts was much more substantial than it was by the time of the Theatre in Crisis movement (the first two chapters of John Fleming's *Stoppard's Theatre* puts this into proper perspective, where Fleming makes clear that *R & G* finally found its way into production as much by chance and circumstance as by resolutely winning over those who read the script).

Moreover, it is worth remembering that by the time of the Theatre in Crisis Conference Stoppard would hardly have felt the pressure that Thatcher's agenda had on the theatre more generally, as by this time his work had already found its way onto the international tourist map and, consequently, actually stood to benefit from the new system. Furthermore, given Stoppard's attitude about success simply being a consequence of producing good and timely material, by this late date in his career it would have been all too easy for him to simply assume that his own success had come about as a consequence of the simple fact that his work provides the public what it wants, while theatre which fails does so only because it is, perhaps, all too intent on finding "a million people with four pence and a conviction that the earth is flat," or is peddling some other such unmarketable nonsense. While this final observation is largely conjecture given Stoppard's silence on this issue, it is reasonably clear that, for all of Stoppard's concern about freedom of expression, the voice of those within the community theatre system struggling to find exposure for their ideas isn't very high on his list of concerns. Moreover, this particular reading of Stoppard's silence resonates in meaningful ways with the most fundamental distinction between playwrights such as Stoppard and Churchill (i.e., their differing epistemological values). For while in her own work Churchill focuses on how all knowledge — even that knowledge presented within her own plays — is constructed according to the dictates of the power elite, Stoppard's work (especially in such plays as *Arcadia* and *Hapgood*), by contrast, suggests that knowledge is something sacred, whose free pursuit can lead to the recovery of truth, beauty, and to the reinvigoration of democracy. To imagine that his own success is, perhaps, dependent upon just how well he tows this very line of thought is, for Stoppard, unthinkable; his plays frequent the national theatre because they belong there.

NANYANG TECHNOLOGICAL UNIVERSITY, SINGAPORE

Notes

1. During the eighteen year tenure of Conservative Party Prime Ministers Thatcher and Major from 1979 to 1997, the arts council budget tripled from 63 million to 186 million, while during the nine year tenure of Labor Party Prime Minister Tony Blair from 1997 to 2006, the budget has more than doubled from 186 million to 410 million. (Arts Council Document accessed at http://www.artscouncil.org.uk/documents/information/HistoryACE_phpJGGeGy.doc on August 14, 2006).

2. See the article "Labour pandering to philistines," BBC News, [Sunday, November 29] accessed at http://news.bbc.co.uk/2/hi/entertainment/224151.stm on April 7).

3. To quote Stoppard at greater length: "It seems to be the case, unfortunately, that despite the government's extremely comfortable majority, they still seem to be super-sensitive to offending the philistine sensibilities of the electorate." (For citation information, see note 1.)

4. It would seem, then, that the real anomaly in this turn of events doesn't reside so much in the fact that Stoppard joined the "Shadow Art's Council" while avoiding the "theatre in crisis" movement, but, rather, that Caryl Churchill signed on to both, especially given her strong commitment to community based social activist theatre evidenced in her work with such groups as Monstrous Regiment and Joint Stock.

5. Except where noted to the contrary, I will be referencing the revised Grove Press edition of 1979.

6. Consider the comments on the aesthetic debate of *Travesties* Stoppard made in interview with Ross Wetzsteon ("Tom Stoppard Eats Steak Tartare with Chocolate Sauce." *Village Voice* (10 Nov. 1975): 121: "Of course I don't want to give any of them shallow arguments and then knock them down. No, you have to give the best possible argument for each of them. It's like playing chess with yourself-you have to try to win just as hard at black as you do with white... But while my sympathies may be divided in that sense, I find Joyce infinitely the most important."

7. In *Tom Stoppard and the Craft of Comedy* (153) Katherine Kelly claims that Stoppard followed this debate closely, and that he would have been versed in the commission's report (Ann Arbor: University of Michigan Press, 1991).

8. For a more thorough discussion of the way in which *Serious Money* is conscious of its own role in the power/knowledge hierarchy, see my essay "*Serious Money* Becomes "Business by Other Means": Caryl Churchill's Metatheatrical Subject," *Comparative Drama* 38:2 & 3 (Summer/Fall 2004).

9. See my essay "Tom Stoppard and 'Postmodern Science': Normalizing Radical Epistemologies in *Hapgood* and *Arcadia*" in *Comparative Drama*. 37 (Spring 2003): 3–35.

References Cited

Bragg, Melvyn. *The South Bank Show*, London Weekend Television, 26 November 1978, reprinted in *Stoppard in Conversation*. Edited by Delaney. Ann Arbor: University of Michigan Press, 1994.

Bull, John Bull. *Stage Right: Crisis and Recovery in British Contemporary Mainstream Theatre*. New York: St. Martins Press, 1994.

Churchill, Caryl. *Serious Money. Plays: Two*. London: Methuen, 1990.

Fleming, John. Stoppard's *Theatre: Finding Order Amid Chaos*. Austin: Texas University Press, 2001.

Gollob, David and David Roper. "Trad Tom Pops In:," *Gambit* 10:37 (1981): 5–17, 15.

Hewett, Ivan. "Ineffable or Just Indefinable." *Prospect Magazine* 41 (May 1999 accessed at http://www.prospect-magazine.co.uk/article_details.php?id=3932 on August 14, 2006).

Kershaw, Baz. "Discouraging Democracy: British Theatres and Economics, 1979–1999." *Theatre Journal* 51:3 (1999): 267–283.

Lavender, Andy. "Theatre in Crisis: Conference Report, December 1988." *New Theatre Quarterly* 5 (1989): 211–213.

McGregor, O. R., Chairman. *Royal Commission on the Press: Final Report*. London: Her Majesty's Stationery Office, 1977.

Stoppard, Tom. *Night and Day*. New York: Grove Press, 1979.

_____. *Night and Day*. London: Faber and Faber, 1978.

9

Metaphor and Semiotics in Text and Movement Dance Performance

Jeffrey Louis Kaplan

Abstract

This paper attempts to develop a visual philosophical model for meaning-making in contemporary dance performance that incorporates spoken text. How do audiences synthesize simultaneous auditory and visual streams of information? To what do they attend? To answer these and related questions, I have conducted a review of relevant theory from semiotics, cognitive linguistics, philosophy of language, and the philosophy of dance. As a result of this research, I was able to conclude that text-based contemporary dance works create webs of metaphorization through the intertwining of texts characteristic of the art form. Although multiple texts are present and interweave in any theatrical event, modern dance that incorporates spoken language uniquely places emphasis on the interface of verbal and body texts. A high level of congruency between these textual domains reads as literalism and a high degree of disconnect abstraction.

In the spring of 2006, I premiered a 30-minute solo performance piece entitled, "The Man Who Planted Trees." Performing outdoors in front of a small grove of trees, I danced while reciting French writer Jean Giono's short story by the same name. Giono sets his story in Provence against the backdrop of the first half of the twentieth century. The protagonist, a traveler, repeatedly encounters a peasant shepherd who redeems the land and finds peace through the daily act of planting trees over a period of decades. I attempted to craft movement evocative of Giono's semi-mythic morality tale. The piece was to be a union of theatrical story telling and modern dance.

After immersing myself in the text and background research for several months, I created movement that I hoped would not only support and inform Giono's words and add to the audience's experience in a substantive way, but

95

also avoid drawing attention to my dancing qua dance. At times I employed visual commentary to alter the meaning of the text and vice versa. Once or twice I utilized gestures to imply a sly irony not present in my vocal intonations or facial expressions, such as doing the chicken dance while speaking about a team of government experts hard at work in the forest and accomplishing very little. At other points in the story, I manipulated the tempo of the movement to convey the main character's experience of time.

Finding the correct tension between text and dance proved to be an exercise in balance. Throughout the process of making the work, I assiduously tried to avoid derivative, pantomimic, or kitsch "interpretive" dancing, but at the same time did not shy away from abstraction or athleticism in my movement choices. Based on audience response, I was successful in creating synchronicity between sight and sound, word and gesture.

As an artist, I arrived at my performance text intuitively. But as a scholar, how am I to understand and articulate the dynamics involved in the various implicit intertexts? A large component of my artistic work involves explorations in a style of modern dance known as "text and movement." In this genre, spoken language and dance coexist to form an overlay of image

The Man Who Planted Trees. Text by Jean Giono. Choreography and Performance by Jeff Kaplan. Texas Woman's University Campus, Denton, Texas, May 5, 2006. Photo by Laurie Sanda.

and words. Simply put, I speak while dancing. Movement and language may support one another, contradict one another, or, perhaps, have no obvious relationship. I am interested in how audiences make sense of performances when confronted with simultaneous visual and auditory modes of representation. To what do they attend? How do they bring differing streams of information together? This paper attempts to model these dynamics.

The Body as Metaphor

William Herlofsky (2003) provides an intriguing point of departure in an apparently parallel problem: Haiku poetry performed in Japanese Sign Language. In this case, meaning emerges on multiple levels. In addition to the literal translation of codified gestures, and the various ways in which these word translations connote associations, the body itself serves as a medium of communication. The presence of the body in Sign creates a bi-directional flow of meaning because, "for the body and other forms of materiality to be graspable via language, linguistic meaning must already have some kind of corporeality" (Ruthrof 2000:vi). Body and text inform one another through the interface of meaning-gestures.

Herlofsky attempts to untangle this web by applying cognitive linguistic models of metaphor. He begins with the assumptions that "the mind is inherently embodied," "thought is mostly unconscious," and that "abstract concepts are largely metaphorical" (2003:43). Of course, definitions of metaphor "vary widely and invariably excite debate" (Haley 1988:8). For Herlofsky, metaphors are the blending of two or more previously unrelated objects, themselves composed of more primitive or primary metaphors.

The distinctness of the source and target domains in the following figure implies a degree of cognitive dissonance. Metaphors reveal truths precisely because of their nonsensical concatenations of qualities. Philosopher Gemma Fiumara notes:

> The boundary between metaphor and nonsense frequently appears to be flexible and permeable for indeed, if read literally, metaphor violates the conditions governing normal application of its terms by joining words whose semantic markers are incompatible [1995:117].

To take a classic example from the philosophy of language (Searle 1979), Romeo's declamation, "Juliet is the sun," is not an astronomical observation, nor flowery poetry, but a statement of fact. Juliet is the center of Romeo's universe, his source of warmth, life, and illumination. Metaphors do not make literal sense, but instantiate deeper truths.

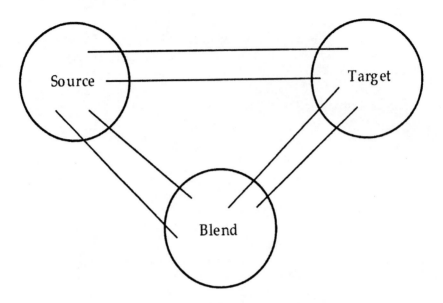

Metaphoric blending (after Herlofsky).

Herlofsky theorizes that performing Haiku in Sign establishes a mapping between visual targets and mental sources, which by definition creates metaphors. For example, signing "The Milky Way [is a] rough sea" evokes, for someone fluent in Japanese Sign Language, associations not just on the poetic level, but also through the shapes of the gestures themselves (Herlofsky 2003:58). The concatenation of signs and words, themselves composed of more primary associations, really makes metaphors of metaphors. A high degree of congruency between multi-tiered mental and visual representation lends a sense of literalism, whereas less iconic targets appear more abstract (Herlofsky 2003:59). Also, because Japanese is a pictographic language, visual resemblances of characters to gestures and/or meanings adds yet another layer of mapping (2003:47–9). All of these mappings contribute to a layered and broadened feeling characteristic of metaphorization.

Although our colloquial understanding of metaphor probably involves mappings between words, source and target domains may be of any kind. This process is in fact what accounts for how multiple streams of sensory information can create metaphorical webs of meaning rather than cacophonous tangles. For example, I witnessed this kind of spontaneous layering in *National Theater for the Deaf*'s 1995 touring production of Dylan Thomas's *Under Milk Wood*. In this production, a narrator read the poem out loud while the others performers silently signed the text in fluid, dance-like movements. I remember wondering how my experience of this performance event might have differed from that of a hearing-impaired audience member. Were we indeed witnessing the same event? I might have had more insight into the piece based on nuances in the spoken words, but a spectator fluent in sign would undoubtedly have seen more than I could in the soft bending of standard sign convention. Either pathway involves the creation of metaphors.

Perhaps metaphor in Herlofsky's sense corresponds to what we think of as truthfulness in performance, or what Susan Melrose calls *"felt specificity"* (2004:8). For instance, in creating my piece to Giono's text, I threw out a great deal of movement in trial and error sessions in the studio because they did not seem particularly "inevitable" or "right." In reciting a given passage, a turn felt no more truthful than a jump. At other times, however, certain gestures or shapes did have an "aha!" quality. They felt as though they were connecting to something specific, hence Melrose's term. At one point, a certain undulating arm gesture did seem connected to fields of wild Provençal lavender, although I could not have said at the time why.

A simplifying aspect in the semiotic reading of sign language-based performance, however, is that sign language gestures map directly onto meanings. This occurs to some extent in any communicative context. Ruthrof claims that, "the linkage between language and our nonverbal construals is at the heart of meaning" (2000:21). Theatrically presented Sign is a particularly vivid instance of these construals, and hence metaphorization. But is this relationship always present in dance? Ruthrof continues:

> The corporeal signified of language, then, is a linguistic signifier activated by nonverbal signs. In this explanation, the signifier acts as a rule agreed upon by a community that sets 'boundaries' for what sort of nonverbal readings are to be selected in each instance as activating signs [2000:104].

"...[A]greed on by a community..." is a pivotal phrase. Unlike gestures in sign languages, the meaning of dance movements, especially contemporary, invented ones, are rarely "agreed upon" by an entire community. Dance gestures, although sometimes capable of allusion or indicating mood or tone, etc., rarely connote similar associations for each audience member. In point of fact, dance gestures do not have to mean anything at all.

Unlike dance, in embodied language such as sign languages, communities agree on the literal reading of gestures, be they abstract or iconic. Fiumara states that, "domains of univocity" are "no more than relatively stable areas of consensual linguistic behavior" (1995:33). These areas are undoubtedly grounded in corporeal experience. "For instance, without a nonverbal imaginative realization of 'acrid,' the word by itself would mean no more than 'x'" (Ruthrof 2000:100–1). Sign language and dance appear similar. But spectators may not share any degree of consensus in their readings because contemporary dance does not contain *a priori* definitions for the meaning of gestures.

Certain specialized instances in dance might convey univocity. For example, the 19th-century audiences for whom classical story ballets were made would have easily parsed the narrative pantomime. Also, emblematic shapes and movements can sometimes encapsulate a dance, career, or even an entire genre. In me piece, a percussive lift of the sternum followed by a deep arch which took me backwards all the way to the ground as I spoke the word "wind" created, for most of the audience, an equivalence between that movement and wind. These are all instances of communally understood meanings.

Contemporary dance movement does not usually follow an isomorphic, or a one-to-one, relationship with meaning, even in the presence of spoken text. Rather, meanings in dances accumulate in an impressionistic manner. They unfold or emerge like photographs in a rinse bath. A seven-minute dance may be "about" the first whiff of a rose. Even my distinctive "wind" gesture altered and changed each time I used it in the story. Dances may refer to "complementarities operating both in a conception of theater and in a conception of the wider 'real out there'" (Melrose 1994:55), but at other times they seem to only refer to themselves. A single movement may convey radically varying tones when used in different dances, unlike a chair in a play, which, whatever other associations it may take on, never ceases being a chair.

The Body as Text

Consequently, our understanding of the relationship between text and movement in contemporary dance requires additional analytical tools. The application of Herlofsky's model seems like a near miss. There is nonetheless a strong intuition that satisfying dances "speak." Another way of making sense of the simultaneous presence of text and movement is to interpret both as texts. In this case, two texts exist: the body text and the spoken text. Dance philosopher Susan Leigh Foster, in her dissertation (1982) and early work (1986), created a framework for understanding how choreographers "write" dances and how audiences "read" them. This approach may have more utility.

Foster formulates how dance events carry within themselves the codes for their own interpretations. Choreographers communicate a context for their works by the choices they make in regards to publicity, type of venue, programs, piece titles, beginning and endings of dances, and dancer focus

(Foster 1986:59–65). Choreographers further frame their dances through modes of representation, "in which dances resemble, imitate, replicate, or reflect something of the outside world" (1986:65). All of these choices orient the audience within the world of the piece.

Once oriented, an audience can begin to read characteristic movement qualities, or even "characteristic use of parts of the body with their various symbolic associations" as "style" (Foster 1986:78). The audience may begin to recognize identifiable movement "vocabulary" within this style (1986:88). Also, audiences may be able to follow compositional choices that create a sense of internal coherence in the dance. These "syntactical rules" within the world and style of the piece tell the audience how to read the work's vocabulary (1986:92).

Foster's model is highly internally coherent, even if twenty years on, some shortcomings now seem evident. For instance, many contemporary choreographers collaborate with their dancers in making work. This is problematic because the line between choreographer and dancers becomes blurred and choreographic intent difficult to pinpoint. Also, Foster's model indicates that there is only one structure per dance. If multiple readings of a dance are valid, then either her model lacks flexibility or else we must assume that those audience members with different views on what they saw did not "get it."

Still, this framework has proven useful and popular in dance scholarship. For example, dance historian Mark Franko (1993) has investigated how to read the text written on and by the Baroque dancing body. Conversely, literary theorists have made extensive use of the body as a metaphor for analyzing text:

> When you look through the catalogues of the leading presses you will note that the body now turns up everywhere. From literary theory and criticism to law and sociology, from gender studies to anthropology and philosophy, the body runs through the titles like an oncoming spring tide [Ruthrof 2000:vi].

Also, frankly, the metaphor of movement as text is reassuring. As dance and performance theoriest André Lepecki notes, "mostly, movement disappears, it marks the passing of time" (2004:128). Yet having "read" a dance, the "reader" has been changed in more ways than witnessing so much abstract movement to a random piece of music might suggest. The idea of writing dances seems less tragically ephemeral than performing them.

If the body may be read as a text, then all of the other elements of theatrical presentation, such as costume, lighting, and set, are texts with stories to tell. These nonverbal texts, what Patrice Pavis calls *"visual discourse"*

(1982:171). While detached from language, these modes nevertheless connect "to structures within the realms of fantasy and imagination" (1982:171). In theatre, spoken text is commonly seen as just one of the many texts that are present (de Toro 1995:36). This way of thinking about performance can radically alter the reading of dances.

A dance as a text is highly context dependent: "If any element of a performance — for example an image, a movement, a sound — can be treated as a 'text,' then each element can be 'read,' singly or in units, through codes on which it draws" (Adshead-Landsdale 1999:9). As codes change, the meanings of texts change. Me (a Caucasian male) speaking and dancing text from Maya Angelou's *I Know Why the Caged Bird Sings* activates very different codes than if an African American woman performs the same text and movement. A naked African American woman performing the same text and movement while being watched by a white man also on the stage says something very different yet again, not to mention the impact of the texts written by the theatre event, such as the racial composition of the audience. Dances cannot be understood solely on the basis of the choreography.

The way that texts inter-relate to create narrative is more obvious in theatre. Patrice Pavis notes that:

> The *mise en scène* is not the putting into practice of what is present in the text. On the contrary, it is the speaking of the text in a given staging, the way in which its presuppositions, its unspoken elements and its enunciations are brought out that will confer on it a particular meaning [1982:18].

But Pavis's quote applies to dance if we equate the "speaking of the text" with dancing and "text" with choreography. The dancing of the choreography in a given context helps determine meaning. Just as in theatre, this context contains all other texts, whether they are set, costume, or abstract dance. One might go as far to say that audiences do not read texts singly at all in theatre or dance, but rather apprehend the interference patterns generated by interweaving texts.

In addition to influence from context and intertextuality, texts are further subject to change due to the collaborative and social nature of their formation. Fiumara points out that, "possible human worlds are collaboratively constructed and transformed through the unbreakable interaction of listening and speaking" (1995:9). Even a soloist rehearsing alone comprises a community of one, speaking and listening to him or her self. Text is a "structure that allows the reader to *generate* meanings, not as a vehicle through which a predetermined meaning can be discovered" (Adshead-Landsdale 1999:16). All this is another way of saying that the audience co-creates the performance event.

While many members of the audience for my Giono piece gave me congruent feedback, certain moments stood out for different audience members in ways that surprised me. A certain circling pattern during a descriptive passage elicited wildly varying responses, whereas giant consecutive standing broad jumps apparently conveyed for nearly everyone an identical sense of the effort required to hike through Provence in the parched summer. As choreographers know, what you intended in a piece may or may not have anything to do with what an audience takes away from the experience.

Foster's analysis is both helpful and unhelpful. If we choose to see dance and speech as kinds of text, it solves the problems raised in trying to apply Herlofsky's analysis: intertwining texts are sites of metaphorization, pure and simple. Text and movement in text and movement dance performance are streams of metaphors that not only operate individually, but also generate metaphorization through iconic mapping onto one another. Herlofsky's model still applies, but now we relabel the domains "words" and "movement."

This model certainly accounts for meaning-making in text and movement dance performance. The obvious problem, though, is that if a text can be anything, what is a text, really? In analyzing dance, "what happens to the distinction of body and text once one critiques the putative distinctions between writing and dancing?" (Lepecki 2004:133). Dance is not the same as spoken text, which is not the set, etc: "Where lie the limits between body and text, movement and language" (2004:124). What additional benefit do we gain from calling dance text? What makes the intertext of speech and dance distinct from other types of intertexts? How does calling a dance a text deepen our understanding of the relationship of movement to words?

The Body as Signifier

Semiotic analysis, especially visual semiotic models, offers a *lingua franca* for combining Herlofsky and Foster's systems into a fully explanatory system. Foster's typology of dances is in fact semiotic in origin (Foster 1986:232). Although semiotics in any form has been characterized as the search for the answer to the question, "what are the minimal units of meaning?" (Parivs 1982:100), graphical models might facilitate the representation of meaning even better, particularly given the visual nature of dance as an art form.

Specifically, Floyd Merrell (2003) offers a graphical explication, notable for its clarity, of the basic building block of semiotic analysis: the semiotic sign. Merrell presents the classical components of the semiotic sign: a semi-otic object (O), its representamen (R), and interpretant (I) as a trefoil loop surrounding a central vortex (Merrell 2003:35). I would like to use this graphic as the basis for subsequent analysis.

Merrell includes the trefoil loop and vortex to indicate that although the triadic structure of signs suggests stability, semiotic signs are in a constant state of flux. Signs can even exist in spaces that are curved or multi-dimensional, "non–Euclidean" or "Hyperbolic" (Merrell 2003:44–45). A representamen may become an object in a different sign. In fact, each part of the triad can become a signifying system in its own right. Semantic reality rests atop an undifferentiated churning soup of open possibility. Signs flow into and out of being and into and out of relatedness to each other. Of course, all language changes over time, but meaning may also change from person to person, culture to culture, and from moment to moment.

Implicit in this model are more interesting ways of seeing text and

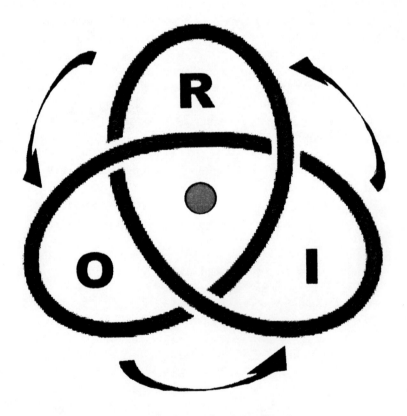

Semiotic knot (after Merrell).

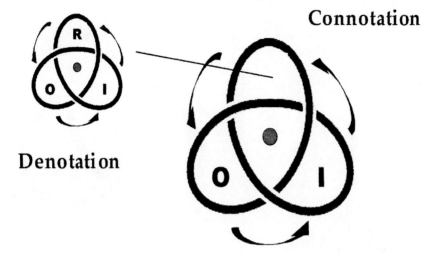

Connotation/Denotation.

movement than the obvious semiotic one of signifier to signified. The straightforward approach would be to interpret a word and a movement performed together as a sign: R = gesture, O = word, I = sense. This is really an equivalent meaning-making process to gestures representing words in sign language. As before, such a dictionary-like approach seems insufficient.

A more promising lead starts with Roland Barthes's (1968) study of connotation and denotation in semiotic systems. Denotation occurs when a referent of one sign expands into a new system (Barthes 1968:89–90). I have translated Barthes's (1968) idea and vocabulary into Merrell's visual system in the above figure:

"Meta-languages" work the same way (Barthes 1968), but occur when the object of the system expands into a new sign.

Of course, multiple layering of connotation, denotation, and meta-language may occur (see figure *Semiotic Webs*). Such layering, Barthes felt (1968), forms variegated systems of signification that convey tone, texture, and themes.

These aggregating webs of interconnectivity seem very dance-like to me. In a dance, as gestures repeat, motifs begin to emerge. During the experience of a dance, movements develop into vocabularies. That is to say, characteristic patterns in space, time, and energy develop giving the work a sense of itself. Characteristic dance movements begin to relate to each other in increasingly textured ways as the dance progresses. Barthe's semiotic webs in Merrell's visual language (see figure *Semiotic Webs*), seems to capture the essence of this process.

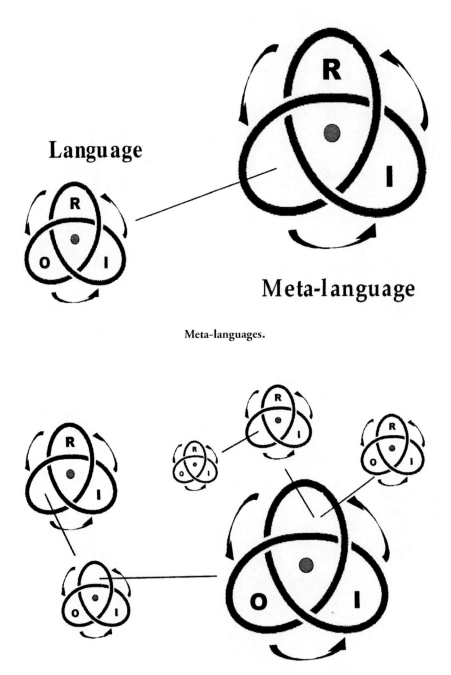

Language

Meta-language

Meta-languages.

Semiotic webs.

Text and Movement as Semiotic Metaphor

To focus more tightly on the way in which text and movement actually interact, we must also translate Herlofsky's ideas into Merrell's visual language. In Herlofsky's analysis, any two domains can blend together to form a metaphor. Here, any connection between two signs, or more likely two clusters of signs, results in metaphor.

Again, clusters may involve a great number of signs. And probably, webs of connotations and meta-languages extend to the point that no two clusters of signs are ever entirely distinct. By the time I use the wind gesture in my piece for the fourth time, the audience has developed a certain history with it. They begin to associate more and more elements with both the gesture and the words surrounding it and perceive increasingly textured metaphors. Or they might get bored!

It is also possible that some signs have the propensity to connect more readily to some types of signs than others. Perhaps the greater the pre-existing number of connections between two clusters of signs, or the greater the propensity for these clusters to connect, the more literal the metaphor will seem.

For example, many connections already exist between the words "blood" and "red" (blood, in fact, is red) so the metaphor seems literal. Alternatively, when an artist connects two domains that do not have many pre-existing connections, the viewer experiences a "semantic shock" (Haley 1988:14). Searle's example of Juliet (1979) is a good example.

"Juliet is the sun" is unexpected. It has few pre-existing connections and hence a high degree of abstraction and shock. In my piece, when I speak of

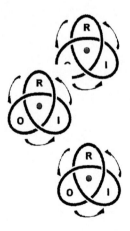

Semiotic metaphor.

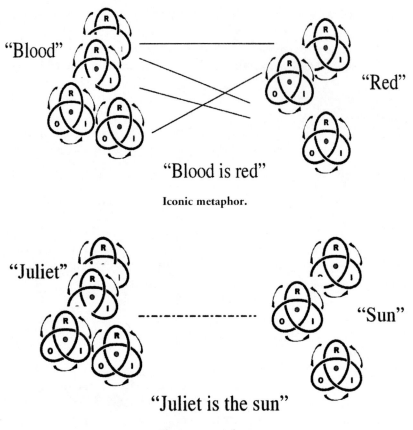

"Blood"

"Red"

"Blood is red"

Iconic metaphor.

"Juliet"

"Sun"

"Juliet is the sun"

Abstract metaphor.

suicidal madness and then begin to allow my hand to tremble violently with the palm exposed to face the audience, the symbolism is vivid and jarring, but unclear.

And in fact, as Haley notes, "not just any fiat of fancy that brings two contrary objects together in an anomalous connection, however imaginative, can qualify as poetic metaphor" (1988:47). The metaphor "Dog 87 (rain-like noise)" hardly even makes sense, at least without context. Strong metaphors are unexpected, but also "instantiate metaphoric truth" (Haley 1988:47). That is to say, the act of naming them creates an "ah, yes, of course!" feeling rather than a "say, what?"

Perhaps strong metaphors do have pre-existing connections between domains, but these connections are hidden in some way or unrecognized until named. Naming the metaphor causes large-scale reorganization in connoted domains. I suspect that there is more than one way that a metaphor may be strong. But in all cases there is some kind of implication. Our knowledge shifts. We see things in a different way. My standing broad jumps across Provence appeared to make a connection that most of the audience was already ready to make. I had apparently made a connection between a gesture and a passage of text that had not yet been associated together, but were highly conducive to this connection.

With some of the dynamics of metaphor now described visually, text and movement in a more general sense may be modeled as in the next figure. As before, semiotic knots represent the basic units of meaning on stage. These knots form patterns through mechanisms such as connotation/denotation/meta-language (Barthes 1968). As patterns become distinct, they may be read as texts. These texts change, depending on context, relationship to other texts, and intertextuality, and differ for each audience member.

Metaphors and motifs of metaphors in the piece may include clusters of signs that viewers are likely to have had access to in the past. In this case, the dance may have a sense of connecting to the outside world. My chicken dance to describe a government expedition amounted to a straightforward

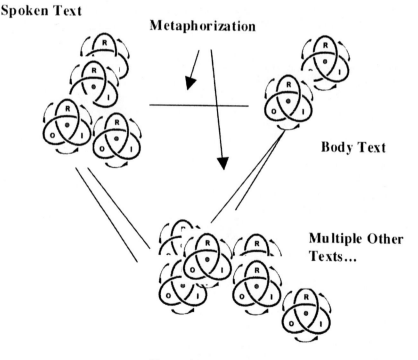

Text and movement.

allusion both to a known gesture and to a common feeling about bureaucracy. Alternatively, dances can develop clusters of signs through repetition and motif exclusively. The dance will seem to only refer to itself. At other points in my piece, I chose to make very specific gestures that did not particularly allude to anything consistently, but served as a recurring motif. Choreographic choices convey a self-referential quality will usually produce a broad range of interpretations.

The accessibility of the piece will depend on the level of iconicity within the spoken text and body text domains. At a certain level of disconnect between dance and speech, the audience will tend to experience confusion, frustration, or even boredom. On the other hand, text and speech that too closely resemble each other will appear mimetic, predictable, and not having much to offer or reveal. Depending on the needs of the piece, the choreographer and performer must find the right balance of abstraction and literalism, of shock value and familiarly to sustain audience interest, give the audience a sense of having taken a journey, and lend a sense of having learned something along the way.

INDEPENDENT SCHOLAR

Notes

Acknowledgments. I would like to thank Texas Woman's University faculty members Dr. Linda Caldwell, Dr. Penelope Hanstein, Ms. Sarah Gamblin, and Dr. Victoria McGillin for their mentorship, editorial advice, and support. I would also like to thank my wife, Dr. Laurie Sanda, for her countless acts of kindness.

References Cited

Ashead-Lansdale, Janet. "Creative Ambiguity: Dancing Intertexts." *Dancing Texts: Intertextuality in Interpretation*, edited by Janet Ashead-Lansdale, 1–25. London: Dance Books, 1999.
Barthes, Roland. *Elements of Semiology.* Translated by Annette Lavers & Colin Smith. New York: Hill and Wang, 1968.
Deely, John. *Basics of Semiotics.* Bloomington & Indianapolis: Indiana University Press, 1990.
De Toro, Fernando. *Theatre Semiotics: Text and Staging in Modern Theater,* edited by John Lewis. Trans. John Lewis. Toronto & Buffalo: University of Toronto Press, 1995.
Eco, Umberto. *A Theory of Semiotics.* Bloomington & London: Indiana University Press, 1979.
Fiumara, Gemma. *The Metaphoric Process: Connections Between Language and Life.* London & New York: Routledge, 1995.

Foster, Susan Leigh. *Reading Dancing: Gestures Towards a Semiotics of Dance.* Unpublished Doctoral Dissertation, University of California, Santa Cruz, 1982.

_____. *Reading Dancing: Bodies and Subjects in Contemporary American Dance.* Berkeley: University of California Press, 1986.

Franko, Mark. *Dance as Text: Ideologies of the Baroque Body.* Cambridge: Cambridge University Press, 1993.

Haley, Michael. *Semeiosis of Poetic Metaphor.* Bloomington & Indianapolis: Indiana University Press, 1988.

Herlofsky, William. "What You See is What You Get: Iconicity and Metaphor in the Visual Language of Written and Signed Poetry: A Cognitive Poetic Approach." *From Sign to Signing: Iconicity in Language and Literature 3,* edited by Wolfgang G. Müller & Olga Fischer, 41–61. Amsterdam and Philadelphia: John Benjamins Publishing Company, 2003.

Lepecki, André. "Inscribing Dance." *Of the Presence of the Body: Essays on Dance and Performance Theory,* edited by André Lepecki, 124–139. Middeltown: Wesleyan University Press, 2004.

Melrose, Susan. *A Semiotics of the Dramatic Text.* New York: St. Martin's Press, 1994.

Merrell, Floyd. *Sensing Corporeally: Toward a Posthuman Understanding.* Toronto: University of Toronto Press, 2003.

Pavis, Patrice. *Languages of the Stage: Essays in the Semiology of the Theatre.* New York: Performing Arts Journal Publications, 1982.

Ruthrof, Horst. *The Body in Language.* London & New York: Cassell, 2000.

Searle, John. *Expression and Meaning: Study in the Theory of Speech Acts.* Cambridge: Cambridge University Press, 1979.

Theatre Hoplology

Simulations and Representations
of Violence on the Stage

Meron Langsner

Abstract

There is a phrase attributed to Picasso that goes, "Art is the lie that tells the truth." While the truth, or the art, of that statement is open to all manner of interpretation, it provides a useful starting point in examining stage combat. What is the "truth" about violence that stage combat tells? How does stage combat "lie" in order to tell us that truth? How is the arrangement of sequences of fake violence in fact an art? Each step in a technique has a very different significance to the actors as compared to the audience. To the actors, each step is either a cue or the mechanical execution of a performance technique; to the audience, each step is part of the story unfolding onstage. Each beat is coded differently depending on the positionality of the receiving party. This study contextualizes stage combat in a framework based on Meyerhold, Baudrillard, semiotics, and both sporting and historical combat practices.

There is a phrase attributed to Picasso that goes, "Art is the lie that tells the truth." This statement provides a useful starting point in examining stage combat. What is the "truth" about violence that stage combat tells? How does stage combat "lie" in order to tell us that truth? How does the craft of arranging sequences of simulated violence fit into the art of theatre as a whole?

Though stage combat techniques have become common convention, there have been few critical analyses of how the techniques actually convey information to the audience. There is a wealth of information in print by high level practitioners and teachers such as Dale Anthony Girard, Richard Lane, J.D. Martinez, and J. Allen Suddeth on production concerns in fight scenes and training techniques for actor combatants, there is also abundant literature concerning application of force in self defense, martial arts and sports, military history, and the history of swordplay, as well as abundant scholarship about the appearance of violence in various forms of media. However, there is as yet very little about what those techniques meant to portray violence onstage have or do not have in common with that which they represent or how those techniques differ in content for the audience as opposed to performers executing the movements.[1]

Violence on the stage is traditionally represented by choreography meant to communicate a sequence of physical events relating to one party attempting to inflict physical harm on another for the benefit of an audience within the context of a stage production. Actors performing this choreography make use of movement, sound (both percussive and vocal), and spoken text to communicate the physical conflict of the characters in a drama.

What is being signified on the stage in these sequences is physical violence. There is a tremendous disparity between the representation of physical violence on the stage and the execution of physical violence in either social competitive situations such as sports (boxing, fencing, wrestling, Judo, MMA, etc), actual physical altercations or assaults, military combat, or other situations in which one party is in fact trying to apply varying degrees of physical force against another.

The relationship between simulated and actual violence is often a distant one. But as modern society most often experiences violence through very controlled prepackaged means, the simulation carries more weight than the real. Baudrillard's comments on the murder of the real by imagery is a useful starting point for beginning to examine representations of violence:

> Thus perhaps at stake has always been the murderous capacity of images, murderers of the real, murderers of their own model as the Byzantine icons could murder the divine identity. To this murderous capacity is opposed the dialectical capacity of representations as a visible and intelligible mediation of the Real [Baudrillard 1983:10].

While Baudrillard's attestation that the Real can be negated through imagery would be naively utopian when applied to images of violence, it is applicable to the discipline of stage combat as it relates to acts of real violence as well as in comparison to martial arts, contact sports, and military practices which either express or mediate the application of force. That images of violence in the world might eliminate real violence is unlikely at best. However, it is arguable that images of simulated violence in various entertainment media create coded systems through which actors and audiences read physical conflict in ways that distantly resemble actual altercations. Stage combat is a discipline of simulation. The discipline has been disseminated so far as to refer to itself and include historical texts relating to violent practices as resources for further simulation. For some actors and audiences, the simulacra is all there is, with no thought for the real.

There is an anecdote passed around stage combat circles about a high level fight director who is also an accomplished martial artist; the story relates that this man once got involved in a bar fight and knocked out his assailant with a single punch. But his body had so assimilated the discipline of simulation that he knapped[2] the punch upon impact. That is, he created the sound effect as used onstage by slapping his non punching hand against his chest. In a moment so rare and so telling as to be worthy of canonizing (whether it occurred or not), a master practitioner of both real and simulated violence simultaneously performed and simulated the same act. In this instance map and territory were indistinguishable.

While a punch to the head in a boxing match or an altercation will make a dull thud and the receiver may or may not react to the impact either psychologically or physically, neither of these conditions (audio and reactive) would necessarily be the case in a stage combat situation. The greatest reason this is so is the primacy of storytelling in the discipline. Stage combat as practiced today is first and foremost a method of communication meant to express character conflict in a drama by physical means. Let us take for example a variation on what is known in American stage combat circles as "The John Wayne Punch," named for the famous movie star. This falls into the general category of non contact blows, meaning that the illusion of impact is created by sleight of hand, as opposed to contact blows, which rely on impact control on the part of the performers and in which a simulated blow does actually land. Like almost all stage combat techniques, the John Wayne punch relies on both parties for effective execution. What the audience should see is one actor delivering a powerful blow to the jaw of another and the actor being hit having a reaction proportionate to the power invested in the blow. The execution is as follows: with two actors facing each other, the attacking actor places both hands on the shoulder of the receiver, the attacker steps back with his right foot and raises his right fist in the air with his elbow bent at a right angle and his fist by his ear. Next, he moves his fist in a diagonal arc that crosses in front of his partner's face by several inches, while the receiving actor turns his head as if struck. The fist is opened and the hand that remained on the victim's shoulder comes up to meet the punching hand and create the clap (known as a "knap"). The punching hand closes into a fist again immediately after clapping, and remains at full extension for an extra moment to complete the image in the audience's eyes. Often, the person receiving the punch will stagger back as well, and place a hand on the side of their face that was meant to have received the blow. If this technique was meant as a knock-out punch, the receiver will act accordingly, and may even end up lying on the stage floor.[3]

Each step in this technique has very different significance to actors and audience. To the actors, each step is either a cue or the mechanical execution of a performance technique, while to the audience each step is part of the story unfolding onstage. In this case, that story being one of one character punching out another. Each beat is coded differently depending on the positionality of the receiving party.

Taken again step by step: the first moment — where one actor places his hands on the other's shoulders — has different readings for both the audience and the actors. For the actors, it is a cue and a safety precaution; it is built into the technique so that the actors can check in with each other and continue the fight safely. The pause serves as a moment for them to prepare for the rest of the technique. For the audience, that pause is a moment where there is a setup for something else to follow. If it occurs at the beginning of a stage altercation, it freezes the action momentarily, preparing them for what is to come. If it is in the end or middle of a longer sequence the effect is similar, but is more of a moment for them to mentally digest whatever has just occurred before the scene continues. Bringing the fist back is again cue from one actor to another, and from the audience perspective it establishes the weapon about to be used. The brandishing of the fist in such a position (in most pairings) creates a moment of tension. In fact, if the action was arrested in this position and dialogue occurred without the technique continuing there would still be the potential for a very powerful moment from the audience perspective. The movement of the simulated punch is a cue for the receiver to begin their reaction. The action of the punch itself and the head turn indicating victim reaction would most likely be lost without the knap and the actions taking place before and after the movement. The knap, a clap in this case, is particularly important because it is that sound that signifies the moment of impact to the audience. That sound acts both as a signifier of impact to the audience and a simulacrum of the highest order in Baudrillard's sense; the sound representing the landing of the punch has replaced not the impact itself, but the empty space where an impact would have been had the "punch" itself existed as a real movement. Dale Anthony Girard explains the importance of this sound in his essay, "Listening to the Language of Violence":

> In addition to the actors' voices, the orchestration of a fight consists of the sounds of body against body, fist to flesh, bone on bone. Such sounds are essential to a fight because they convey not only that contact has been made but the strength or degree of that contact as well. Whether these sounds are

> created manually or mechanically, they must create the impression of truth [Girard 1999:91–92].

The last step of the technique, the momentary freezing of the attacker and the continued reaction of the victim (overlapping the previously mentioned physical reaction during the punching motion), help the audience to make sense of all that they've seen before. Often in performing this technique, the victim will turn their body completely away with the twist beginning at the head and continuing through to the feet, and continuing into a fall. Delivered properly, the entire sequence is perceived as one character delivering a powerful blow to another.

It is useful to examine such sequences within the framework of Meyerhold's biomechanical concept of the acting cycle, broken into three segments: intention (*otkas*, also translated as "rejection" as it typically indicates moving away from the intended action), realization (*pasil*), and reaction (*stoika*). Meyerhold explains his own concepts best, as quoted by Braun in *Meyerhold on Theatre*:

> The *intention* is the intellectual assimilation of a task prescribed externally by the dramatist, the director, or the initiative of the performer. *The realization* is the cycle of volitional, mimetic and vocal reflex. *The reaction* is the attenuation of the volitional reflex as it is realized mimetically and vocally in preparation for the reception of a new intention (the transition to a new acting cycle) ... [Meyerhold, V.M. Bebutov and I.A. Aksyonov, *Emploi aktyora*, Moscow, 1922, 3–4] [Braun 1969:201].

Much of stage combat works on identical principles, as illustrated by the steps of the John Wayne Punch. Drawing the fist back is the intention, delivering the false blow is the realization, and the rest is the reaction. Similarly, the opposite side of the story is told in the movements of the victim's reaction, which in turn works with the attack to form a complete symbolic sequence on the stage. As the separate steps of the punch carry semiotic weight, and the entire technique carries another, fuller significance than the separate parts, it is important to break down the steps in order to understand the illusion, or rather, the construction of the agreed upon fiction.

In his book, *On Killing: The Psychological Cost of Learning to Kill in War and Society*, Lt. Col. Dave Grossman describes the study of lethal violence in today's society as "a world of virgins studying sex" (Grossman 1996:2). It can be assumed that this is an accurate assessment of most theatre audiences watching a fight sequence. While modern society on the whole is sufficiently separated from first hand experiences of violence on regular basis,[4] simulated violence on television and in cinema is omnipresent. A punch to the head does not make the same sound as two hands clapping, but if the dull thud of actual impact of fist to head were to make it onto a stage, the sound would be unlikely to carry into the back row. This is to say nothing of actual injuries that might be sustained by both puncher (broken knuckles) and victim and the effect that such an event would have on a performance. We have the exaggerated sequence of the John Wayne punch that exists as a simulacrum of a real punch, performed using a discipline created to communicate signifiers of violence in complex sequences that exist as simulacra of the "real" event. In actuality, the simulacrum is more real than the real for stage purposes. Furthermore, any substitution of real violence for the simulacra, either by accident or misguided design, would compromise the entire production on both a practical and aesthetic level. Leslie Pasternack offers an explanation of why this is so:

> Now, if an apple onstage is exactly like an apple offstage, that likeness will probably not interfere with its ability to perform as a signifier. The audience might be aware that, in addition to signifying an edible fruit, the onstage object actually is an edible fruit, but that knowledge will probably only minimally affect the reception of the overall signification. The audience might feel hungry or wonder if an actor is really going to eat the apple. But the use of real violence onstage has at least three immediate results which will damage the signification:
>   1) The victim will experience pain, which could certainly stop the performance completely or which could require improvisation to allow the victim time to recover sufficiently to continue the performance. At the very least, the pain will split the victim's focus and disrupt the trust between the fight partners.
>   2) The attacker will suffer split focus: he/she will wonder if the victim has been hurt, perhaps feel guilt or a lack of control, and will feel pressed to think forward to later actions in the same scene which might need to be improvised to prevent further injury.
>   3) The audience will, in that moment of actual injury which is immediately obvious to most spectators, be wrenched from its concern for the character to a concern for the actor — a transfer of attention from the signifier, the idea of a victim, to an unexpected signified, an actual victim. The semiotic unit of actor-as-victim is suddenly signifying him or herself [Pasternak 1993:9–10].

Pasternack's analysis of what happens when the real either replaces the fake in terms of an accident, or worse, is used either out of ignorance or in the interests of "realistic" staging, illustrates the importance in stage combat of signifying a series of events which *never actually happen*. It is arguable that all of theatre signifies events which do not in fact occur, but there is an important distinction in the case of stage combat. An actor saying a line that a character says is in fact saying the line, two characters dancing the tango are signified by actors who are in fact dancing the tango, but two characters engaged in a life or death physical confrontation cannot and must not in the interests of safety be signified by actors who are in fact actually fighting.

The idea of the audience being pulled out of the play by the intervention of the "real" in the stage violence highlights the importance of the simulacrum. The audience insists on the simulation in order to enjoy the play, the moment this simulation cannot withstand an assault by the "real." The John Wayne Punch is pure simulation: all the actions are designed to create a simulacrum of a punch within the codes of realistic theatre. No contact is ever made and both performers are operating in complex temporal and spatial relationships to create the signifiers read by each other as cues and by the audience as an act of aggression and a physical reaction to same.

The area of stage combat where the simulacra are most complex is where it has no current model: swordplay. Though fight directors conduct in depth research on historical fencing, all they really have to refer to is other stage combatants and sport fencing. While fencing is an active practice, it is itself a simulacra which, though it evolved more directly from the actual combative practices, evolved in an entirely different direction. Period fencing manuals are essentially instructions on how to kill. The practice of rapier fencing evolved into smallsword fencing, from which the foil, the mainstay of sport fencing, evolved as a training weapon. Modern fencing evolved according to Baudrillard's model:

> This then would be the successive phases of the image:
> –it is the reflection of a basic reality
> –it masks and perverts a basic reality
> –it masks the *absence* of a basic reality
> –it bears no relation to any reality whatever: it is its own pure simulacrum
> [Baudrillard 1994:6].

The history of sport fencing is important when discussing stage combat as coaches were hired to create stage fights: much of early to mid 20th century sword work for the stage descends from saber fencing. When the shape of stage combat as we know it today came to solidify, fight directors cared far more for the older fencing for blood than the current fencing for sport. Capo Ferro, a master who wrote in the early 1600s, was given precedence over Barbasetti, who wrote in the 1930s. There are fight directors who see modern actors as the heirs of the great fencing masters of the Renaissance — a Baudrillard field day. If the simulacrum of Italian rapier fighting is the modern equivalent of that tradition, what is to be done with the Japanese martial tradition? Are those who choreograph *Rashomon* the heirs of legendary samurai such as Musashi, Tesshu, and Tsnunetomo? Would anyone who has done so make such a claim in the presence of a Kenjitsu instructor? How would we measure a simulacrum against the living tradition that it is meant to simulate? There is a question of what would in fact be murdered in such an encounter, the image or that which it means to simulate.

In the case of swordplay for the stage, what is the final image? The first difference between fencing as a conflict and stage fencing is the difference between opponent and partner. One faces an opponent in open conflict. One works with a partner with the shared goal of simulating conflict for the audience. The clearest example would be the case of feints. A feint is a false attack meant to draw a parry towards a specific line of defense, thus opening another line for a real attack. In the case of fencing for sport, the feint is a specific semiotic device through which one combatant attempts to lie to another, getting the other to act upon that lie and thus open themselves up to an attack. In the case of the stage, the feint tells the story of a lie to the audience. It is in effect, a lie about a lie, but, it is an agreed upon lie.

Let us take a feint to the head followed by an attack to the flank. In the case of sport fencing, this move would be a matter of a split second. If the attack lands it is registered by an electronic scoring device and the point is scored. In the case of the stage, the feint to the head is a cue for one's scene partner to raise their sword up to parry. It must be obvious enough both for the other actor to see it coming and act accordingly, and to be clear to the audience that one character tried to mislead another with that movement. Using Meyerhold to examine the next step, the intention (*otkas*) is the cue, which prepares both audience and partner. The cue is given by bringing the sword level to the target and drawing back for the cut. The realization (*posil*) is the cut itself, which ideally travels on an arc that expends all of its energy and stops several inches away from the other actor's body. And the reaction (*stoika*) is the choreographed result of that cut, possibly either a parry by the other actor or a landed blow. The overall dramatic effect of the feint attack is one of narrow escape and quick reflexes if the parry is made.

The audience sees deception, agility, and a narrow escape from death by a three foot long piece of sharpened steel (or rather, a prop signifying as much). But the sequence of events as it actually occurs would be as follows: First, eye contact is established between actors. The attacker breaks eye contact and looks up at the crown of the defender's head. He brings his blade in line to begin the attack, then moves his body. The defender follows first the attacker's eyes, then his blade, stepping back and raising his own blade into a head parry ("parry of five" in fencing jargon). The attacker, before his own blade makes contact with the parry, draws it back a bit and realigns it with the defender's flank, then steps forward and makes the cut. The defender follows the attacker's eyes and blade, and moves backward as the attacker moves forward. He brings his own blade into position to parry the flank cut, and after both parties have stopped moving their bodies the blades connect.

Clausewitz wrote that war is a continuation of diplomacy by other means. This is true of violence on the stage in the sense that it is a pursuit of character objective by means other than dialogue. Characters pursue their objectives. When the best or only means of pursuing that objective is physical violence that is what will appear on the stage. This may be explicitly stated in the dialogue or a stage direction, or it may come from a director's impulse. Either way the actions themselves communicate very specific circumstances to the audience.

Stage combat, then, is a discipline through which actors communicate violent circumstance by way of a system of signs. These signs signify attacks, defenses, injuries, and the attempts to make the preceding events occur. The system as a whole is a simulacra in the sense of Baudrillard. Though it refers to physical altercations, it merely simulates them and serves as an index to those occurrences. These simulations have overtaken the actual events in the eyes of the audience, and the "real" would be unacceptable for aesthetic reasons on top of safety concerns. Audiences are acculturated to images and sounds of violence, but those images and sounds are not necessarily accurate representations of the real event. In *Simulations*, Baudrillard refers to the story by Borges in which imperial mapmakers create a map so detailed that it covers the entire empire. In the case of stage combat as simulacra of actual violence, the map has not only covered the territory, the map has expanded far beyond it. The challenge now is not so much about understanding the tension between the real and the simulated as relocating the real so as to better understand that which has come to represent it.

TUFTS UNIVERSITY

Notes

Acknowledgments. The author would like to thank Professor Downing Cless for his help and guidance both in the writing of the original paper and in its preparation for publication.

1. The author's background in stage combat includes training with and membership in the Society of American Fight Directors since 2001, teaching stage combat at Tufts University, Boston University Opera Institute, and various workshops, and fight directing dozens of shows in various venues throughout New England and New York City. In addition, he holds a black belt in Matsubayashi Shorin-Ryu Karate and has also trained in other Asian martial arts including Judo, Kali, and Jeet Kune Do. He also has a background as a competitive fencer and has worked as a women's self defense instructor for IMPACT.

2. A "knap" is a stage combat term describing the sound made by the actors to signify the impact of a strike. This is usually done by clapping one's hands or slapping part of the body. It can come from either or both actors involved in a stage fight, or from a third party. It is generally masked from the audience's view.

3. Of course, all directions would be reversed for a left handed punch and the male pronoun is arbitrary.

4. Self defense experts such as Peyton Quinn and Luciano Silvera apply sociological and psychological methods based on research on how assaults happen to their training programs. Very little of their work even remotely resembles what their students may have been led to expect by a lifetime of exposure to simulated violence in the media, though some of their principles have been studied and adapted by various fight directors for their own work.

References Cited

Barbasetti, Luigi. *The Art of the Foil,* E. P. Dutton & Co., 1932, Barnes & Noble Books, 1998.

Baudrillard, Jean. *Simulations.* Semiotext[e], MIT Press, 1983.

_____. *Simulacra and Simulation,* Ann Arbor: University of Michigan Press, 1994.

Braun, Edward. *Meyerhold on Theatre,* New York: Hill & Wang, 1969.

Capo Ferro, Ridolfo. *The Grand Simulacrum of the Art and Use of Fencing.* Siena, 1610. Translated and edited by Jared Kirby, Pennsylvania: Stackpole Books, 2004.

Girard, Dale Anthony. *Actors on Guard: A Practical Guide for the Use of Rapier and Dagger for Stage and Screen,* New York: Routledge, 1997.

_____. "Listening to the Language of Violence: The Orchestration of Sound and Silence in Fights for the Stage and Screen," in *Theatre Symposium Volume 7,* University of Alabama Press, 1999.

Grossman, Dave, Lt. Col. *On Killing: The Psychological Cost of Learning to Kill in War and Society,* New York: Little Brown and Company, 1996.

Lane, Richard, *Swashbuckling: A Step-by-Step Guide to the Art of Stage Combat and Theatrical Swordplay,* New York: Limelight Editions, 1999.

Martinez, J.D. *Combat Mime: A Non-Violent Approach to Stage Violence,* Chicago: Burnham, 1982.

Pasternak, Leslie. *Moving Violence from the Page to the Stage: Stage Combat in Theory and Practice,* MA Thesis, University of Texas at Austin, 1993.

Quinn, Peyton. *Real Fighting: Adrenaline Stress Conditioning through Scenario Based Training,* Boulder, CO: Paladin Press, 1996.

Silvera, Luciano. *The Moment of Truth: How to Physically, Mentally, and Legally Survive a Street Fight,* VHS Video Produced by Luciano Silvera, Boulder, CO: Paladin Press, 2000.

Suddeth, J. Allen. *Fight Directing for the Theatre,* Portsmouth, NH: Heinemann, 1996.

Acting Lessons at the Comédie Française

Nivelle de la Chaussée and the Theatricalization of Bourgeois Morality

Jeffrey M. Leichman

Abstract

As a privileged site of contact between social groups in the rigidly stratified society of ancien régime France, the theatre of the Comédie Française was at the center of a constantly evolving debate over decorum, taste, and social class throughout the eighteenth century. In the 1730s, Nivelle de la Chaussée introduced a new theatrical genre, the comédie larmoyante. For the first time on France's most prestigious stage, non-noble characters are presented as the protagonists of a serious, emotionally charged action. At the same time, La Chaussée figures the private sphere of the bourgeois household as a public space of representation, proposing that skillful acting is a necessary attribute of the morality championed in his plays. By associating acting with virtuous conduct, La Chaussée revokes the nobility's monopoly on self-representation and redefines the ideals of behavior of the French middle class as it prepares to step onto the stage of European history.

"Les Français sont les comédiens ordinaires du bon dieu."
— Heinrich Heine

"The French are the good lord's official actors" (Sammons 1986:623). Commenting on the mores of his hosts in 1830, Heine memorably remarked on the self-conscious theatricality of polite society in France as an explanation of the excellence of its national stage. The French treated everyday comportment as a role to play; both public and private interactions were characterized by an awareness of acting a part for an ever-present audience of peers on the great stage of the modern city. I contend that this fundamentally modern conception of individual subjectivity and social interaction draws on a theatrical tradition that had begun a hundred years earlier on the stage of the Comédie Française. In the first half of the eighteenth century, Nivelle de la Chaussée's extremely popular *comédies larmoyantes* (weeping comedies) proposed that self-theatricalization was both a virtue and a social necessity for the rising middle class. At the same time that plays began to depict non-noble characters as the focus of the dramatic action, French commoners increasingly looked to the stage for models of correct comportment. The theatre's central importance in French cultural and intellectual life during this period, as well as its broad social appeal, made it the ideal medium to demonstrate how acting could be both socially advantageous and morally laudable.

This article will explore the theatricalization of the bourgeois subject in eighteenth-century France as articulated in the influential early plays of Nivelle de la Chaussée. Through both formal and thematic innovations, La Chaussée uses the stage of the Comédie Française to prepare the ground for the spectacularization of private life that will achieve its greatest intensity during the French Enlightenment. As existing generic categories did not allow for a serious bourgeois protagonist, La Chaussée's plays propose a middle term between tragedy and comedy in order to address an audience whose evolving tastes demanded a new form. Thematically, the plays advance a vision of virtuous private interaction as a staged performance. La Chaussée instrumentalizes acting, an activity associated with immorality and vice, in the service of the social needs of a bourgeoisie seeking access to the polite society of the nobility without compromising its rigorous morality. I will argue that the incessant depiction of non-nobles self-consciously "playing" themselves in works that espouse a bourgeois morality situates acting as an essential modality of virtuous conduct for the French middle class. This movement towards the theatricalization of the bourgeois subject initiated on the stage of the Comédie Française in the 1730s contributed to the revolution of the social imaginary that was a prerequisite for the French Revolution, and the introduction of the modern era.

Genre and Class

Pierre Claude Nivelle de La Chaussée is principally known as the inventor of a theatrical genre known as the *comédie larmoyante*, defined by Gustave Lanson as "an intermediate genre between comedy and tragedy, which presents characters of private condition [...] in a serious, grave, occasionally pitiable action" (1903:1).[1] These were not laugh-provoking comedies in the style of Molière and indeed, as the name suggests, were often sentimental and serious in tone. The generic shift embodied in these plays responded to a social deficiency inherent to the binary classical aesthetic of comedy and tragedy. The rules governing tragedy, as established in France during the seventeenth century, limited it to the depiction of the nobility in momentous and life-threatening situations. Only the comic genre allowed the representation of non-aristocratic characters, but the model established by Molière, which continued to dominate the French stage long after his death, used the bourgeois character exclusively as a source of ridicule. Non-nobles in Molière's comedies are notable for their identicalness to themselves, their inability to escape from an inherent baseness of character dictated by their blood. The stain of *la roture* (low birth) clings to the title characters of *Le bourgeois gentilhomme* and *George Dandin*, whose essential *gaucherie* is most humorous precisely when they attempt to pass as aristocrats. The *comédie larmoyante* falls between these two poles, portraying private citizens in emotionally wrenching situations, while retaining the "happy end" of a well-assorted marriage. La Chaussée's sentimental "comedies" begin to address the social ambitions of the non-noble spectators, who could at last see themselves depicted as the central focus of a serious dramatic action.

Luigi Riccoboni,[2] commenting on negative critical responses to La Chaussée's first play, *La fausse antipathie*, attributes them to the discomfort occasioned by unsatisfied generic expectations. "Spectators came to know, more than ever before, that tears and laughter could be nobly brought together in a comedy [...] the tears have triumphed to such an extent that they ignited the indignation of the spectators [...] it seemed to them that they should not feel it [tragic pleasure] in a comedy" ([1777]1970:194). For Riccoboni, La Chaussée evokes tragic sentiment more effectively within the framework of comedy than would have been possible had he adhered to the generic requirements of a tragedy. The mixing of genres offers not only a much-needed possibility for renewal within the French theatre, but gives the playwright access to new levels of affectivity beyond what could be achieved within the traditional forms. While some spectators might resent being manipulated into tears when they had a right to expect light entertainment, for Riccoboni the strong emotional appeal of these works is central to the moralizing project of the La Chaussée's theatre:

> It is much easier to correct morals by plays of this nature than by tragedies; in the latter, one only shows on stage people who seem to us to be composed and to think differently than the majority of men, and that we would never dare to imitate, because we believe them fantastical or supernatural. [...] When we see it shine in characters who are only above us by a single

degree, we are made aware to what extent it would be easy for everyone to possess and make a habit of virtue [1970:210].

The noble sentiment of tragedy is allied with the civilizing mission of comedy in order to impart a lesson that aims for the heart, more than the head, of the middle-class spectator: the road to social advancement lies in the imitation of virtuous actions on stage.

Riccoboni's emphasis on the issue of imitation is extremely pertinent in this instance, and calls attention to an important sociological development within the theatrical world of the *ancien régime*. After Louis XIV's death in 1715 the Regent renewed royal patronage of the arts, and his court's orientation toward Paris increased the importance of the city audience. When Louis XV assumed the throne in 1723, his indifference to the theater and the court's retreat to Versailles meant that the crucial arbiters of theatrical success remained the spectators of the capital despite the fact that the three major theatres in Paris (the Comédie Française, the Comédie Italienne, and the Opéra) remained under the direct tutelage of the crown. As the officially sanctioned mimetic representation of reality, theatre (and especially the Comédie Française) retained its very public function of defining and refining the conduct of French subjects. Forward-looking theorists such as Riccoboni correctly sensed that comic form, with its depiction of private citizens, had far greater potential for instilling new behavioral models now that playwrights were no longer speaking directly to the court. He saw in La Chaussée's hybrid form "a kind of comedy for which we have been waiting for several centuries" (1970:212), which brought the emotional power of tragedy to bear on situations with which "bourgeois" audiences could easily identify.

A Taste for the Bourgeois

La Chaussée addresses the relationship between literary genre and social class in the *Prologue* that precedes his first play, *La fausse antipathie*. One of the only theoretical statements that we have from him on the subject, it demonstrates a keen awareness of the political assumptions implicit in the discussion of genre in the theatre. The *Prologue* insists on the specifically class-based desires of audiences, and the difficulty of satisfying the diverse tastes of a socially heterogeneous theatre-going public. La Chaussée frames his argument in a brief allegorical satire that implicates the actual audience in an otherwise technical discussion of dramaturgical practice.

The main character, "Le Génie de la Comédie Française" (The Spirit of the French Theatre), is looking for a play to perform, but wants first to assure himself of "*le goût du public*" ("the public's taste") (La Chaussée [1777]1970:17).[3] Because playwrights worked within highly regulated forms, inherited from racinian tragedy and molieresque comedy, the choices for new entrants into the field were severely limited. Any formal innovation had to overcome the inertia of an officially sanctioned *goût* that responded to the desires of a court-oriented public. Tension over the respect for the rules governing traditional forms versus the desires of an increasingly non-noble urban public to see themselves represented on stage served to discourage authors from writing for the theatre. In a period when the audience (and in particular, the *parterre*, or pit, composed principally of non-noble spectators) was accustomed to noisily signaling its approbation or disapproval of a play[4], La Chaussée attempts to make the case for a third genre by giving voice to a string of audience stand-ins, each of whom will weigh in on what constitutes a valuable piece of theatre. The *Prologue* caricatures the opinions of a public that is conscious of the socially determined nature of taste, presenting archetypes of the Admirer, the Critic, the *Précieuse* (snob), the Bourgeois, the *Petit-Maître* (fop), and the *Homme Sensé* (man of reason). In the end Thalia, the muse of comedy, arrives and hands Le Génie a new work, *La fausse antipathie*. While she abstains from pronouncing a verdict on how to satisfy the diversity of audience tastes, the play she recommends is significantly labeled a *comédie*, the genre with a vocation to portray non-aristocratic characters.

While not the first to apostrophe his public before presenting a new play, La Chaussée's insistence on the class-based divisions of good taste is particularly interesting, given the very public forum in which they are addressed: the audience is the subject of a representation that calls attention to its social fault lines. Furthermore, the monopoly on good taste is not reflexively attributed to the aristocracy, but to a "true public (*véritable public*) [...] the least numerous of them all, and the most redoubtable" (La Chaussée 1970:17). This elite class of spectators is not defined by its social station, but by its penchant to do "what it pleases" and "what it must" as well as its discernment of true comedy versus base farce: "it never blushes at what makes it laugh" (1970:17). La Chaussée's idealized public has no appetite for the vulgar or the obscene, establishing moral rectitude, rather than noble birth, as the fundamental prerequisite to aesthetic discernment.

La Chaussée presents the Bourgeois as a crass, materialistic boor for whom presence at the theatre is a social acquisition, but who has no appreciation for dramatic art. His only pleasure is "full-throated laughter"; as for serious works, "I yawn while admiring them" (1970:18). The Précieuse rejects out of hand anything that appeals to the Bourgeois; the mere fact that the

Bourgeois might enjoy laughing at the theatre is sufficient reason to banish laughter entirely. "Joy belongs to the base (*La joie est tombée en roture*)" (1970:18) she declares. This attitude also reflects the behavioral restrictions inherent to *le bon ton*, a kind of unflappable evenness of demeanor that dominated polite society at this time. The moniker "*précieuse*," with inevitable reference to Molière's *Les précieuses ridicules*, has a distinctly negative connotation[5], undermining the authority of this character's opinions. The *Prologue* mocks both the Bourgeois and the Précieuse, suggesting that neither can be relied upon in matters of taste.

The character of the Bourgeois appears to contradict La Chaussée's championing of what I characterize as "bourgeois" values in his plays. Sarah Maza provocatively asserts that "the French bourgeoisie did not exist" in the eighteenth century as an organized political entity that made claims for itself; rather, it was "a myth which served (and possibly still does) to define negatively France's deepest social, cultural, and political ideals" (Maza 2003:6).[6] La Chaussée's use of the term here certainly falls into Maza's rubric of the bourgeois as a figurative other, a not-us onto whom cultural anxieties could be projected by an increasingly threatened aristocracy, as well as by the upwardly-mobile middle class, so as to avoid their stain. As a rhetorical tool, the category of bourgeois allows for a kind of provisional truce between the social orders in what was supposed to be a rigidly hierarchical society. The nobility could heap its disdain on an empty category of *roturiers* (non-nobles) without offending the industrious city-dwellers whose accumulated wealth and purchased titles made them — to all outward appearances — social equals.[7] However, if La Chaussée subscribes to a frequent usage of the period, he nevertheless remains engaged in the rehabilitation of core values that directly oppose, and strongly rebuke, the license of aristocratic mores. In his plays, La Chaussée skirts the semantic question by abstaining from making any claims in the name of a "bourgeois" class. Instead, he incessantly alludes to the humble origins of the most virtuous characters and presents their carefully constructed behavioral refinement as a model to be emulated by the aspiring members of the audience.[8] Though still politically diffuse, the bourgeoisie at this time was far from a "lackluster understudy to the nobility" (Maza 2003:100), and indeed was poised to displace the aesthetic and moral dominance of the gentry by taking the lead role at the Comédie Française.

The last allegorical character to appear on stage in the *Prologue* is the Homme Sensé, the man of reason, who alone is not identified as to his class origins. An ideal spectator for La Chaussée's project to reform the theatre, he pays close attention to what the play says, both for its entertainment value as well as for the lesson it imparts: "I seek amusement, and instruction even more" (La Chaussée 1970:21). He is against excessive stylization and exaggerated character traits, stating that "The true, the natural have certain charms for me. [...] An exaggerated ridiculousness / Makes one laugh, and yet corrects nobody" (1970:21). In an important statement of dramatic principles, and a rebuke to the molieresque style that dominated the comic genre, La Chaussée advocates a naturalistic representation that allows the *hommes sensés* in attendance — the *"véritable public"* — to identify easily with the characters on stage, so that they might apply the lessons of the theatre to their own lives. L'Homme Sensé's desire to see an image of himself on stage, his indifference to the sublime beauties of tragedy (of which he makes no mention), and his willingness to draw a moral lesson from the play all point to a drive for individual self-improvement that, while utterly foreign to the aristocracy, is characteristic of the French middle class and coincides with Nivelle de La Chaussée's theatrical aims.

During this period, theoretical texts are beginning to articulate a polemic around the nature of acting, and the degree to which an actor must truly invest him or herself in the emotional life of the role[9]; and at the same time, "comic" theatre becomes preoccupied with the notion of self-representation in a social context. The newly urgent question of how to *act* one's social status in society is a natural subject of anxiety in a society that increasingly requires its private citizens to conceive of their interpersonal relations in terms of public performance. The *comédie larmoyante*, by expanding the possibilities of the kinds of actions and characters that could be represented on stage, both responded to the public's changing social and esthetic needs and revolutionized the standards of taste in France's most prestigious theatre. Thematic innovation accompanied formal changes, as play plots increasingly focused on the theatricalization of individual comportment. It was in watching these plays that the French public received its first lessons in acting the *comédie* of everyday life.

Performing Fidelity in La fausse antipathie

In 1736, Nivelle de La Chaussée, at age 44, had had just two successful plays presented at the Comédie Française, *La fausse antipathie* and *Le préjugé à la mode*. Despite the slightness of his oeuvre, he was inducted that year into the Académie Française, which to this day remains the highest literary honor that France bestows on its authors. La Chaussée's inclusion in this august body is all the more remarkable for the extraordinary speech that was delivered on his behalf by the Archbishop of Sens, Languet de Gergy, in which the eminent prelate rejected centuries of official condemnation of the theatre and its practitioners by admitting "without difficulty that there is a certain affinity between he who condemns our theatres [i.e., the Archbishop] and he who attempts to correct them" (de Gergy [1777]1970:400).[10] While these remarks ignited an immediate scandal in the religious community,[11] they nevertheless give an indication of the important social impact of La Chaussée's first two works for the stage, which explicitly link ostentatious morality with the adaptation of acting techniques to everyday life.

La fausse antipathie (*The False Antipathy*) was Nivelle de la Chaussée's first publicly presented play. Premiered at the Comédie Française on 2 October, 1733, the three-act verse comedy was an immediate popular success. The characters Léonore and Damon have met and fallen in love at the home of Léonore's uncle. Unbeknownst to both of them, they are actually married. Twelve years earlier their union had been arranged against their will, but when a duel erupted at the church door moments after the ceremony was completed the new husband was obligated to flee as a result of having killed his opponent. The couple, neither of whom wished to marry in the first place, was separated after having just met for the first time. As a result, at the opening of the play, respect for their still-valid marital commitment (even though it was entered into involuntarily) obliges Léonore and Damon to hide their true feelings from a lover that neither one of them recognizes as their spouse. The play ends with a recognition scene — a hallmark of La Chaussée's theatre — in which it is revealed that Léonore and Damon (real names: Silvie and Sainflore) have every right as husband and wife to publicly, and virtuously, avow their feelings. As in many of La Chaussée's plays, the major theme is that characters are not who they seem to be — that they are, in essence, *acting* in order to adhere to social expectations. This dissembling in defence of the sanctity of the marriage vow casts acting in a morally positive light. Their feigned distaste for each other (the "false" antipathy of the title) showcases acting as the guarantor not only of acceptable decorum in polite society, but also of socially legitimate emotional satisfaction and release.

The capital importance of correctly interpreting social acting is addressed by characters that stand outside of the love interest, acting as audience surrogates to guide viewers through the labyrinths of performance that the play proposes. Nérine, Léonore's chambermaid, broadcasts the central theme from the first scene, announcing that "*les femmes ne sont pas tout ce qu'elles paroissent*" (La Chaussée 1970:23) — "women are not all that they appear to be." Léonore and Damon carefully maintain a façade of mutual indifference, although the "*détours*" (ruses) they use to hide their true feelings more closely resemble the conduct of the nobility (as depicted in a long tradition of "libertine" literature) than the intimate exchanges of respectable middle-class citizens. While servant characters frequently have recourse to disguising and trickery throughout the classical canon, the reward for such subterfuge, even when undertaken at the behest of a master, frequently amounts to a solid beating. By contrast, La Chaussée's comedies introduce feigning to the "honest" bourgeois character, whose recompense is improved social standing. In classical comedy, the non-noble's most salient feature had always been a fundamental identity with him — or herself. La Chaussée's theatre, however, posits self-theatricalization as the basis of all interactions between men and women with pretensions to a certain social standing.

Nérine understands how to read Damon's *feinte* (fakery), discerning his real emotion through the outward signals of his indifference: "I have discerned, I tell you, behind his courtesy, / Stifled sighs, sidelong glances, / A troubled silence, against his will; / Desires, respects, discomfort, intrigue, / A secret interest, a special care. / An indifferent man is much more cavalier" (1970:24). Nérine recognizes Damon's overt respectfulness, his silence, and his deference as components of a self-conscious performance. At the same time, he is not able to fully subordinate Sainflore's true emotions under the decorous exterior required of the role of Damon. Nérine instructs Léonore in the vocabulary of poorly-concealed desire (stifled sighs, troubled silence, great care in every gesture), providing a lesson for the men in the audience in how to behave as what she significantly calls an "*amant honnête homme*" (an upstanding lover) (1970:24), as well as guiding female spectators in how to correctly read such a performance. This delicate balancing act, caught between a convincing outward portrayal and an invitation to see behind the mask, marks the introduction of a *virtuous strategy for seduction* predicated on a shared understanding of the codes of self-theatricalization.

Orphise, Léonore's aunt, wishes to marry her daughter from a previous marriage to Damon, who is a guest in her house. She seeks to enlist the help of Léonore who, unaware that she is married to Damon and much attracted to him, has so carefully hidden her true feelings that everyone is convinced of her distaste for him. The older woman broaches the subject delicately, however, in full awareness that even within the enclosed space of a wealthy home, the most intimate exchanges are carried out as if acted out on the stage of a Paris theatre: "I am well aware that a woman of your age, / Does not care to play a minor role. / She would rather that everything be centered on her, / To be the only goal, the perpetual object, / Towards which all hearts, eyes and ears reach out" (1970:28). Orphise could just as well be describing an actress on stage: the object of multiple gazes, eroticized and narcissistic, whose actions dictate the unfolding plot. Female desire is figured in theatrical terms, even in the very private domain of romantic love. Henceforth, skill in acting will determine control of the scenic space in a newly theatricalized domestic sphere.

All the World Is Staged:
The New Paradigm of Social Acting

La Chaussée's next play, *Le préjugé à la mode* (*The Fashionable Preju-dice*), continues and develops the themes of acting introduced in *La fausse antipathie*. A five-act verse comedy, *Le préjugé* was first played on 3 Febru-ary 1735, and went on to be La Chaussée's greatest success during his life-time. The plot demonstrates, even more explicitly than in the previous work, the indispensability of self-theatricalization to virtuous conduct in a social world increasingly conceived of as a public space of representation. Durval and his wife live in the same château, but at opposite ends. For years, his philandering has forced her to maintain in public the unhappy role of the devoted wife to an inconstant husband. When the play begins, he has redis-covered his love for her; however, the prevailing aristocratic fashion dictates that he suppress these feelings. In the end, the levels of deception and counter-deception conspire to reveal the "true" feelings of husband and wife, confirming the sanctity of the marriage vow. Constance, in particular, fore-grounds her performance as "contented wife," sacrificing her personal satis-faction on the altar of her social duty to maintain a harmonious domestic sphere. Her sentimental crisis speaks directly to a feminine audience, under-scoring the necessity of emotional ruse to win back errant husbands and pre-serve the integrity of the family unit in the eyes of an ever-present and deeply "prejudiced" public. Acting techniques equip women in polite society to virtuously subordinate their individual desires to the demands of a (bour-geois) system of values that privileges marital and domestic groupings as the essential guarantors of their social standing.

Throughout the play, characters call attention to the socially marked character of the marital fidelity that Constance cherishes, as well as the class-based stigmatization of this virtue that prevents Durval from embracing it openly.[12] Sophie, Constance's cousin, here fulfills the function formerly held by Nérine in *La fausse antipathie*, that of an outside observer of the "false enmity" between husband and wife and a commentator on the acting tech-niques that will be used to overcome it. A more effective audience surrogate than a mere *suivante*, Sophie is herself contemplating marriage to Durval's friend and confidant, Damon. Unlike what we find in many of Molière's comedies (e.g., *L'école des femmes*, *Tartuffe*, *Sganarelle*), masculine rather than feminine infidelity poses the greater threat to marital stability in La Chaussée's theatre: women, despite their penchant for disguising their emo-tions, are the standard-bearers of matrimonial faithfulness. Sophie fears being cuckolded by Damon, and expresses her skepticism about the institution of marriage in explicitly class-based terms: "I have noticed that it's no longer in style / To love a companion to whom one is bound. / It's a practice kept up only amongst the bourgeois (*Cet usage n'est plus que chez la bourgeoisie*): / Everywhere else conjugal love has been made / Utterly ridiculous, an unparalleled gaffe" (1970:45). Sophie understands that the "bourgeois" stigma attached to marital fidelity guarantees that, should she agree to marry him, her noble lover Damon will imitate his friend Durval's inconstancy. Indeed, in aristocratic circles few insults carry the same crushing force as being associated with *arriviste* commoners, and the anxiety over dispelling this perception drives the action of *Le préjugé* as well as several other of La Chaussée's plays (especially *L'école des amis*, *L'école des mères*, and *L'homme de fortune*). Just as the Précieuse in the *Prologue* to *La fausse antipathie* refuses to laugh once "*la joie est tombée en roture*," the nobility's definition of itself has less to do with bloodlines than with a model of comportment that is defined negatively with respect to the numerically superior, and economically ascendant, middle class.

While the term "bourgeois" carries a negative valence, its metonymic equivalent (monogamy) represents the ideal to which the play seeks to inspire the audience, and a "practice" that Sophie, and the forlorn Constance, clearly hold in great esteem. Whereas Sophie early on expresses her despair that any aristocrat would dare flout the expectations of his caste, she later redefines class status by conflating it with emotional commitment: "Without a husband's love, we are without luster: / His heart is our title and gives us our rank" (1970:54). In La Chaussée's aristocracy of sentiment, the lowest can accede to the nobility of love while many a marquise's luster (*éclat*) is tarnished, and her rank (*état*) diminished, by the adventures of a philandering husband. Conjugal love bestows title and rank; in its absence, Constance, despite her marriage to Durval, is "Reduced, for all wealth, to a name that she shares / With an unfaithful man: what a worthless advantage!" (1970:54). Sophie rejects this "prejudice," and refuses to wed Damon until Durval demonstrates that he is capable of a faithful relationship with his wife — until, that is, he proves his worth by adopting "bourgeois" values.

The plot hinges on Durval's own conversion to the cult of conjugal love. He gives an insight into his true feelings by extolling for Sophie the virtues of marriage: "Marriage alone can give infinite pleasures; / One enjoys them without pain or worry: / Spouses make for each other a happy habit / Of respect, acceptance, and the most tender care. / If there is a happy fate, it's that of the husband" (1970:51). While he can express his admiration for the institution of marriage on behalf of others, Durval, as a man of wealth and title, cannot bring himself to buck publicly the expectations of his station, which include a carefree disrespect for monogamy. La Chaussée does not make any explicit reference to Durval's social status, as he is careful to do for the protagonists in all of his subsequent plays. However, having clearly aligned himself with the social mores of the aristocracy, the resolution of the conflict depends on his embrace of values pointedly identified as "bourgeois." This reversal of the imitative order, with a self-proclaimed noble ("My rank attracts to me here a thousand bothersome respects" [1970:49]) striving to live up to the moral precepts of the middle classes, represents a significant reversal of the hierarchy of values that has dominated French theatre until this time.

The two gossipy marquis who arrive at Durval's estate, Clitandre and Damis, embody the aristocratic disdain for marriage. They recount the story of Sainfar, a well-known seducer who, to his enduring shame, falls in love with and marries one of his conquests. The upstanding Damon, aware of Durval's secret love, rails against this prejudice, defending the "bourgeois" institution of marital love: "For whom then is this story so laughable? / For inconsequential, conceited people, / Who believe that the whole public is none but themselves (*Pour des évaporés, des gens avantageux, / Qui croiroient composer tout le public entr'eux*)" (1970:52). Damon's rebuke of the values of a frivolous "public" draws on both senses of the word in the eighteenth century. He is speaking both of a theatre audience (the ridiculousness of Sainfar has been memorialized in a comedy entitled *The Husband in Love with His Wife*) and of the nobility. In his *Prologue* to *La fausse antipathie*, La Chaussée underlines that these two publics are no longer identical, as they largely were in the time of Molière: with the marked increase in middle-class theatre-going in the early eighteenth century, the spectators of his plays are a socially heterogeneous group. La Chaussée addresses his plays to an idealized Honnête Homme, encouraging him to stand up to the "conceited people" (*gens avantageux*) who arrogate to themselves the exclusive right to pass judgment on taste and morals.

The play that has been made of Sainfar's adventure, and which Clitandre and Damis propose to stage at Durval's estate, underscores the growing indistinguishability of intimate affairs and public performances. The vogue of the *théâtre de société*, the private theatricals staged in the châteaux and "*hôtels particuliers*" of the upper bourgeoisie and the nobility, epitomized the *théâtromanie* of eighteenth-century France. As plays became a popular pastime, the ability to act convincingly became doubly necessary, required to participate in sophisticated recreation as well as for managing a social image or persona in polite company that may not conform with a person's true feelings or character. "Perfect politeness consists in ceasing to be one's self, at any time when the 'I' lives, feels, and suffers most intensely, to hide completely behind a mask of cold elegance" (Lanson 1903:194). In polite company, nobility of comportment demands maintaining an utter equanimity in the face of even the most acute adversity. "The courtly aristocracy could not prevent — indeed, through their contacts with rich bourgeois strata whom they needed for one reason or another, they assisted — the spreading of their manners, their customs, their tastes and their language to other classes" (Elias 1982:257). Theatre, both in private residences and in the public spectacles at the Comédie Française, was a crucial site of inter-class contact, and of the appropriation of a "noble" comportment by the rising middle class. Mastering this social performance was one of the great accomplishments of the French middle class in the eighteenth century.

The threat to Durval's precarious social acting comes in the form of a stage-play, which allows La Chaussée to address questions of legibility in social performance by relating them to the legibility of an explicitly avowed performance within a fictional drama. For Durval, in particular, the prospect of performing the play reinforces the anxiety he feels about "performing" his role of the insouciant, philandering husband: he is assigned the role of the husband who loves his wife, which is to say he is being asked to betray his carefully constructed *social* character in order to portray his true feelings on behalf of a *fictional* character on stage. The risk of this role is that a surfeit of "reality" will spill out of the fictional frame and undermine his social performance: "I will betray myself / All will see that I feel everything that I say / I will put, despite myself, too much love in my part / I would lose myself (*Je me perdrois*)" (1970:53). Durval's fear of "losing himself" ("*je me perdrois*") touches on the two crucial concerns of social acting. First, there is the danger of the subject literally losing sight of his true nature beneath the layers of artifice that he carefully maintains. The other meaning of *perdre*, in reference to a person, is the destruction of that person's reputation. Thus by acting, Durval risks not only self-alienation but also incurring the ridicule of his peers in the process; compounding the problem, Constance plays the role of the object of his desires, both in life and within the proposed play.

Durval's fear of going too far in his portrayal of a character relates back to the questions of legibility that were first sketched in *La fausse antipathie* and which are expanded upon in *Le préjugé à la mode*. Durval's situation makes explicit the connection between acting for the stage and playing a social role, but he is not alone in his concern over being too convincing. Sophie serves as both acting coach for Constance and an interpretive guide for the audience. As with Nérine's perceptive reading of Damon/Sainflore, Sophie sees beneath Constance's placid surface, where "I have recognized the tracks of your tears; / At the bottom of your heart, I have spied your pain" (1970:45). But just as Durval fears too completely identifying with his assigned part, Sophie advises Constance against a too thorough investment in her "character" of the accepting wife: "One might interpret in a strange way / All of your care to project a happy appearance / One might impute it to your indifference" (1970:46). The social acting advocated by the *comédie larmoyante* is predicated on an incomplete identification; appearances must be outwardly maintained, but the most intimate spectators must nonetheless be able to see behind the representation to the true feelings of the "actor."

Spectators at the theatre are privy to the emotional disguises of characters on stage. La Chaussée's dramaturgy proposes an extension of this dramatic irony into the domain of private relations: for social acting to have its desired effect, a portion of the domestic "audience" must be aware of the ruse, and thus of the "true" feelings that lie beneath. This layering of social roles on stage corresponds to the changing function of the characters within a play's economy. Anne Ubersfeld's semiotic analysis of theatre highlights how such layering can be achieved by a use of "*adjuvants*" and "*opposants*" (respectively, characters who help, and characters who oppose, the "subject's" quest to attain the "object"), a transformation frequently effected in La Chaussée's theatre through characters' manipulation of social acting. As Ubersfeld points out, "*actants* who are at once *adjuvants* and *opposants* [...] in general have indicators that are immediately perceptible by the spectator" (1996:53). In order to signal these transformations to the public, the *comédie larmoyante* frequently has recourse to asides signaling the character's duplicity: "*feignons*," "*faisons-nous violence*," etc. But while the audience is aware of the game on stage, within the fictional frame these different levels of communication prove difficult for the characters to manage. By emphasizing their inexperience in social acting, the plays demonstrate how techniques of affect-control developed for stage acting can effectively guide the outcome of real-life social situations. Thus when Durval is convinced of Constance's indifference, Damon must correct his misreading of her performance: "Ah! don't fool yourself; it's but an outward calm / And for a virtuous heart, it is the greatest effort" (1970:57).

Damon's observation goes to the heart of a different *préjugé* that La Chaussée's theatre redresses by depicting acting as a buttress to virtuous conduct in contemporary society. Constance's ability to convincingly act the role of indifference does not detract from her inherent virtue, despite the deeply ingrained French prejudice against the morality of acting and actors. Domesticating acting technique in the service of legitimate social achievement (Constance must keep up appearances in order to preserve the integrity of her household) flies in the face of received ideas about the sexual and moral depredations of female actors. This disdain erupts in Act IV, when Durval becomes convinced that Constance has taken Clitandre as her lover. Despite Damon's reproach, he attributes "this too-true calm, that I thought was affected" not to "the fruit of her prudence, / the effects of her love, the effort of her reason" but to her "treason" (1970:62). He convokes the members of the household to serve as an audience for his accusation, expressing a contempt for her actions that is compounded by her apparent skill as an actress (her calm being interpreted in this instance as a supreme effort to rein in her lascivious nature): "Recognize the error that disposed all of you / in favor of a woman instructed in the art of feigning" (1970:63). The "art of feigning" (*l'art de feindre*) permits the actor to dupe the credulous spectator; introducing that art into the domestic sphere runs the risk of destabilizing the family unit when all parties do not equally understand the acting codes being used. For the men in the *parterre* as much as for the women peering over the banisters of the balconies, La Chaussée underscores the necessity of observing the performances of the opposite sex with the same circumspection and care that they must put into constructing their own social roles. Inasmuch as acting is only effective for a public that knows how to interpret its signs, the *comédie larmoyante* presents acting and informed spectatorship as two aspects of the same socially vital skill.

Exemplary Actors

The play that Damis and Clitandre bring to Durval's estate, *L'époux amoureux de sa femme*, is never actually performed within the course of the action of *Le préjugé à la mode*. Whereas the Baroque theatre reveled in the mise-en-abime of the play-within-a-play, La Chaussée's refusal to see the trope through to its consummation serves to mark a rupture with this increasingly archaic worldview. In the last act of *Le préjugé*, Durval and Constance are dressed "*en domino*," the traditional garb of the masked ball and the *théâtre de société*, with cape, hood, and half-mask, costumed to take the stage in a play that neither of them wishes to perform. The disguising of the actor's body and face harkens back to traditional forms of theater[13], and to the fear that the action on the stage might somehow call into question the stability of the surrounding reality. The othering of the fictional character assures its status as a construct that can exist only within the frame of the stage space, and safeguards the "reality" of the world outside of the play. For Durval, the mask provides a necessary distance between his social self (the persona that he projects) and his character who will, paradoxically, be allowed to express the true feelings that Durval hides behind his socially necessary performance. This alienation permits him to disavow the very real emotions from which he will construct his "fictional" acting. At the beginning of the recognition scene (act V, scene v), the name "Durval" does not appear on the page of the printed script, replaced instead by "*Le masque*," with its reference to the etymological root of "person" (both the English and French derive from the Latin *persona*, which originally denoted a theatrical mask). The complete disappearance of Durval (textually and theatrically) behind Le Masque reinforces the play's central theme of social beings as theatrical performances. Durval has constructed a role that pits him fundamentally against himself; the mask allows him to enter into a character more aligned with his desires and goals. Constance, on the other hand, has all along played a part intended to reconcile her actual situation (neglected wife) with her desires (monogamous marriage), and as such appears on stage without a literal mask. While in order to conceal her true feelings she has had to do some violence to herself, acting remains for her a means to take control of her social situation rather than submitting to its inevitability. The play-within-a-play of Baroque theatre reinforced the predetermination of human actions by showing them as scripted for the pleasure of an unknowable audience. But by the end of *Le préjugé à la mode*, Durval has understood that this need not be true. The *domino* provides the necessary crutch for him to express his true feelings, but also reminds him that masks (both a literal face-covering and a social performance) can be removed when convenient, exchanged for others, or discarded entirely.

This highly theatricalized exchange between Durval and his wife is their most honest communication in the entire play. No irony is intended here: henceforth, this will be the mask that Durval wears, and thus he can remove the *domino* and show his "real" face. The double recognition (Constance realizes that Durval, rather than an impertinent *petit-maître* has been courting her; Durval recognizes himself in the mask) of this scene obviates the need for actually presenting the play-within-a-play, as both characters realize how the structural resemblance of "real" domestic space to theatrical fiction allows them to use their acting skill in the service of virtuous ideals. If there were any lingering doubt as to the explicitly exemplary intent of this dénouement, Durval dispels it by addressing the small audience of friends that assembles after this scene (the same public that he had convoked in act IV to accuse his wife of acting), and speaking through them to the spectators gathered in the rue Saint-Germain: "Perhaps my example will have greater credit: / You can imitate me (*On pourra m'imiter*)" (1970:68). La Chaussée offers his parable of the usefulness and moral uprightness of acting as a defense and illustration of a new dimension of social interaction for the emerging French middle class.

The justification for comedy was always that it would serve as a moral lesson; its ridicule would show audiences how *not* to act. Having removed the ridicule, La Chaussée's plays indicate that the behaviors depicted are apt for imitation, publicly proclaiming the legitimacy of a serious bourgeois subject and the moral imperative of acting in society. Lanson, once again, brushes the surface of this truth before pulling back into an accusatory posture: "When one prides one's self on bringing real life to the stage [...] one must show private life, not the masquerade of private life" (1903:188). I contend, to the contrary, that La Chaussée's plays precipitate the convergence of "private life" and "masquerade" (an entertainment where the participants wear masks), insisting that the real itself is another category of performance. In so doing, they provide an early articulation of a distinctly modern paradigm of theatrical self-conception which posits that "ordinary social intercourse is itself put together as a scene is put together, by the exchange of dramatically inflated actions, counteractions, and terminating replies" (Goffman 1997:106). Once the world is acknowledged as a mutable play-script, individual actors are empowered to take advantage of the formal limitations of the social world's play-like structure in order to secure their own personal goals. By attaching this awareness to a narrative thread that privileges conservative values such as monogamy and familial stability, La Chaussée's theatre stops far short of a revolution in morality. However, by validating acting — the portraying of a character not one's own, in society if not on stage — as a legitimate tool for attaining social advancement for the emerging bourgeois class, La Chaussée's theatre opens the door to a host of social and psychological changes that will shake the very foundations of the *ancien régime*.

YALE UNIVERSITY

Notes

1. Lanson's monograph, *Nivelle de la Chaussée et la comédie larmoyante*, originally published in 1887, remains the standard reference work on La Chaussée. All translations from French are my own.

In a footnote to his definition of the *comédie larmoyante*, Lanson asserts an equivalence between the *drame*, as later articulated by Diderot, and the *comédie larmoyante*. I maintain, however, that La Chaussée's use of verse and his continued reliance on the vocabulary of classical French tragedy argue for a formal distinction between the two genres. (See also Pierre Trahard, *Les maîtres de la sensibilité française au XVIIIe siècle*, vol. 2. Paris: Boivin & Cie., 1932, and Félix Gaiffe, *Le drame en France au XVIIIe siècle*. Paris: Armand Colin, 1910.) By contrast, Diderot's *Entretiens sur le fils naturel* and his *Discours sur la poésie dramatique* define a poetics of his proposed serious genre, whereas no such statement of esthetic principles exists for the *comédie larmoyante*. Finally, while the *comédie larmoyante* reflects a latent obsession with class status, it stops well short of overtly embracing the notion of bourgeois ascendancy in the representational frame. This inherent conservatism differs from Diderot's explicitly political dramatic agenda, which seeks to instrumentalize the theatre in service of moral and social reform. As W.D. Howarth points out in his introduction to *Mélanide* (Brighton: Sussex reprints, 1973), La Chaussée never embraces Diderot's proposed imitation of middle class speech and surroundings, opting instead for an emotional mimesis, substituting parallels of *sentiment* for a realistic interpretation of everyday life.

2. Luigi Riccoboni, called Lélio, was the leader of the troupe of Italian actors sent by the Duke of Padua (at the request of the Regent, Philippe d'Orléans) to take up residence in Paris in 1716. An actor, director, and active critic of contemporary European drama, Riccoboni was also an enthusiastic early supporter of La Chaussée's innovations. The 1777 edition of Nivelle de la Chaussée's *Oeuvres* includes Riccoboni's "Lettre à M. le docteur Muratori." The letter dates from 1737, after the première of La Chaussée's third play, *L'Ecole des amis*.

3. The 1970 Slatkine Reprints edition contains all five volumes of the 1777 *Oeuvres* in one volume. On each numbered page of the reprint, four pages of the original appear; all references are to the 1970 pagination.

4. On the importance of the parterre in making or breaking a play, as well as its theatrical sophistication, see Jeffrey Ravel, "*La Reine Boit!* Print, Performance, and Theater Publics in France, 1724–1725" *Eighteenth-Century Studies* 29:4 (1996): 391–411.

5. *Les précieuses ridicules* (1659) mockingly portrays the excesses of *salonnières* who prize an exaggerated nobility and specious erudition above all else. Their spurned lovers resolve to avenge themselves by passing off their valets, Mascarille and Jodelet, as learned aristocrats. The caricature of the aristocracy acted by the two buffoons charms and seduces the ladies, until the lovers return to reveal the ruse and correct the snobbish posturing that infects high society.

6. Maza's well-argued analysis is persuasive but fails to take into account the valorization of mores specifically identified as "bourgeois" both in La Chaussée's theatre and in the theoretical writings of Diderot on the *drame*. Rather, she asserts that the sentimentality that characterizes the family romance in eighteenth-century theatre transcends class concerns, serving as a stand-in for national sentiment. While this may also be true, the marked vocabulary of class in works that present the ultimate triumph of bourgeois values suggests that, even if they did not make political claims in the name of a middle class social group, many authors of this period nonetheless embraced the "bourgeois" as an avatar of national decency and moral uprightness.

7. The difficulty of distinguishing between social strata manifests itself in the anxiety over class miscegenation represented by marriage prospects between old-blood aristocrats and the newly wealthy "bourgeoisie." This theme that appears repeatedly in La Chaussée's works, including in *L'école des mères*, *La gouvernante*, and *L'homme de fortune*.

8. All of the late plays (with the exception of *L'école de la jeunesse*) associate humble origins with moral uprightness. This is the case for Monrose's uncle and Ariste in *L'école des amis*, the title character in *Mélanide*, Monsieur Argant and Doligny *père* in *L'école des mères*, the Président Sainville in *La gouvernante*, and Brice *père* in *L'homme de fortune*.

9. The declamatory style that dominated French theatre in the seventeenth century hewed to fixed rules of physical expression of emotion inherited from clas-

sical rhetoric. (See Angelica Goodden, *Actio and Persuasion: Dramatic Performance in Eighteenth Century France.* Oxford: Clarendon Press, 1986, and Dene Barnett, *The Art of Gesture: The Practices and Principles of 18th Century Acting.* Heidelberg: Carl Winter, 1987.) However, the modern debate in France over the appropriate degree of emotional investment can be traced back to Bishop Bossuet's 1696 anti-theatrical screed, *Maximes et réflexions sur la comédie*, in which he decries the dangers of assuming the emotions of a character in order to give a convincing performance. L'Abbé Dubos suggests an incomplete identification between actor and character as a prerequisite for effective tragic acting in his 1719 *Réflexions critiques sur la poésie et la peinture*, and Luigi Riccoboni champions emotional investment in his 1738 survey, *Réflexions historiques et critiques sur les différents théâtres de l'Europe.* (The actor Maillet-Duclairon specifically addresses the acting problems raised by the *comédie larmoyante* in his 1751 work, *Sur la conaissance des Théâtres français*, cited in F.C. Green, *Minuet: A Critical Survey of French and English Literary Ideas in the Eighteenth Century.* London: J.M. Dent & Sons, 1935, 25.) The watershed event, however, is the 1747 publication of Rémond de Saint-Albine's *Le comédien* (translated into English in 1749 by John Hill as *The Actor*), which prescribes a total fusion of the actor with the character. This work, coupled with François Riccoboni's 1750 response to it, *L'art du théâtre à Mme.* ***, both contribute directly to the French enlightenment's most lasting contribution to the theory of acting, Diderot's *Paradoxe sur le comédien.* See also Joseph Roach, *The Player's Passion: Studies in the Science of Acting.* Newark: University of Delaware Press, 1985.

10. Languet de Gergy's welcoming speech is reprinted in the 1777 edition of the *Oeuvres* of Nivelle de la Chaussée.

11. As a result of this reaction, de Gergy's speech welcoming Marivaux into the Académie in 1744 sharply censured both the playwright and the theatre as a whole. For an account of this incident, see d'Alembert's "Eloge de Languet" in his *Oeuvres complètes*, vol. 3. Paris: A. Belin, 1821.

12. The nature of the plot makes this play, and in particular the role of Constance, a surprising choice for Louis XV's mistress, Mme de Pompadour (*née* Poisson). The fact that she chose to play it several times at her private *Théâtre des petits-cabinets* testifies to the appeal of La Chaussée's theatre for even the most rarefied of eighteenth century audiences.

13. The half-mask remained in use at the Comédie Italienne throughout the eighteenth century for servant characters, including the many incarnations of Arlequin in Marivaux's oeuvre.

References Cited

de Gergy, Languet. "Réponse de M. l'Archevêque de Sens, au discours de M. de la Chaussée." In La Chaussée, *Oeuvres*, 400. Geneva: Slatkine Reprints, 1970.

Elias, Norbert. *Power & Civility.* Trans. Edmond Jephcott. New York: Pantheon Books, 1982.

Goffman, Erving. *The Goffman Reader.* C. Lemert and A. Branaman, eds. Malden, MA: Blackwells, 1997.

La Chaussée, Pierre Claude Nivelle de. *Oeuvres.* Geneva: Slatkine Reprints, 1970 (1777).

Lanson, Gustave. *Nivelle de la Chaussée et la comédie larmoyante.* Paris: Hachette, 1903.

Maza, Sarah. *The Myth of the French Bourgeoisie.* Cambridge, MA: Harvard UP, 2003.

Riccoboni, Luigi. "Lettre à M. le docteur Muratori." In La Chaussée, *Oeuvres*, 401–406. Geneva: Slatkine Reprints, 1970.

Sammons, Jeffrey L. "Heine as Weltburger: A Skeptical Inquiry." *Modern Language Notes* 101:3: 609–628.

Ubersfeld, Anne. *Lire le théâtre I.* Paris: Belin, 1996.

12

Excavating Multiple"Troys"

An Embodied Deconstruction of the Scenario of Conquest through "Teatro de Vivência"

Carla Melo

Abstract

For a period of four years, ending in July of 2006, the southern Brazilian theatrical company Oi Nóis Aqui Traveiz, *famous for its political commitment and aesthetic investment, staged* To Those Who Will Come After Us: Kassandra in Process, *which was their intertextual and interactive version of Christa Wolf's feminist novel,* Kassandra. *Through Teatro de Vivência—a radical reinvention of environmental theater—this performance deconstructed and multiplied the scenario of conquest in the Trojan War by transferring it to various postcolonial contexts. I examine how Oi Nois's highly articulate gestural and scenic languages destabilized the binaries that make up the logic of conquest.*

Never was I more alive then now, in the hour of my death [...]. Slowly I reach with longing the years prior to the war, the time when I was a priestess — a white block. Further back: the girl–here I am caught by the word "girl" and caught all the more by her form; by its beautiful image. I have always been caught by images more than by words. And everything will end with an image, not with a word. Words die before images.

(To Those Who Will Come After Us: Kassandra in Process 51)[1]

What can images conjured by the visions of a Trojan priestess convey about war in our neo-imperialist and globalizing world? A daring theatrical piece staged in the south of Brazil posed this question to the participant-witnesses of this drama of prophetic wisdom. At the end of a narrow corridor, participants ran into a shaky wooden stairwell that led into a room with moving walls. In this room, the Trojan King reminded his daughter, Kassandra, of her brother's death at the hands of Achilles. Suddenly, one of the four walls slid open to an actual staging of the battle, and the participants watched the fatal duel between the two warriors on a level below. Those audience members who were next to the moving wall stepped rapidly away from it, afraid of falling from the twenty-foot-high loft. As they moved back, their sense of direction and of the actual size of the entire space had been severely altered.

These were some of the scenic strategies in *To Those Who Will Come After Us: Kassandra in Process*, a three-hour production by the legendary Southern Brazilian theatrical collective *Oi Nóis Aqui Traveiz*.[2] The name of the group literally translates as "Here We Are Again," but its use of broken Portuguese lends it a lower class connotation that reveals its dedication to popular theatre. Born during the struggle for democratization that took place in late 1970s (when the military dictatorship that ruled the country since 1964 had slightly loosened its hold), the group has now become one of the most important and politically engaged popular theatre companies in the country. From 2002 to July of 2006, the group staged their interactive version of Christa's Wolf's feminist novel *Kassandra* (1983; English trans.1984). *Oi Nóis* adopted Wolf's novel as a point of departure for its intertextual interpretation, which also included excerpts from Native American[3] and Hindu mythology, as well as texts by Pablo Neruda, Heiner Muller, Samuel Beckett, Albert Camus, Peter Handke, George Orwell, and Euripides.[4] Yet, it was *Kassandra* that set the structure, tone, and overall theme of the production; the other texts were inserted as fragments into the narrative. Like the novel, the production explored the subjectivity of Kassandra, the priestess of Apollo and prophet-seer, who warned her compatriots that if they engaged in war with the Greeks, Troy would be destroyed. All Trojans, including her father, the King of Troy, deemed her a mad woman and a traitor, ignoring her prophecies. Troy, after a ten-year war, was indeed conquered and destroyed.

In *Kassandra in Process*, the collective strategically employed this "scenario" to question the persistence of male-driven violence in our contemporary world. As the thirty to forty participants followed the action through a number of different rooms varying in shape and size, their spatial awareness, orientation, and corporeal boundaries were challenged. In this group's reinvention of the environmental theater tradition, which they call *Teatro de Vivência*, or "Theatre of Lived Experience," not only are the boundaries between actors — who call themselves "agents" — and "participants" blurred, but also the relation between bodies and space is constantly shifting, inciting explorations of myriad affective possibilities. Participants are often encouraged to interact physically with the agents and with the environment through the activation of other senses, such as smell, taste and touch. As a fine example of *Teatro de Vivência*, this production was staged in a warehouse that measured between 2,000 to 3,000 square feet and which had been transformed into a kind of metamorphic labyrinth. Once inside of the performance space, the participants could not escape the multiple temporalities and corporeo-spatial disjunctions that constituted this episodic journey through Kassandra's non-linear memories and visions of the Trojan War. In the production, this war functioned as a thread weaving 1200 BCE to various historical contexts. While both the seminal novel and the production performed a feminist critique of physical and epistemic violence,[5] exposing female exclusion from political participation in times of war, the production took the critique further. By "excavating" characters that have been submerged in the ruins of numerous fallen "Troys" across the twentieth and twentieth first centuries, it staged, deconstructed and multiplied the signification of the scenario of conquest in the Trojan War. Through highly articulate gestural and scenic languages, the production engaged the notion of conquest as an embodied practice that primarily entails gender and racial colonization. The various theatrical languages in *Kassandra in Process* enacted corporeal, spatial, cultural and textual disjunctions that working along the axes of Self/Other, East/West, and male/female, destabilized the binaries that make up the logic of conquest.

Wolf's "Chrissandra"

Through the novel *Kassandra,* the East German intellectual Christa Wolf, critiqued a pivotal narrative in the establishment of patriarchal dominance as based on the notion of heroic violence. She seemed to foresee, like the mythic heroine Kassandra, the fall of the German Democratic Republic (GDR) for which Troy served as a trope — a fall that for the author, signified a problematic, yet perhaps inevitable conquest of the first world over the second.[6] Published seven years before unification, Wolf's *Kassandra* reflected on the oppression of female subjectivity and the silencing of the female voice during times of political conflict. She also indirectly reflected on the possibility of global destruction as a result of the Cold War (Wolf 1984:228–229). If, at first, the parallels between the Trojan War and the Cold War, as well as between GDR and Troy seemed to reinforce the binaries of East and West, according to Karen Jacobs, it is clear that her critique of male violence and misogyny was applied to both Trojans and Greeks.

Jacobs adds that Wolf constructed a "composite voice, a 'Chrissandra' [...], one that aspires to occupy and encode multiple historical and political positions" (Jacobs 2001:2).

The Scenario of Conquest

The Kassandra as embodied in *Oi Nóis's* performance, through her intense corporeal language, became a medium that was also "possessed" by multiple voices. As she chanted, moaned and whispered words that denounced the complicity of Troy in prolonging an endless and meaningless war, she also warned Aeneas: "The new masters will dictate the laws over all survivors. The earth is not big enough for us to escape" (*Oi Nóis* 2004:108). As her body became the site of competing discourses, it acted out in a quasi-schizoid dance between compulsive repetitive movements, frozen images, and absurd gestures. The corporeal and textual disjunctions embodied by Tania Farias in the role of Kassandra permeated the production as a whole, heightening the friction between what Diana Taylor calls "archive" and "repertoire," that is, between official narratives and embodied knowledge[7]— a friction already found in the novel[8]. Besides staging dissociation between text and movement and presenting contradictory texts, *Kassandra in Process* also enacted what I will call "cultural and spatial disjunctions." These multiple disjunctions not only unsettled the narrative flow but also the actual phenomenology of reception. As the audience became a participant-witness who inhabited the same space as the "agents," the Trojan War became more than an allegory — it became a "scenario." According to Taylor, a "scenario" is more than narrative; it is narrative and space, setup and action, and thus requires live bodies for its reenactment (2003:28–29). The twenty-three scenes that made up this reenactment shifted between past and present, moving from Troy to Greece to moments of more recent history. Since all conjured events shared a colonial logic, the scenario could be specified as a "scenario of conquest." What made *Oi Nóis's* reenactment of the scenario of conquest unique was the way in which disjunctions between different theatrical elements intensified the scenario's deconstruction. For instance, the non-realistic corporeal language, which often resisted the text, made the collage-like construction of the script more evident. In the same manner, the apparent permanence of the aesthetics of space juxtaposed with the impermanent nature of the architecture blurred the lines between past and present, while the dialogue between costumes and languages engendered a sense of cultural hybridity. All these juxtapositions worked towards challenging individual, racial, gendered, and geopolitical boundaries.

The production began with Kassandra's arrival at the Mycenaean portal as a slave to Agamemnon after the fall of Troy, and developed as a journey through her memories and visions during the few hours before her execution. After the arrival scene the participants were led as witnesses through a "memory corridor" that took them into her non-linear reenactment of events up to the fall of Troy. In Wolf's novel, the historic/mythic war between Troy and Greece becomes a trope for the East/West divide. The production radically destabilized this binary as it foregrounded the masculinist seduction of violence and the greed, racial hatred and national (city-state) pride that fuel war, genocide, and torture. These "characters" of the Trojan War, as fictionalized by Wolf, were shuffled and recombined in the performance to conjure up other "scenarios of conquest" such as the endless ethnic-religious conflict over territories that constitutes the Israeli-Palestinian conflict, the imperialist drive of Nazi Germany and the Holocaust, as well as the U.S. invasion and occupation of Iraq. The latter example presented a similar reasoning for waging war since in both cases pretexts, i.e., "Helen" and "weapons of mass destruction," covered up political and economic interests.

Yet, perhaps the most poignant reactivation of the scenario of conquest took place when the women who played Kassandra's doubles entered the sand-covered battle field, (a 25' by 15' space on the ground level of the warehouse) singing an old German song that exalted a German soldier, as if they were little girls. They circled Kassandra, who then started to sing along with them. From a wooden box Kassandra took a ball of red yarn and "drew" a Star of David on the floor with the yarn. She partly took on the identity of the "Others" of the Nazi, as she lay on the floor and recited in German: "Thousands of communists killed. Thousands of homosexuals killed. Thousands of gypsies killed. Thousands of Jewish killed" (*Oi Nóis* 2004:106). As she got up the other women blindfolded her. Then she delivered a text borrowed from Heiner Muller's play, entitled *Germania 3 Death in Berlin*: "You have fertilized this earth with blood. You have filled this industry with human bodies. [...] Humanity is a sad material. Material humanity. Ants under your boots. Yesterday for your tomorrow" (106). Following this monologue, she sang a Hebrew song as she blindly tried to embrace the participants. Then, a voice-over of a female voice singing and wailing in Arabic overlapped her voice. Embodying both the perpetrators and the victims of violence (The Nazi and their victims), this scene also alluded to the broader context of the cycle of violence between Israelis and Palestinians. As the Arab presence was constituted only through the voice, it seemed to suggest the invisibility of Arab women within this scenario. This scene also confirmed Taylor's theorizing that a scenario "is not necessarily mimetic." The notion that a scenario "works through reactivation rather than duplication" and that "all scenarios have localized meaning, though many attempt to pass as universally valid," seems to apply to the strategic cross-cultural and transnational equations that took place in the metamorphic stage of *Kassandra in Process* (Taylor 2003:28–32).

While these equations seemed to correspond to different scenarios — racial genocide, preemptive wars, neo-imperialist occupations, terrorism — the scenario of conquest's underlying logic can encompass these various kinds of armed conflict. If Jill Lane is correct in asserting that following early sixteenth century scenarios of conquest, new versions of these "became recast as scenarios of conversions [...] in effort to mitigate the violence of the entangled projects," and that "conquest, as a term rather than a project was out," then it is possible to theorize a transferring of this scenario into modern and postcolonial contexts (qtd. in Taylor 2003:31). In other words, the impetus behind territorial control central to conquest is still active in more recent history; it has simply been disguised and/or substituted by other forms of control. In this sense, conquering does not necessarily entail territorial occupation, creation of a colony, neither complete extermination or absorption of the Other into one's culture, although many times one or more of these can occur. Whichever its goal or method, central to the logic of conquest is the physical and epistemic violence along with exoticization or demonization of the Other. This othering usually entails racial and gender domination — of one side against the other and within each side of the struggle. *Kassandra in Process* deconstructed the logic that underpins the scenario of conquest by foregrounding the subjugation of women that occurs in times of armed conflict, by refusing to demonize the Other, and by destabilizing geopolitical binaries.

The feminist perspective of the production criticized the masculinist drive to power as not necessarily limited to the male gender. In other words, women can also become perpetrators of violence as they adopt a masculinist approach in order to gain a sense of power. Kassandra immediately understood this when she first encountered Clytemnestra:

> She was exactly as I imagined her. Full of hatred. [...] The same smile appeared on our lips. It wasn't cruel or suffered. Too bad that destiny didn't put us on the same side. [...] She's also going to become a victim of the blindness that surrounds power [*Oi Nóis* 2004:75].

This recognition of oneself in the Other was not solely restricted to women. As "Kassandra" walked towards the hands of the conqueror who had burned down her city and who had taken her as a slave, she exclaimed:

> How much they look like my Trojans! Who am I to look at them as only the winners and not those who will continue to live? Who must keep on living so that what we call life may go on. They, who must live for all those they have killed, if they know how to stop winning, their city will survive [77].

In a way, this refusal to demonize the Other retained an echo of the archive, since one of the praises of Homer's *Iliad* is its sympathetic treatment of the enemies.[9] Nonetheless, the production deconstructed the most popular archival narrative of the Trojan War (present in the *Iliad*, as well as on Euripides' *Trojan Women* and Aeschylus' *Oresteia*) by presenting its own adaptation of a lesser-known version of its causes. The production followed Wolf's adaptation of a version of the myth,[10] which stated that "Helen never returned to Troy with Paris and that the Trojans honestly told the Greeks of her absence" (Gilpin 1989:361). In adapting this version of the story, Wolf chose to have the Trojans not tell the Greeks that they didn't have Helen in order to save their honor since she had been stolen from Paris by the King of Egypt.

When Kassandra confronted her father Priam on the absurdity of the war and on his unwillingness to avoid it by telling the Greeks the truth, Priam responded: "Kassandra, what the Greeks want is our wealth and the free access to the Black Sea" (*Oi Nóis* 2004:53). Priam refused to deny the pretext because he knew that it would not stop the Greeks. Besides, he had his own thirst for revenge since Achilles had killed one of his sons. Thus, Helen was really a pretext for both sides to engage in war. While the scenario of conquest generally downplays economic and political motivations in favor of masculinist codes of honor and duty, as Trojans and Greeks became interchangeable, the binarism of the scenario of conquest was subdued and the real causes for waging war were made explicit. As this destabilized scenario was juxtaposed against modern and contemporary historical contexts, this particular deconstruction suggested that one must not think only in terms of "us versus them" and that the causes of conflict are often more complex than official history allows.

This friction between the different versions of history as well as between those versions and the embodied knowledge of conquest was heightened by what I call "cultural disjunction" or "strategic orientalism." The orientalism, which was clear from the very first scene, was "strategic" in the sense that it utilized a mysterious and exotic collage of decontextualized and invented aesthetic elements with a general oriental/ancient flavor while undoing the binarism that, according to Edward Said, is central to the orientalist project (1979:201–205). As the thirty participants entered an approximately 15' × 15' room, they may have read in the program notes that this room represented the Mycenaean Portal. As they entered this sand covered space with two walls covered with relief sculptures, they were saluted along with the two arriving characters (Kassandra and Agamemnon) by three women who are wearing burkas, singing in a language that mixes Greek, Hebrew and Arabic, playing musical instruments such as sitar, and through their only exposed body parts — their hands — creating mudras in reference to South-Indian dance.

This collage of cultures can be seen as "de-orientalizing" in that it mixed Greek language, characters and Greek-inspired sculptural relief and masks with Semitic and Arabic languages, traditional Islamic clothing and South Indian codified gestures. By engaging in such collage, *Oi Nóis* politically aligned the portrayal of Kassandra with revisionist histories of the ancient Mediterranean world that argue that an overlooked "Afro-Asiatic" element was an important component in the ancient Greek ethnic make up.[11] Arguably, one could assert that the myth of Aryan dominance is an important factor in legitimizing Greek culture as a cradle of the Western culture. Thus, to challenge this paradigm by affirming the hybridity of the ancient Greeks is one strategy that challenges the very foundation of the East-West divide. *Oi Nóis* representation of the Oriental Other, given its blatant employment of collage, works as long as it does not intend or pretend to present an authentic image of one particular culture. On the contrary, the blatant hybridity of their representation presented a fusion of diverse cultural elements that intentionally complicates not only the East-West divide, but also the North-South axis. The East-West divide was here conflated with the North-South axis, not only because the performance was located in Latin America and made clear references to the imperialism of the North, but also because through its "strategic orientalism," it also merged Oriental aesthetics with a generalized Native American aesthetic. Although all these conflations and equations, which I am calling "cultural disjunctions," might seem highly problematic from a postcolonial perspective, the strategy here seemed to connect multiple temporalities, spaces, and cultures in order to call for a coalition among those who have a subaltern condition in this globalizing world. In such permutation of the scenario of conquest, the collage may point to a reclaiming of the potential agency of cultural hybridity.

Kassandra as a central subject and the women who embodied her doubles suggested the centrality of Third World women as agents of resistance against the inherent violence in the scenario of conquest — a resistance that was mainly articulated through the body as a multiple field of signification. The cultural disjunctions discussed earlier were combined with corporeal and textual ones that continued to destabilize certain binaries that organize the scenario of conquest. Yet, it was not corporeality alone that enacted this

Tania Farias in the role of Kassandra. Photograph by Claudio Etges

resistance; verbal language was not less important, since it also assumed a corporeal quality. As the body dissociated from language and as language took on corporeality and rhythm, these disjunctions were punctuated by moments of utter coherence and a sense of integration between movement and words. To make this clear we must visit the second scene once more. As

Kassandra confronted her father Priam and asked him to negotiate with the Greeks in order to avoid the war, her head was facing the ground as she raised her right fist as if to point to the sky. Then, with the other hand, she pointed to the right one and recalled: "This is the oldest image I have, my daddy's favorite; myself liking politics more than my brothers; it was allowed for me to sit close to him" (Oi Nóis 2004:52). There was a great degree of dissociation within the gestural language as well as within the verbal text itself. She pointed to an image that she didn't initially look at; the logic of the sentences had a coherence of their own; the rhythm of the delivery didn't stress words that should be stressed. This dissociation between words, delivery, hands and head was emphasized by the way the image was formed. It was as if the pointing finger of authority — the pointing finger of interpellation — was leading her as opposed to it obeying her will. Then, in one beat, the short and frail body of "Kassandra" seemed to fill the space as she raised her head and, combining authority and coherence, pointed to her father in confrontation: "There is no Helen. [...] This war is absurd" (52). Her words also took on a corporeal presence as she played with musicality and repetition in a way that worked alternatively with and against the meaning of the text.

The power of Kassandra's presence was primarily drawn from the tension between integration and dissociation, which was further emphasized by the fact that the body was not always decodable. Her gestures assumed a language quality, which, due to its obscure content, placed us in the position of the Trojans who were not able to understand her message. Most of the time, she engaged in a repertoire of her own, in a corporeal language that no one else shared. These gaps in translation further engaged us in the meaning making process. In contrast, what we did translate pierced us not only emotionally but also physically, whereby the performance truly assumed the power of what Diana Taylor calls an "act of transfer," that is, the power to transmit knowledge (2003:2–3). At this point of identification, Kassandra's vision of terror and the inability to avoid it became an exhausting burden that was shared among the "witnesses." The very rhythm of this shift between speaking and not being heard, seeing and not being seen, and the moments of silent communication, brought a sense of relief and signified an utter resistance that even defied the tragic ending. Kassandra died but her image remained due to its attempts at deconstructing the very polarization that many find necessary for engaging in resistance. The power of her corporeal language lay in betraying decoding attempts that sought to disable it. As her words humanized the enemy and encompassed divergent positions within her society, her corporeal language of disjunction intensified this effect, effectively challenging the boundaries between Self and Other.

From the very beginning of the "journey" Kassandra also addressed another set of boundaries as she emphasized the notion of embodied memory: "I take the pain test as a doctor that pinches the muscle to know if it is anesthetized. I pinch my memory. Maybe the pain will die before my own death" (*Oi Nôis* 2004:50). Thus, the goal was to find the junction between body and mind, movement and memory, and the disjunctions constituted a strategy of finding pathways to the junction. Additionally, the juxtaposition of her excessive presence (engaged in rescuing memories inscribed into the body) with the narrative of the Trojan War, created another point of junction/disjunction between official narratives and embodied knowledge. This point of junction/disjunction is due not only to the fact that the second deconstructed the meanings of the first, but also to how the performative elements embodied that which is absent from the official narratives. The dilemma of the character was that her corporeal language seemed to be trying to communicate through a language that was not always understood, and therefore the repertoire seemed to fail as an act of transfer. Except that here, that which was trying to be communicated was the very "untranslatability" of her burden: the gift of prophecy.

This "gift" also assumed greater signification because it seemed to derive from historical awareness. This signification transpired from the apparent gestural archeology that "Kassandra" was engaged in. Her visions came through a trance-like state in which she seemed "possessed" by past memories that had been blocked. In spite of the association with the future, she was engaged in retrieving a memory-of-the-vision-of-the-future, which then constituted the present, or rather: a contingency between past, present, and future, which simultaneously she tried to grasp and grasped her. While, as Taylor points out, "archival memory succeeds in separating the source of knowledge' from the knower," on the metamorphic stage of *Oi Nôis*, it was the body of the knower that represented the source of knowledge (2003:19). As participants, we were caught trying to decode Kassandra's frenetic gestures that choreographed the future of the past. We were also moved, both emotionally and literally — as the topography continued to shift — to decode the implied historical contingencies, especially in terms of what drives us towards demonization of the Other, violence, and even self-destruction.

The emphasis on constant shifting was translated into the very topography of the performance. This shifting constituted spatial disjunctions that highlighted the centrality of violence in the scenario of conquest. The very condition of not being able to leave the space and of being led from one room to the next may have generated in the participants a feeling of vulnerability and claustrophobia. The spatial disorientation caused by the changing boundaries not only made them fall prey to the imminent violence, but also reflected Kassandra's subjectivity in the sense of feeling imprisoned and confused by the burden of knowing too much — possibly furthering the participants' identification with the heroine. Yet, unlike Greek tragedy, this identification did not lead to a catharsis or any kind of closure because our experience as participants was not vicariously lived through the character; in this *Teatro de Vivência*, our experience was fully embodied and engaged in the action. We were often given the choice to be physically touched and to drink from the same cup as "Kassandra." Yet it was not only our interaction with the actors that created this participatory experience; we constantly had to make choices regarding our level of interaction with other participants, our spatial positioning and our boundaries.

If, according to Diana Taylor "the scenario places us within its frame, implicating us in its ethics and politics," due to the tactics of spatial disjunction of *Oi Nóis's Teatro de Vivência* we were placed literally inside of the frame, thereby enhancing the ethical implication. And while Taylor asserts, "the frame is basically fixed and, as such repeatable and transferable," the transferability of the scenario of conquest, in this case, had to do more with the relationship among characters than with the frame itself (2003:33). Thus, it was not surprising that the literal frame — the physical space was constantly shifting. This constant shifting heightened our level of engagement both at the physical and the ethical levels. Taylor adds that, as we are forced to witness, the scenario "precludes a certain kind of distancing" (2003:33). Yet at certain moments, such as when the participants were walking through the memory corridor, whoever was towards the end of the line could not see Kassandra, who was delivering a monologue at the far end of the corridor; they could only hear her and depending on the commotion created by the experience, only vaguely so. This distancing signified that being part of an event does not necessarily provide one with specular mastery over the environment; instead it seemed to turn one's spatial positioning into a metaphor for culturally constructed ideologies. In other words, where "we stand" dictates what we are allowed to perceive and how we perceive; the cultural assumptions of each location, nation, and geopolitical region are always at play. Thus, instead of simply erasing distance, the staging of the multiple scenarios of conquest created a choreography that played with a sharp contrast between distance and intimacy. This dance between distance and full immersion triggered criticality and empathy alternatively.

After three hours of being immersed in a shifting space that affected one at every sensory level, including smell, taste, and touch, one's senses became awake and alert. Following the serving of a sacred drink during the scene of Kassandra's initiation, which took place inside of a cave-like room filled with the scent of moss, the participants were harassed by soldiers who pointed strong flash lights on their faces and corralled them out of the cave.

Although the sense of enclosure and vulnerability present in this radical rein-vention of the environmental theater tradition may prompt a feeling of lack of immediate agency upon the environment, the intensity of this feeling may create a desire for agency in the participant. If the possibility of "cognitive mapping,"[12] as Fredric Jameson postulates, is intrinsically connected to a sense of agency, it may just be that an intensification of its lack may trigger a desire for remapping — for being able to see oneself as part of the map, and thus as one who cannot avoid being engaged in shaping social reality (1991:51–54). The polysemic corporeality in the figure of Kassandra allied to the affective intensity of the performance constructed a complex subjec-tive perspective on violence as an integral part of the scenario of conquest. The use of orientalist images, though arguably problematic in their decon-textualized staging, was actually strategic. The "Orient" in this case, exhib-ited a welcoming hybridity. If Wolf's Kassandra proclaimed the end of an era, the end experienced by both "agents" and participants in this produc-tion was, at the same time, hopeful and dystopian. Valmir Santos's descrip-tion of the audience's response made explicit that the absence of applause I had experienced during the several times I attended must have been the stan-dard:

> In over ten years of journalistic theater criticism, I had never witnessed such a disturbing silence as the one that invaded our senses at the end of *Oi Nóis Aqui Traveiz's* new production. [...] After three hours of performance, we had no energy to bring a hand close to the other — a mix of impotence, indignation and rapture [2004:123].

Although "impotence" could definitely have been one of the responses, it was exactly this "mix," that made the piece so complex and powerful. I would argue that impotence was the first layer of response and it came with the realization that there is not space outside of this scenario from which one can have an objective perspective. No longer can we escape the "system" as we dreamed of in the sixties. The "cognitive mapping" as theorized by Jame-son entails this realization and requires that we move beyond it, charged by the "indignation" and the "rapture." This affective effect is related to the sense that, in spite of transporting us through several geographies and histories, the action was forcibly rooted in the here-now. The set of corporeal, tex-tual, cultural and spatial disjunctions not only engendered a sense of imme-diacy and urgency, but also operated with and against each other creating a friction between that which is perceived as stable — the hegemonic culture — and that which is seen as ephemeral, collectively improvised. Ultimately, these disjunctions turned the scenario of conquest into a space where the necessity for resisting practices and cultural agency becomes the only way out of self-destruction. Yet, what was made evident is that this resistance can only come through a coalitionist approach from groups that understand their complicity with the framing of this scenario. Like Wolf's "Chrissandra," *Oi Nóis's* Kassandra was positioned at a turning point in history in which we, as participants and witnesses to her journey, were also reminded of our role as historical agents. In *Oi Nóis's To Those Who Will Come After Us–Kassandra in Process*, we realized that, if we accept for a moment the idea that we are to some extent "those who came after them," it is up to us to listen and to give credit to what Kassandra, as a double for *Oi Nóis* was trying to tell us — and we must not expect simplistic solutions.

UNIVERSITY OF CALIFORNIA, LOS ANGELES

Notes

1. Although the play premiered in September of 2002, the book *Aos que Virão Depois de Nós: Kassandra in Process— O Desassombro da Utopia* (*To Those Who Will Come After Us: Kassandra in Process—The Fearlessness of Utopia*), edited and compiled by Valmir Santos was published only in December of 2004 (Porto Alegre: Oi Nóis na Memória, 2004). It contains the script, which was collectively created out of a collage of several texts, as well as several critical essays that examine this specific production and the group's entire trajectory. I have translated all the quotes from the script and have cited the group as the author, since their collages have often adapted the original source. The central source is ChristaWolf's *Cassandra; A Novel and Four Essays*, written in 1983 and translated into English in 1984 (New York: Farrar, Straus and Girroux, Inc., 1984).

2. The name also connotes a playful element of surprise, constant mobility, collectivity and resistance, in which the "here" is never fixed, and the "againess" alludes to the collective's persistent and quasi-utopian 28 years of activism in the streets of Porto Alegre — the capital of Brazil's furthest southern state. Their survival has been made possible — not without extreme difficulties — with minimal support both from private and public institutions. The current collective has a core group of 13 members and although only one, Paulo Flores, is a founding member, others have been with the company for as long as 20 years. As many Latin American popular theater companies, they are influenced by European modern theater, more specifically, by the ideas of Bertold Brecht, Antonin Artaud, and Jerzy Growtowski. However, they also draw extensively from Brazilian folklore and performance traditions. Throughout its career the group has managed to balance its street theater activities with free pedagogical activities for low-income communities and with the staging of more private *Teatro de Vivência* performances.

3. Excerpts were taken from Native North American texts, more specifically from Sioux and Cheyenne, while props and musical instruments were inspired by Native South American tribes such as Mapuchi and Caingangue.

4. The texts from Euripides are not specified. References only mentioned that the script utilized more than one tragedy. Other texts that were used in the script

include excerpts from the *Mahabharatha*, Pablo Neruda's *General Song* (1950), Heiner Muller's *Germania 3 Death in Berlin* (1978), Samuel Beckett's *What Will Be the Word?* (1989), Albert Camus's *The Just* (1949) and *State of Siege* (1948), Peter Handle's *Kaspar Hauser* (1967), and George Orwell's *1984* (1949).

5. "Epistemic violence" is what constitutes the colonial subject as an Other, often as a demonized Other. Michel Foucault introduced the term which is now widely used in postcolonial studies. It basically refers to the notion that violence can be of a discursive nature.

6. Christa Wolf revealed in her correspondence with another East German writer: "I waited anxiously to see if they (the censors) would understand the message of Kassandra that the decline of Troy was inevitable." Taken from article on the magazine *Aplauso*, quoted in the book *Aos que Virão Depois de Nós: Kassandra in Process—O Desassombro da Utopia*.

7. While the repertoire encompasses all embodied performance practices that are usually "thought of as non-reproducible knowledge," the archive is intrinsically connected to writing and thus to power, but it also includes all forms of record keeping such as video recordings and photographs. If, at first glance, the relationship between what Taylor calls the archive and the repertoire seems to be constituted as a binary, a closer reading clarifies that either can be used in the service of power and that both are in a constant dialogue, usually filled with productive tension.

8. Although the reinterpretation of Greek mythology is a process largely invested in what Taylor calls the "archive," the friction between the archive and repertoire that is evident in the production can be already found in Wolf's *Kassandra*. The book is composed of a novel followed by four essays entitled "Conditions of a Narrative." These essays meditate on the mythic prophet-seer within her historical context as well as on the narratives the context generated. They fulfill a highly self-reflexive function as they meditate upon the author's identity and her own politically divided world. In the same vein, they also address male dominance in literature and the necessity for a female voice to provide a counterbalance. As the intertextuality of the novel and Kassandra's allegorical function is made explicit through the essays, the non-linear novel (at times) conflates the author/narrator with Kassandra, thereby, as Heidi Gilpin has noted, engaging the reader in a more active/performative manner (357). But the obvious tension between archive and repertoire lies in Wolf's rewriting the canonical archive both in terms of content and form, that is, through a performative writing that gives a minor and disregarded female character a major role, she constructs a feminist version of the narrative both in aesthetic and conceptual terms. The very reclaiming of the figure of Kassandra — the one whose words did not deserve the official legitimacy bestowed by the archive (within the mythical/literary narratives themselves)–signifies a reclaiming of the power of the repertoire. Kassandra's concern with the transmission of knowledge and the realization that access to the archive will be denied to the female characters of her time finds in the repertoire of oral transmission a way to keep the collective memory alive. This is exemplified at the moment when Kassandra, knowing that her final moments are approaching, begs Clytemnestra: "Send me a scribe, or better yet a young slave woman with a keen memory and a powerful voice. Ordain that she may repeat to her daughter what she hears from me. That her daughter in turn may pass it on to her daughter, and so on. So that alongside the river of heroic songs this

tiny rivulet, too, may reach those faraway, perhaps happier people who will live in times to come" (Wolf 1984:81).

9. Although Homer's Iliad did not depict Trojans as noble as the Greeks, the first were definitely treated as sympathetic. One illuminating example can be found in book 22 line 475ff in which Andromache begs her husband Hector not to go to war.

10. This version of the myth, which is also used in Euripides's Helen (412 BCE) is credited to 6th century Greek poet Stesichorus, and, in Herodotus opinion, even Homer knew that version.

11. I am referring to Martin Bernal's *Black Athena; The Afroasiatic Roots of Classical Civilization*, which has a very strong Afrocentric perspective on the issue. I am not suggesting that the theater artists were in any way applying his theories, first, because that is not part of their methodology, second, because African references are not prominent in the production. The Orient that is merged with the Occident is Middle Eastern and south East Asian (London: Free Association Books, 1987).

12. Frederic Jameson in his seminal book *Postmodernism and the Logic of Late Capitalism* applied Kevin Lynch's work on spatial perception of urban spaces, which posited that alienation in a city (the grid city being the best example) was proportional to people's inability "to map their own position or the urban totality" to a political and global dimension (London: Duke University Press, 1991).

References Cited

Bernal, Martin. *Black Athena; The Afroasiatic Roots of Classical Civilization*. London: Free Association Books, 1987.

Gilpin, Heidi. "Cassandra: Creating a Female Voice." *Responses to Christa Wolf; Critical Essays*. Ed. Marilyn Sibley Fries, 342–380. Detroit: Wayne University Press, 1989.

Jacobs, Karen. "Speaking 'Chrissandra': Christa Wolf, Bakhtin, and the Politics of the Polyvocal Text." *Narrative*. 9:3 (October 2001): 1–36.

Jameson, Fredric. *Postmodernism and the Logic of Late Capitalism*. Durham and London: Duke University Press, 1991.

Oi Nóis Aqui Traveiz. *Aos que Virão Depois de Nós: Kassandra in Process. Aos que Virão Depois de Nós: Kassandra in Process— O Desassombro da Utopia*. Edited by Valmir Santos, 49–119. Porto Alegre: Oi Nóis na Memória, 2004.

Said, Edward. *Orientalism*. New York, Vintage Books, 1979.

Santos, Valmir. "O Resto é Silêncio, Dor e Reflexão." *Aos que Virão Depois de Nós: Kassandra in Process— O Desassombro da Utopia*. Ed. Valmir Santos, 123–127. Porto Alegre: Oi Nóis na Memória, 2004.

Taylor, Diana. *The Archive and the Repertoire; Performing Cultural Memory in the Americas*. Durham and London: Duke University Press, 2003.

Wolf, Christa. *Cassandra; A Novel and Four Essays*. Translated by Jan van Heurck. New York: Farrar, Straus and Girroux, Inc., 1984.

13

Philosophical Investigations
Will Eno's *Thom Pain* and the
Wittgenstein Effect
Doug Phillips

Abstract

As a spectator of Will Eno's recent Thom Pain *(based on nothing), you can't help but feel at risk: far from the security of a fourth wall, you're likely to be insulted by both the play's premise and by Thom Pain himself who might as easily call you on stage as call you a cunt. Described by one critic as "Beckett for the Jon Stewart generation," the eponymous Thom Pain spends the better part of an hour musing on all things existential. Indeed, it seems as though we have come to the theatre to witness a man teach, and perhaps more interesting than what Pain has to say is how exactly he goes about saying it—that is, his method, his pedagogy, his, in the words of Ludwig Wittgenstein, perspicuous representation. More, then, than a monologue on the meaning of life,* Thom Pain *enacts the difficulty of communicating the deepest truths about life, while at the same time giving to those of us who try our hand at it in the classroom each day a pedagogical performance that relies as much on showing as anything that might be said.*

As a spectator of Will Eno's recent play *Thom Pain (based on nothing)*, you can't help but feel at risk: far from the security of a fourth wall, you're likely to be insulted by both the play's premise (to educate you about pain — and *Pain*, the play's only character — in a way that necessitates, well, your pain) and by Thom Pain himself who might as easily call you on stage as call you a *cunt*. What passes for improvisation, however, is in the end rehearsed: you've been had, by both Eno and the plant sitting next to you. The play though is no joke, or at least not entirely so. Described by one critic as "Beckett for the Jon Stewart generation" (Isherwood 2005), the eponymous Thom Pain spends the better part of an hour musing on all things existential, even cataloging at one point the themes of his performance: "fear, boyhood, nature, hate, the nature of performance and vice versa, the heart of man, of woman, et cetera" (16). How it is that both Pain and we — the audience — are included as part of the play's dramatis personae is never made clear; nor is the occasion we have for showing up at a theatre where, the text tells us, the play is set. One possibility, however, is that we have gathered to learn from someone, say, a professor or a philosopher or perhaps even a patient, who wishes desperately to communicate something, Siddhartha-like, that is true about himself and, by extension, true about ourselves. Indeed, it seems as though we have come to the theatre to witness a man teach, and perhaps more interesting than *what* Pain has to say is *how* exactly he goes about saying it — that is, his method, his pedagogy, his, in the words of Ludwig Wittgenstein, *perspicuous representation*: in other words, the kind of understanding that comes with seeing connections.[1] For as Wittgenstein himself remarks in *Culture and Value*: "A thinker is very much like a draftsman whose aim it is to represent all the interrelations between things" (12e). More, then, than a monologue of musings on the meaning of life, *Thom Pain* at once enacts the difficulty of communicating the deepest truths about life, while giving to those of us who try our hand at it in the classroom each day a pedagogical performance that relies as much on *showing*— on perspicuous representation — as anything that might be *said* directly.

In order to preempt any confusion, I should make clear from the outset that Eno's Thom Pain is not the Revolutionary of the same if differently spelled name; in fact, Eno's Pain bears little if any resemblance to the author of *Common Sense*, with the exception perhaps of the American pamphleteer's reputation for indiscretion and hot-temperedness. Outfitted in Woody Allen-evoking eyeglasses and a rumpled, professorial-looking dark grey suit, Thom Pain, standing alone on a bare and dimly lit stage, is a decidedly modern figure, whose confessional and seemingly extemporaneous mode of expression recalls, on the one hand, the ranting of Dostoevsky's Underground Man, and, on the other, the influential and much imitated pedagogical styling of Wittgenstein. And while Eno makes no specific reference to Pain's occupation, he appears to be a man who, like Wittgenstein before a classroom of spellbound students, is working through a problem of great philosophical import, the gist of which is *fear* in its many life-impeding manifestations. Fear, in fact, is a point of departure for Pain, just as it was for Ionesco who remarked in *Notes and Counter Notes*:

> To discover the fundamental problem to all mankind, I must ask myself what *my* fundamental problem is, what *my* most ineradicable fear is. I am certain, then, to find the problems and fears of literally everyone. That is the true road, into my own darkness, our darkness, which I try to bring to the light of day [92].

It is also perhaps the overriding emotion among members of the audience, as the direction of Pain's multi-layered narratives is, from the get-go, uncertain and often confrontational: what he might ask or demand of those seated in the theatre is anyone's guess.

"We should define some terms here," begins Pain's initially conventional approach to teaching as he tries to get hold of the word "*fear*" via a rather fuzzy entry in the *New Century Dictionary of English*:

> Quote, "Fear:
> 1. Any of the discrete parts of the face, as in the eyes or mouth, or eyes.
> 2. The capital of Lower Meersham, in the north central southeast corner. Pop. 8,000,001, approx.
> 3. Fear
> 4. See three.
> 5. There is no seven. (*pause*). Colloquial. Archaic. A verb. Or noun. Depends." End quote [13].

Clearly, the definitions provided are inadequate to the task; his attempt to define *fear* fails because the definitions are, ultimately, senseless or tautological. The dictionary does not provide the *value* of fear, the only explanation it seems worth remarking — the only explanation of *any* value. And what is of value, Wittgenstein reminds us, cannot be articulated, cannot be *said*, only *shown*, which is why he makes the case again and again that only art is capable of expressing our most important truths, and only the artist can teach the things that matter most in life.[1] In short, Wittgenstein, like Nietzsche before him, argues for the emergence of the artist-philosopher — the artist-teacher. For as George Steiner argues in *Lessons of the Masters*, "the only honest, verifiable license for teaching, for didactic authority, is by virtue of example... Exemplary teaching is enactment... Valid teaching is ostensible. It shows" (4).

Similar to the start of *Thom Pain*, Wittgenstein's *The Blue Book* opens with the interrogation of a particular word, in this case the word "*word*" itself: "What is the meaning of a word?" (1), Wittgenstein asks. The answer, he explains, "can, *very roughly*, be divided into verbal and ostensive definitions... The verbal definition, as it takes us from one verbal expression to another, in a sense gets us no further" (1). An ostensive definition, on the other hand, *shows* us what a word means. Thus, as Steiner explains, Wittgenstein was "profoundly intent on escaping from the spiral of language... [He] compels us to wonder whether reality can be *spoken of*, when speech is merely a kind of infinite regression, words being spoken of other words" (1986:21). In lieu, then, of an adequate verbal definition of fear — and with it the "spiral of language into infinite regress" — Pain promises an ostensive definition, "a little story," he says, one that will quickly morph into multiple narratives, each playfully and at times dramatically intersecting the other as he attempts — through showing, through performing — to make sense of his subject and, as Wittgenstein would have it, "to bring words back from their metaphysical to their everyday use" (1953:41e). In this way, Pain's pedagogy mirrors in many respects Wittgenstein's own style of writing and teaching, about which Wittgenstein himself said: "I ought to be no more than a mirror, in which my reader can see his own thinking with all its deformities so that, helped in this way, he can put it right" (1980:18e). Moreover, says Wittgenstein, "working in philosophy is really more a working on oneself. On one's own interpretation. On one's way of seeing things" (16e). After all, he says, "nothing is so difficult as not deceiving oneself" (34e). Thus, as Michael Peters has observed, "Wittgenstein's *Investigations* might be said to embody ... a way of doing philosophy that no longer conforms to the Platonic search for final essences or final truths but rather attempts to shift our thinking in a never-ending process of mutual edification" (186).

The same can be said of *Thom Pain*, which enacts a similar process of mutual edification with its audience through a kind of transference whereby Pain's anxieties, fears, and disappointments becomes the spectator's own. Not unlike Wittgenstein's own students, we become involved. This transference, however, is not always guaranteed to occur, as Wittgenstein himself knew quite well, going so far as to write in the preface to the *Tractatus* that the purpose of the book "would be achieved if it gave pleasure to one person who read and understood it" (3). Similarly, when asked whether people sometimes did not "get" *Thom Pain*, actor James Urbaniak (who played the role of Pain in both the London and initial New York productions) replied "there are pockets of people now and then who don't," which he then followed with an admission of disbelief: "I thought to myself: you mean your entire childhood, family and romantic history is without ripples? There's been no tension?" (Steinberg 2005). This lack of identification, however, is *always* a potential failing of a performance-based pedagogy, when, that is, the bond between performer and spectator, between teacher and student, does not take — a point emphasized early in *Thom Pain* when a seemingly disgruntled member of the audience (who, by the way, is "planted" as part of the script) rustles together his shopping bags and unceremoniously stomps out of the theatre. For those enthralled, however, there is good reason — the result of what I call the "Wittgenstein Effect."

In his biography *The Duty of Genius*, Ray Monk's account of Wittgenstein's method of instruction effectively describes what is meant by the "Wittgenstein Effect," which serves also as an accurate depiction of Thom Pain's presence on stage:

> His lecture style ... seems to have been quite different from that of any other
> university lecturer: he lectured without notes, often appeared to be simply
> standing in front of his audience, thinking aloud. Occasionally he would
> stop, saying, 'Just a minute, let me think!' ... Wittgenstein's impassioned and
> syncopated performance left a memorable impression on all who heard him
> [289–90].

Jay Parini, in the *The Art of Teaching*, adds:

> He [Wittgenstein] always had a specific philosophical problem in mind as
> he walked into the lecture hall, his face hardened into thought, his eyes
> expressionless, as though cutting off the sensory world from his brain. He
> would worry the problem of the day aloud, as if the shutters of his mind—
> an awesome thing in itself—were flung open, and the class could look into
> the whirring mechanism of his brain. This was, in his own term, a process
> of "showing" or "ostentation." This was teaching in its root sense: *techen*,
> which in Middle English means "demonstrate" or to point in a direction.
> Wittgenstein was the ideal teacher in many ways, one who showed students
> what it meant to think. He didn't give them answers; he presented a way, a
> technique, for finding answers to problems [129].

It is through this ostentation, this *techen*—this dramatic demonstration—
that Thom Pain, in the footsteps of Wittgenstein, has something to show us
about the efficacy of a certain kind of pedagogy, one that is at root *performative*: a body-centered practice which invokes a healthy sense of risk for
both teachers and students through the use of improvisation (or, at least the
sense of improvisation), contingent dialogue, experimentation, reflection,
agitation, irony, parody, and jest.

In her essay, "Teaching Is Performance: Reconceptualizing a Problematic Metaphor," Elyse Pineau outlines four key words in relation to performative teaching: *poetics, play, process*, and *power*—all of which, to one degree
or another, are employed by both Wittgenstein and Pain. The first, *poetics*,
recognizes that "educators and students engage not in 'pursuit of truths,' but
in collaborative fictions — perpetually making and remaking worldviews and
their tenuous positions within them" (10). This, in so many words, defines
Wittgenstein's notion of language games, as well as echoes the narrator in
Eno's play *The Flu Season* who strikes a very Wittgenstein-like chord with
the observation that "Life is a word game. I don't know what else" (41). But
it especially applies to Thom Pain who, in order to make his points, to show
just what he means, relies on scarcely disguised autobiographical narratives,
which he doesn't hesitate to amend, embellish, truncate, or leave unclosed.
As John Glavin has observed:

The magnetic teacher tells a lifestory.... The teacher both models and describes that lifestory. And students recognize it as (really, deeply) about themselves, often unexpectedly, but almost immediately, and with a joyous clarity that feels like truth, and that certainly works like romance.... In the winning teacher's story, we joyously recognize ourselves as having — perhaps for the first time — the chance of narrative, the possibility of history" [16–17].

In this way, says Pineau, "performance reframes the whole educational enterprise as a mutable and ongoing ensemble of narratives and performances, rather than a linear accumulation of isolated, discipline-specific competencies" (10). Wittgenstein made roughly the same claim, saying "my thoughts were soon crippled if I tried to force them in any single direction against their natural inclination" (1953:ix).

The second keyword, *play*, refers to the playful nature of performance. Pineau explains, "the concept of play, with its attendant implications of experimentation, innovation, critique, and subversion, breaks open conventionalized classroom practices" (14). Dwight Conquergood adds that "playful impulse promotes a radical self-questioning critique that yields a deeper self-knowledge, the first step towards transformation" (qtd. in Pineau 14). Thom Pain's own sense of play is evident throughout his performance, especially when he addresses the audience directly. For example, at one point he compliments a woman in the audience for what he perceives to be her individuality. He then asks her:

> Maybe you could meet me, later on? We'll get a drink. Should your bright and ladylike ways give way to those of a drunken, cold, and repetitive pig, that's all right, I'll still love you, but not in any way you'd notice. Still, depending on the state of your life and its degradation at your own hands, I could be a good move for you [23].

Elsewhere Pain recounts the details of a failed romance, which includes having awakened "one fine week ... to cold sores tearing through our lips" (29). "Love cankers all" (29), he tells us. In all, the form of the play *Thom Pain* is not unlike that of Wittgenstein's *Investigations*, described by Terry Eagleton as:

> a thoroughly dialogical work, in which the author wonders out loud, imagines an interlocutor, asks us questions which may or may not be on the level. Like the Freudian analyst, we suspect that he has some answers but is keeping them up his sleeve, forcing the reader [or spectator] into the work of self-demystification ... but running the odd ring around us into the bargain [9].

Like Wittgenstein, Thom Pain's own pedagogical method necessitates that "one travel over a wide field of thought, crisscrossing in every direction and often approaching the same point from different directions" (Heaton 9). This, in effect, is what Pineau means by her third term, *process*. "Performance," she says, "privileges the fluid, ongoing, often contradictory features of human experience that resists reification and closure." Furthermore, "it acknowledges that identities are always multiple, overlapping ensembles of real and possible selves who enact themselves in direct relation to the context and communities in which they perform" (15). This, of course, is not without its dangers, as Pain knows quite well when, on the subject of a failed romance, he tells us: "I disappeared in her and she, wondering where I went, left" (30).

Pineau's last term, *power*, simply acknowledges that performances, whether inside or outside the classroom, are (according to Dwight Conquergood) "a site of struggle where competing interests intersect, and different viewpoints and voices get articulated" (qtd. in Pineau 18). This suggests the fundamentally dialogical nature of performative teaching, though not necessarily in the Socratic sense of deriving a single truth; rather, it is "the notion of dialogue as conversation, which emphasizes edification (or education) rather than truth" (Peters, 185)—a practice common to both Pain and Wittgenstein. In *Philosophical Investigations*, for example, Wittgenstein poses some eight hundred questions to his imagined audience. In Eno's short play of twenty-five pages, Thom Pain poses more than sixty questions to the audience, only a quarter of which he presumes to answer himself.

Wittgenstein's famed if enigmatic conclusion to the *Tractatus*—whereof one cannot speak, thereof one must be silent—is a point of departure, if not a point of conclusion, for much of modern drama, Beckett and Pinter's works most certainly, and Will Eno's *Thom Pain (based on nothing)* most recently. The question for educators then is how to reach beyond the silence, how to show, in the words of Wittgenstein, "the fly the way out of the fly bottle," especially if philosophers and mystics agree that wisdom, unlike knowledge, is fundamentally incommunicable. Wittgenstein, like Freud and Socrates before him, routinely if ironically professed the impossibility of teaching, despite the legions of students who clamored to attend his lectures. Little did he know perhaps that the content of what he had to say was only slightly more interesting than how he went about showing it—that is, his performance. Perhaps the same can be said about Thom Pain.

HILL-MURRAY SCHOOL

Notes

1. In *Philosophical Investigations,* Wittgenstein explains: "A main source of our failure to understand is that we do not *command a clear view* of the use of our words. Our grammar is lacking in this sort of perspicuity. A perspicuous representation produces just that understanding which consists in 'seeing connections.' Hence the importance of finding and inventing *intermediate cases.* The concept of a perspicuous representation is of fundamental significance for us. It earmarks the form of account we give, the way we look at things" (42e). For a detailed analysis of Wittgenstein's notion of "perspicuous representation," refer to John M. Heaton's *Wittgenstein and Psychoanalysis* (2000).

2. In *Wittgenstein's Vienna* (1973), Alan Janik emphasizes Wittgenstein's ethical position in the *Tractatus:* "Only art can express moral truth, and only the artist can teach the things that matter most in life" (197). In *Culture and Value,* Wittgenstein himself writes: "I think I summed up my attitude to philosophy when I said: philosophy ought really to be written only as a *poetic composition*" (24e).

References Cited

Eagleton, Terry. *Wittgenstein: The Terry Eagleton Script.* London: British Film Institute, 1993.

Eno, Will. *The Flu Season.* New York: Dramatist Play Service, 2005.

_____. *Thom Pain (based on nothing).* London: Oberon Books, 2004.

Glavin, John. "The Intimacies of Instruction." *The Erotics of Instruction.* Edited by Regina Barreca and Deborah Denenholz Morse, 12–27. Hanover: University Press of New England, 1997.

Heaton, John M. *Wittgenstein and Psychoanalysis.* New York: Totem Books, 2000.

Ionesco, Eugene. *Notes and Counter Notes: Writings on the Theatre.* Translated by Donald Watson. New York: Grove Press, 1964.

Isherwood, Charles. "Life's a Gift? Quick. Exchange It." *New York Times.* February 2, 2005. March 26, 2006. http://theater2.nytimes.com/2005/02/02/theater/reviews/02pain.html

Monk, Ray. *Ludwig Wittgenstein: The Duty of Genius.* New York: Penguin, 1991.

Parini, Jay. *The Art of Teaching.* New York: Oxford University Press, 2005.

Peters, Michael and James Marshall. *Wittgenstein: Philosophy, Postmodernism, Pedagogy.* Westport: Bergin & Garvey, 1999.

Pineau, Elyse Lamm. "Teaching is Performance: Reconceptualizing a Problematic Metaphor." *American Educational Research Journal* 31:1 (1994): 3–25.

Steinberg, Katherine. "Talking to James Urbaniak." March 24, 2005. March 26, 2006. http://www.culturebot.org/archives/2005/03/24/TalkingToJamesUrbaniak.php>

Steiner, George. *Language and Silence.* New York: Atheneum, 1986.

_____. *Lessons of the Masters.* Cambridge: Harvard University Press, 2003.

Wittgenstein, Ludwig. *The Blue and Brown Books.* Oxford: Blackwell, 1958.

_____. *Culture and Value*. Ed. G.H. Von Wright. Translated by Peter Winch. Chicago: University of Chicago Press, 1980.

_____. *Philosophical Investigations*. Translated by G.E.M. Anscombe. Oxford: Blackwell, 1953.

_____. *Tractatus Logico-Philosophicus*. Translated by D.F. Pears and B.F. McGuinness. London: Routledge, 1961.

Foreign or Domestic Drama?
Osanai Kaoru and Modern Japanese Theatre

M. Cody Poulton

Abstract

The Tsukiji Little Theatre, often called Japan's first truly modern theatre, opened within a year of the Great Earthquake of 1923. The opening of this new theatre excited considerable interest among the Tokyo intelligentsia. Osanai Kaoru (1881–1928), one of the theatre's founders and a protean figure in the movement to modernize Japanese theatre, created an uproar when he stated at a meeting held prior to its opening that the Tsukiji Little Theatre would not, "for the time being," stage any original Japanese plays. His decision was immediately attacked by dramatists like Kikuchi Kan (1888–1948) and Kishida Kunio (1890–1954). This clash between Japan's pre-eminent stage director and two of its most accomplished playwrights was indicative of the frustrations Japanese playwrights experienced in creating an indigenous modern drama. Osanai's address also reflected the intense debate over the relationship between dramatic text and performance in the creation of a modern theatre art in Japan.

Standard accounts paint the history of modern Japanese theatre as a history of the adoption of Western theatre in Japan. The story begins in the 1880s, with tentative efforts to reform kabuki (then Japan's most vibrant and most popular theatre art) and debates over incorporating "modern" (European) theatre architecture and dramaturgy which would have eliminated some of those very elements that defined the kabuki: the *hanamichi* ramp that runs through the audience to the stage, incidental *geza* music and, most importantly, the female impersonator (*onnagata*). By all accounts, kabuki and other increasingly "classical" theatres were vessels that could not accommodate the new wine of modern theatre and, slowly and painstakingly, efforts were made to build new theatres, train new actors (actresses too by the 1900s), and learn the latest techniques from the West of directing, stage design and lighting.

Drama also played a vital, but somewhat belated role in the creation of a new theatre movement. From the 1880s onward, many of the preeminent figures in the Japanese literary and theatre circles — men like Tsubouchi Shôyô (1859–1935), Mori Ôgai (1862–1922), Shimamura Hôgetsu (1871–1918), and Osanai Kaoru — devoted much of their time and talent to the translation of Shakespeare, Ibsen, Strindberg, Hauptmann, Maeterlinck, Shaw, Chekhov, and Gorky, to name just a few. Indeed, by the first decade of the twentieth century, in the case of contemporary playwrights, the time lag between the first performance of a major European play and its publication in translation in the pages of a leading Japanese journal was often a matter of only months. Similarly, key works of criticism were being quickly read, discussed and translated into Japanese. The ideas of Edward Gordon Craig and William Archer, for example, were hotly debated. (Japan still remains well ahead of the English-speaking world in the translation from other European languages of scholarly and critical texts.)

For obvious practical reasons, staging European drama in Japan took more time than the publication of works in translation, but most critics trace the beginning of the so-called New Theatre (*shingeki*) movement to the establishment of two companies largely devoted to the staging of Western plays: Tsubouchi Shôyô's Literary Society (Bungei Kyôkai, 1906) and Osanai Kaoru's Free Theatre (Jiyû Gekijô, named after Antoine's Théâtre Libre, 1909). For a number of years the two troupes competed with each other in staging many of the cardinal works of modern Western drama. In particular, productions of two Ibsen plays — *John Gabriel Borkman* by the Free Theatre in 1909 and *A Doll's House* by the Literary Society in 1911 — were cultural sensations of their day, alerting Japan's intelligentsia to drama as a powerful medium for the expression of new ideas. In particular, Osanai's efforts to promote and stage modern European drama had a galvanizing effect on a generation of young playwrights, and in the second and third decades of the twentieth century, literally dozens of magazines published new plays and articles on theatre, not only the so-called general magazines (*sôgô zasshi*) like *The Central Review* (Chûô kôron), *The Sun* (Taiyô), *Literary Annals* (Bungei shunjû) and others that were and still are read by Japan's intelligentsia, but also journals devoted to the stage, like *New Theatre Arts* (*Shin-engei*) and *Theatre Arts Illustrated* (*Engei gahô*). Two journals stood out as particularly strong advocates for new Japanese drama: *New Currents in Thought* (*Shinshichô*) and *New Currents in Theatre* (*Engeki Shinchô*); Osanai Kaoru was on the editorial boards of both. A number of major collections (*zenshû*) were also published, including the eighteen volume *Anthology of Modern Drama* (Kindaigeki zenshû, Daiichi Shobô, 1927–1930) and the massive, fifty volume *Anthology of Japanese Drama* (Nihon gikyoku zenshû, Shun'yôdô, 1927–29).

Even so, Osanai's legacy was a dubious one if we are to consider not the introduction of Western drama, but the creation of an indigenous drama in Japan as the defining moment in modern Japanese theatre. As we shall see, he prevented much Japanese drama from being staged. His first trip abroad (1912–1913) seems to mark a turn toward what he would later call a "true age of translation" (*ma no hon'yaku jidai*) that frustrated many who had hoped the Free Theatre would remain a forum for the presentation of Japanese drama. With the rise of *shingeki*'s emphasis on translation, the Japanese assim-ilation of Western culture also became less a matter of adaptation than adop-tion, an attempt to import whole new ideas and modes of expression. Gioa Ottaviani has remarked that *shingeki* (a form increasingly associated with Osanai) was faced with a "twofold learning process" whereby not only did its Japanese practitioners have to acquire new forms of expression, but on a more fundamental level, they had to try to embody the cognitive universe of West-erners, acquire their sensibilities and behavior (Ottaviani 1994, 226). This was a nigh impossible task and, arguably, it presented a powerfully inhibit-ing effect on the development of native theatrical expressive forms, to say nothing of a truly Japanese expression for the experience of modernity.

The Taishô era (1912–26)[1] has been called an "age of drama," but while venues existed for the publication of new Japanese plays, getting them staged presented a whole other problem. Most playwrights considered themselves lucky if their work was performed by kabuki or *shinpa* (a melodramatic the-atre that retained many elements of kabuki) troupes, but the patterned act-ing styles of these more traditional theatres did not make them the best venues for new ideological and artistic experiments. In the meantime, Osanai increasingly focused his attention on the development of acting and direc-torial skills at the expense of the text.

The Great Kantô Earthquake in 1923 marked a watershed year for Japa-nese theatre. Practically every major theatre in Tokyo had been destroyed in the quake and fires. The relaxation of building codes for the post-disaster reconstruction made it possible to build on a shoestring the Tsukiji Little Theatre (*Tsukiji Shôgekijô*), which opened less than a year after the disaster, on June 13, 1924. One of the theatre's founders, Hijikata Yoshi (1898–1959), had rushed home from Europe when he heard of the earthquake and enlisted Osanai Kaoru's support in building what Brian Powell has called "Japan's first modern stage" (1975:69–85). Another who would become a key *shingeki* figure, Kishida Kunio, had returned from France only a couple of months before, to attend to his family on the death of his father. He had spent the previous two years studying at Jacques Copeau's Le Vieux Colombier and hoped to make his mark in the Japanese theatre world.

The opening of this new theatre excited considerable interest in the

Tokyo theatre and literary worlds. A meeting was held at Keiô University on May 20, 1924 to discuss the event. Presentations were given by Tsukiji Little Theatre associates (*dôjin*) Wada Sei (who spoke on the theatre's stage and auditorium design), Hijikata, and by playwright and Keiô lecturer Kubota Mantarô (1889–1963); another playwright, Mizuki Kyôta (1894–1948), acted as emcee. Osanai Kaoru spoke last. He began innocently enough, first, addressing the building itself:

> There are many theatres that can cram in the audiences, but not one that is worth accommodating theatre. Our Tsukiji Little Theatre is a crude sort of building, like a packing case, but it's a vessel that can take any sort of theatre without anything spilling out ["Tsukiji Shôgekijô to watakushi" / The Tsukiji Little Theatre and I, in Sugai 1965:43].

The Tsukiji Little Theatre was to be a "laboratory" (*jikkenshitsu*) for new theatre in Japan. In contrast to audiences of the past, who came to the theatre for a good time, "our audience must be students," Osanai asserted. He admitted that he himself was "groping in the dark":

> I was twenty-nine years old in 1909 when I founded the Free Theatre ... and, fumbling around in the dark, I made a mess of things. Now, fifteen years later, I find myself with a new group of people, groping around in the dark again. Which is to say, I deny my past. In fact, I used to be proud of what I'd accomplished, but I discovered recently that none of it served me any good. Here I am, back to where I was when I was twenty-nine, groping around in the dark, throwing myself right into it, actually. This may sound out of place, but one can't really say that the future of Japanese theatre looks very bright [Sugai 1965:43].

Then Osanai dropped a veritable bombshell:

> For the next couple of years, anyway, we plan to stage only Western drama. Why won't we do Japanese plays? I have a simple answer. We directors haven't been inspired to do anything by contemporary Japanese playwrights — and I'd have to count my own work as well.[2] If there were a play we felt like directing, we'd certainly plan on doing it, no matter what country it came from. [...] We're not averse to Japanese plays, nor are we trying to ape the West. We're staging [Western drama] simply because there aren't any Japanese works that whet our desire to direct them [Sugai 1965:44].

This in fact was news to Hijikata, who had been planning to stage a couple of Japanese plays himself.[3] Apparently Osanai had not consulted his colleagues. He concluded his speech with an admission that his remarks would "unavoidably alienate some old friends."

Indeed, his old friends on the board of the leading theatre magazine of the day, *New Currents in Theatre*, were stunned.[4] Kikuchi Kan (then Japan's most popular writer of new drama and, as editor of *Literary Annals* (Bungei Shunjû), a powerful political force in Japanese letters) had reservations about a theatre that refused to get its hands dirty with popular drama and, in a roundtable discussion published in the July issue of *New Currents in Theatre*, called The Tsukiji Little Theatre, ironically enough, a "coterie magazine" (*dôsô zasshi*) and Osanai's decision to stage only Western drama "asinine" (*bakabakashii*). Translation is necessarily a transitional art, so it is stupid to insist on doing only Western plays, Kikuchi added:

> Even if he said he wanted to do one of our plays, I'd tell him "no." My idea of theatre is completely opposed to Osanai's. [...] It's a waste of time having short-legged, yellow-faced Japanese trying to pass themselves off as Europeans [*Engeki shinchô* 1:7 (July 1924): 30–31].

Doing Western drama was like eating the Japanese version of Western food (*yôshoku*): it may look European, but it doesn't taste European, Kikuchi concluded (31). Kubota Mantarô was more conciliatory, chiding Osanai more on how he had phrased his remarks. One could take it wrong and think he meant there was no value in staging Japanese plays, he suggested. Nagata Hideo (1885–1949), one of Ibsen's Japanese epigones, thought Osanai made too much of the role of director and Yamamoto Yûzô (1887–1974), like Kikuchi an influential playwright and novelist, expressed bemusement over the choice of programming. There seemed no consistency in the selection of plays the theatre had opened with: Chekhov's *Swan Song*, Émile Mazaud's *Holiday* (both directed by Osanai) and Reinhard Goering's expressionist *A Sea Battle* (directed by Hijikata).

Osanai's appearance before the editorial board for another roundtable discussion the following month (it was published in the August issue of *New Currents in Theatre*) was rather like willingly showing up for one's own lynching, said one critic (see Fujiki 1977:9). Osanai tried to preempt their attack with a prepared address, called "For What Does the Tsukiji Little Theatre exist?" The theatre had three purposes, he stated: theatre itself (*engeki*); the future; and the people. The first is the most germane for what ensued:

> Tsukiji Shôgekijô, like all other theatres, exists for theatre (*engeki*).... It does not exist for drama (*gikyoku*). Drama is literature. Literature has its own organs — newspapers, magazines, books — things that are printed. [...] We'll leave the literary critics to determine what value Tsukiji Shôgekijô's drama will have.[5]

What follows is a digest of the main points of the ensuing debate:

KIKUCHI: It's odd that you'll rely on contemporary audiences but not on contemporary playwrights.

OSANAI: You can't do good theatre unless you lead the people into the future. Kabuki and *shinpa* are fine insofar as they are able to express the common tastes of people today, but that isn't the aim of the Tsukiji Little Theatre.

KIKUCHI: If the quality of drama selected is not an issue for the Tsukiji Little Theatre, does that mean it's all right to perform bad plays?

OSANAI: The quality may not be up to scratch from a literary standpoint, but theatre is another matter.

KIKUCHI: So, what are the Tsukiji Little Theatre's standards?

OSANAI: We haven't established any particular artistic ideologies or beliefs at the Tsukiji Little Theatre yet.

KIKUCHI: But you can't do theatre without ideals or principles of some sort.

OSANAI: It's wrong to be ideologically bound. I may have no abiding theories, but I do have an objective, and that is "first the performance, then the drama" [*Engeki shinchô* 1:8 (August 1924), 24–27 ff.].

In effect, Osanai was reversing the formula that his own mentor, Mori Ôgai, had put forth a generation before: "first the drama, then the performance."[6] Osanai wanted to assert that theatre was an art form independent from literature. This may have been a noble idea, but curiously, it seemed like a step back to the aesthetic principles of the traditional theatre, particularly kabuki, in which the text was always subordinate to the performance and the playwright was subservient to the actor. It was an idea that ran counter to the central importance of the playwright and the written text in modern drama.

Beginning to weaken from the attacks of his former friends, Osanai began to backtrack. "When I said we would do Western drama, I didn't mean we wouldn't do Japanese plays. It's not that I'm picky," he claimed. Kubota Mantarô replied, "But I really wished you had phrased your remarks a bit more generously" (39). Kikuchi continued to attack Osanai, this time for directing a minor play by Chekhov. Osanai remarked that Hijikata would not do Chekhov because he thought the Russian playwright old hat. The differences in Osanai's and Hijikata's tastes, as many have noted, reflect the times when they visited Europe: Osanai in 1912, and Hijikata after the 1917 Russian revolution. Osanai's model was still Stanislavsky's Moscow Arts Theatre, while Hijikata had been impressed with the expressionism of Reinhart and Meyerhold. Yet Osanai himself seemed to be coming around to the opinion that Chekhov was passé. "But just because something belongs to the present day doesn't make it better than what came before. You're too tolerant of novelty," countered Kubota, who urged him to be a bit more consistent and suggested that a denial of the past — particularly one's own old ideals — was a kind of self-denial. "What do you rely on if not yourself?" asked Yamamoto. "I can't help it if I change," protested Osanai (40).

The debate ended with Osanai finally incapable of defending himself with any consistent theory or ideological program for the Tsukiji Little Theatre, except for an expressed aversion for "decadent," art-for-art's sake drama. In the end, it was the mild-mannered Kubota, and not the strident and bitter Kikuchi, who appeared to deal the *coup de grâce*. The chief problem with Osanai and the Tsukiji Little Theatre's programming was a lack of an abiding vision for the theatre. Osanai was a passionate and charismatic figure, but he was often tactless and dogmatic, and his dogmatism ran especially at odds with his tendency to change his opinions on fundamental artistic matters such as the style of theatre he wished to promote. There is a sense in reading his essays that Osanai's mind was in permanent revolution. His views were changing radically during this time, but what views he had he tried to defend tenaciously. Yet was this how a modern man should live? Where was the bedrock of his identity? Perhaps part of his charisma lay in the way Osanai seemed to embody the unhinged nature of modernity itself. Perhaps, too, Osanai was attempting to defend not only his own principles, but Hijikata's as well. The two had conflicting visions for their theatre, visions that would eventually split the Tsukiji Little Theatre into two ideological camps, one strongly leftist and the other professedly apolitical.

Osanai himself was sensitive to the shifting winds of ideological change that were blowing in from the West, especially in this volatile period after the Great War and the Russian Revolution. The Tsukiji Little Theatre, Osanai said, would exist for the "future" and the "people" (*minshu*). It was the latter, especially, that would distinguish Tsukiji from the elitism of the Free Theatre, which he had founded some fifteen years before. He wanted, he said, to make theatre as necessary to the common people as bread or rice, but perhaps it was too much to expect them to enjoy a solid diet of European meat and potatoes. Soon enough, people would long for the comfort of kabuki and other popular performance. Politically or otherwise, *shingeki* was becoming increasingly didactic: audiences were there to learn, not so much to be entertained. But this was not a good box-office formula.

It was Osanai's insistence on the stage as a testing ground for ideas that distinguished his vision most from the traditional theatre, but he shared with kabuki the notion that drama was neither more nor less than a pretext for the theatrical event. It was the latter, especially, that pitted him against a generation of writers who were trying to create new drama in Japan, men (for the most part) who were eager to see their work staged by the most modern of Tokyo theatres and then were bitterly disappointed by Osanai's insensitive remarks. Taishô writers had worked hard to establish drama as a literary genre, and while a few might have been interested in the form as a purely literary exercise, most were eager to see their works staged — eager, in short, to play their part in the creation of a new theatre.

The *New Currents in Theatre* playwrights certainly had doubts about the criteria used to select drama at the Tsukiji Little Theatre. Much of it seemed hardly superior to what they were writing. During their first round-table discussion in June 1924, Yamamoto Yûzô mentioned that "a friend who had spent quite some time in France" had remarked that one of the three plays presented at Tsukiji's premiere, Mazaud's *Holiday*, was a bad translation of a mediocre play. It had bombed in France, he said. The friend was Kishida Kunio. Kishida, who had made his debut as a playwright just months earlier with *Old Toys* (*Furui omocha*) in the March 1924 issue of *New Currents in Theatre*,[7] had every reason to want to be on Osanai's good side, but he was already being cast as an antagonist.[8] In fact, he shared Osanai's low opinion of many Taishô plays, and would write in the December 1924 issue of *New Currents in Theatre* that "the hundred flowers that were supposed to have blossomed in this so-called age of drama presented in fact a veritable, broad daylight parade of pandemonium" (*gikyoku jidai wa hyakka ranman sono jitsu wa hyakki chûgyô no jidai de aru*). Taishô was "an age when pseudo-drama was rampant. Novels are hard to write, so everybody writes plays instead" (quoted in Fujiki 1976:44). But he was squarely in the *New Currents* camp when it came to emphasizing the importance of the text. The second production at the Tsukiji Little Theatre hardly inspired more confidence. Why had the theatre selected *Wolves*, wondered Kishida. Romain Rolland's play was, in a negative sense, the more "literary" and, by the same token, the most "anti-dramatic" (*higikyokuteki*) of plays:

> What I mean when I say "anti-dramatic" may have nothing to do with what the Tsukiji Little Theatre considers the "theatrical." Not "may"— in fact, I'm sure it doesn't. A drama, no matter how dull it is, can be turned into superb theatre in the hands of a great director — it's not necessary to harp on this, really. Besides, the Tsukiji Little Theatre has taken greater pains in selecting its programming than other theatres. But if that's the case, how on earth can this be a drama that whets your desire to direct? How can it possibly live up to the "ideal theatre" that you are striving for? [Kishida Kunio 1989:83; for another account of Kishida's views, see Rimer 1976:68–69].

Ultimately, it seemed quixotic to try and make great theatre out of poor drama. Far more to the point was picking good scripts, because great drama will always inspire a great director. Moreover, an important part of the director's job was precisely in selecting such plays.

It seemed that ideological criteria (*Wolves* was about the French revolution) trumped artistic ones. But the two were increasingly harder to distinguish in the politically charged climate of the 1920s. Perhaps nothing indicated this more than Osanai's changing views of realist theatre. He had been one of the first to champion this style and his directing was still patterned after Stanislavsky, but when the Tsukiji Little Theatre opened, he was changing his tune. Kikuchi Kan, the king of realism, was still Japan's most successful modern playwright, but in 1924, both he and his style of theatre seemed poised to decline. Ever alert to new trends, Osanai had already written an attack on realism and Kikuchi in 1922:

> From the standpoint of world art, realism is already finished. You won't find realism in any of the finest works of art now: not in painting, or sculpture, or literature, or theatre. And this is, of course, true for music and dance as well. But Japanese playwrights still insist on realism and Kikuchi Kan, who unfortunately is still stuck in this style, continues to be held in high respect. In the coming years, the winds of a new aesthetic, which began to blow before the Great War and then erupted all over Europe when it ended, cannot help but wipe out our Japanese realism (which I believe is an element of our bourgeois literature) [Osanai, "Shôgekijô to daigekijô" (Little theatres and big theatres), quoted in Ôzasa 1987:400].

It is no wonder, then, that it was Kikuchi, more than any of the other *New Currents* playwrights, who lashed out at Osanai. Both he and Yamamoto would increasingly devote their considerable literary energies to fiction and editorial activities.

As Brian Powell has noted, the Tsukiji Little Theatre "prepared for the first production of a Japanese play [...] divided within and attacked from without" (Powell 1975:85). [9] By late 1925 the theatre was already casting around for Japanese plays to stage, and the December issue of their house newsletter, *Tsukiji Shôgekijô*, solicited ideas from its readers. Top of the list, with thirty-eight votes, was the newcomer Kishida. Several of his plays, including *Old Toys*, *Autumn in Tyrol* (Chiroru no aki), *Paper Balloon* (Kami fûsen) and *The Swing* (Buranko), were suggested. Second most popular was Mushanokôji Saneatsu (1885–1976), with thirty-four votes. The distinguished novelist Tanizaki Jun'ichirô (1886–1965) was a distant third, with twenty-two votes, followed closely by Yamamoto Yûzô, with twenty. Kikuchi Kan matched leftist playwright Akita Ujaku (1883–1962), with thirteen votes, followed by Kubota Mantarô and Suzuki Senzaburô (1893–1924) with twelve each. Osanai himself ranked lower, matching the eleven votes accorded to the leftists Fujii Masumi (1889–1962) and Kaneko Yôbun (1894–1985). The list represented a cross-section of Taishô drama, by the very writers whose plays Osanai had shown little interest in producing.

Osanai's ultimate choice was a play no one had considered, Tsubouchi Shôyô's *En the Ascetic* (En no gyôja), which in the ten years since its publication in 1916 had never been staged. His choice sparked another round of shock and intense debate. Many thought the subject matter, about a semi-legendary, seventh-century mountain recluse, was arcane and its kabukiesque style dated. Akita Ujaku thought the theme irrelevant to contemporary life (*Engei gahô* 20:5 (1926): 34, quoted in Keenan 1989:299). Some considered the play a veiled allegory of Shôyô's own battle with his erstwhile disciple Shimamura Hôgetsu, who left the Literary Society with his mistress Matsui Sumako (1886–1919) to establish the Arts Theatre (Geijutsuza). Osanai saw *En the Ascetic* as a drama about humanity's struggle with nature and the supernatural. It was an odd choice for a decidedly rationalist director who had been Shôyô's chief rival at the end of the Meiji era, and some suggest that it was an overture of good will to the grand old man of modern Japanese theatre. (Shôyô would go on to translate all of Shakespeare's plays and is memorialized by a theatre museum in his name at his alma mater, Waseda University.) Osanai, however, also considered the play a technical challenge for his actors: the tension of downplaying *En the Ascetic*'s kabuki tendencies ("Reject kabuki, forget tradition. Don't dance, walk. Don't sing, speak," he instructed his actors in rehearsal; Osanai, "*En no gyôja* no daiichiya wo oete" (Finishing *En the Ascetic*'s first night), in Sugai 1965:271) would be theatrically interesting.

En the Ascetic was a great box office success. The production pulled the Tsukiji Little Theatre out of the doldrums, drawing back audiences that had become sated with the solid diet of Western drama.[10] They extended the run for another week and revived it the following year, in November 1927, in a much larger venue, The Imperial Theatre. Critical reception was mixed, however. Critics were impressed with the special effects, but "the acting left much to be desired, and the grand scale of the play required a significantly larger stage than what the Little Theatre had to offer," Linda Keenan notes (1989:299). *New Currents in Theatre*, typically, attacked the play for being "full of bluster" and "too preachy" (Keenan, 300). Worse, its playwright, Shôyô, hated it. "First two acts generally good; third act no good, a complete misinterpretation," he wrote in his diary, and the Imperial Theatre production, which attempted to do the third act according to Shôyô's conception of it, "was worse than the first time" (cf. Keenan, 284–285, 298).

En was the forty-fifth production at the Tsukiji Little Theatre. Until Osanai's death, on Christmas Day, 1928, the theatre staged twenty-seven Japanese plays by thirteen playwrights; only twenty percent of the plays staged by the Tsukiji Little theatre were not foreign, a record for producing domestic drama that was worse than the Free Theatre's.[11]

The only plays the Tsujiki Little Theatre chose to do that were recommended by the theatre's subscribers were by Akita Ujaku, Mushanokôji Saneatsu and Osanai himself. The theatre staged as many as six plays by Osanai, four plays by Mushanokôji and only one by Ujaku. One critic suggests that Ujaku was selected because he and Osanai had both been invited to the Soviet Union in 1927 for celebrations of the tenth anniversary of their revolution (Fujiki 1977:13). Fujimori Seikichi (1892–1971; another leftist, he had not made the list of desired playwrights) made a successful debut with his sensational *What Made Her Do It?* (*Nani ga kanojo o sô saseta ka*).[12] The Tsukiji Little Theatre's selection of Japanese plays was inconsistent and arbitrary, but could be divided into roughly three categories: "safe" works by well established writers like Shôyô, Mushanokôji, Tanizaki and Nakamura Kichizô (1887–1941); proletarian drama by people like Fujimori; and plays by Osanai and his protégés, people like Kitamura Komatsu and Ueda (Enchi) Fumiko (1905–1986), a distinguished novelist who made her debut as a playwright, with *Banshun sôya* (Wild night in late spring).[13] Completely missing from the list of plays the Tsukiji Little Theatre actually staged were works by Kishida Kunio, Kikuchi Kan and Yamamoto Yûzô, the three playwrights Osanai had greatest cause to snub. In any event, Hijikata Yoshi and Aoyama Sugisaku (1891–1956) directed most of the Japanese drama.

Osanai's disparagement of drama, particularly from his old comrades at *New Currents in Theatre*, succeeded in driving yet another wedge between those who did theatre and those who wrote literature, and over the coming decades, drama would seem a less and less appealing challenge for aspiring writers, critics and scholars. The face the Tsukiji Little Theatre presented both to the world and to itself reflected yet another ground for contention, between those who saw drama as a medium for political discourse and others whose criteria for evaluating a work, they professed, were entirely artistic. After Osanai's rejection of Japanese plays in 1924, Kikuchi Kan led a campaign to stage domestic drama with a rival troupe, the New Theatre Society (Shingeki Kyôkai), which produced its work in a larger hall just behind the Tsukiji Little Theatre. (The company would fold in 1927 after Kikuchi pulled out his financial backing because he objected to his associate Hatanaka Ryôha's desire to stage Western plays as well as Japanese.) After Osanai's death in 1928, the Tsukiji Little Theatre split along ideological lines. Leftist directors, actors and playwrights like Senda Koreya (1904–1996), Yamamoto Yasue (1902–1993), Kubo Sakae (1900–1958), Murayama Tomoyoshi (1901–1977) and Miyoshi Jûrô (1902–1958) established politically committed companies like the New Cooperative Troupe (Shinkyô gekidan) and the New Tsukiji Troupe (Shin-Tsukiji gekidan). At the same time, a more bourgeois style of psychological realism came to dominate the plays of the apolitical and "literary" school of dramatists in the late 1920s and '30s. Some Tsukiji Little Theatre alumni like the brilliant actor Tomoda Kyôsuke (1899–1937) and his wife, the equally talented Tamura Akiko (1905–1983), felt increasingly disenchanted by the encroachment of politics on artistic decisions; they would found companies like the Tsukijiza. It was the latter company that Kishida and others would gravitate to in the 1930s, and after Tomoda was killed in action in China in 1937, Kishida, together with playwrights Kubota Mantarô and Iwata Toyoo (1893–1969) and actress Sugimura Haruko (1909–1997), would establish the Literary Theatre (Bungakuza), one of the only troupes allowed to perform after the government crackdown on leftist theatres in 1940.[14] The venues for staging new plays by Japanese dramatists remained limited, however, and Osanai's decision initially to stage only Japanese plays at the Tsukiji New Theatre effectively closed a chapter in which drama was an important genre for practically every Japanese writer; thereafter, only the very dedicated would devote themselves to writing for the stage.

Osanai stood squarely at the center of every key debate that raged in Japanese theatre circles in the early twentieth century. What was theatre's purpose in a modern world? Was it as an agent of social change, or as a place to explore the human soul? Was it a venue for the introduction of Western ideas and ways of thought and action, or for the production of new dramatic texts written by the Japanese themselves? In both cases, Osanai stood for the former and strenuously resisted the latter. As theatre scholar Sugai Yukio has pointed out, Osanai's legacy served to distort modern Japanese theatre by excluding from its active participation the very playwrights who could have contributed so much to its development (Sugai 1979, 155). Dramatists like Kishida had to go elsewhere to see their plays produced. At the same time, notes J. Thomas Rimer, *shingeki*'s emphasis on translated drama would ensure for decades to come that modern Japanese theatre "would remain an intellectual rather than an emotional experience" (Rimer 1976:96). Osanai and his colleagues wanted to reach the people, but the means they used appealed to a narrow audience of mostly leftist cognoscenti. The general public was increasingly presented with improbable and alien ideals of thought and comportment and was less able to see itself presented onstage as it really was. Paradoxically, then, the rise of modern drama coincided with the gradual decline of theatre as a popular art in early twentieth-century Japan.

If, however, Osanai is cast as the villain in this play, we nonetheless need to give this devil his due. He himself was not responsible for the increasing ideological polarization that was occurring in Japanese culture, especially the theatre, during the 1920s and '30s; it was a global phenomenon in which, both as artist and arbiter of modern culture, he felt a duty to take a stand. And this political position was also related to a legitimate aesthetic concern:

if, as Lukacs and Szondi have suggested, modern drama came more and more to emulate the novel in its probing of the inner soul of the individual at the expense of its portrayal of social dynamics, modern drama in Japan may have represented a betrayal of the native, sociable theatricality of traditional Japanese culture. Osanai sensed that one strain of modern drama — an eminently literary, indeed private and interior form of expression — was anathema to theatre's physical and social essence. As he would remark in a critique of Kishida's *Autumn in Tyrol* (Chiroru no aki, 1925):

> To be sure, this work manages somehow to flourish within the confines of the so-called "playhouse." But if we were to take it outside, into the environment people like us live in today, it would wither just like a flower taken out of a hothouse. [...] Theatre's fundamental nature is to head for the outdoors ["Engeki ni taisuru kôsatsu (Deliberations on theatre)," quoted in Ôta 1976, 140].

In order to preserve what he considered the essence of the theatrical experience, Osanai felt a need to expunge from it anything that smacked of being too "literary," too bourgeois. If modern culture severed the word from the human body, Osanai reasoned that, in order to reclaim physicality in its new, "modern" form, theatre had to distance itself from anything too resolutely textual. Hence his dictum: "first the performance, then the drama." The leftist theatre to which Osanai and his epigones increasingly aligned themselves arguably attempted to create a new image of community, one which they felt could compensate for a traditional sense of solidarity lost to the modern, alienated self. It is ironic, however, that the impetus for this was an intellectual one, and its effect remained cerebral and not sensual. In the politically charged ferment of 1930s Japan, it is also a bitter irony that the more "literary" dramatists, people like Kikuchi and Kishida who had in turn felt alienated by Osanai and his comrades, later collaborated with the militarists. But that is another story.

UNIVERSITY OF VICTORIA, CANADA

Notes

1. "Taishô" refers to the reign of the emperor Yoshihito, a physically and mentally weak and ineffectual ruler. The period, sometimes called the "Taishô democracy," witnessed the rapid urbanization and industrialization of Japan, much political and social unrest, and the rise of an energetic and inventive popular culture. Leftist and feminist movements, which were spawned during this period, were crushed under Hirohito's regency (from 1921) and reign, which began in 1926.

2. Osanai himself had written several plays, which he or others directed.

3. See Fujiki (1977:9–10). Inoue Yoshie (1999:240, note 3) similarly cites Hijikata's wife as recalling her husband's shock at Osanai's pronouncement.

4. Besides Osanai, Kikuchi Kan, Yamamoto Yûzô, Kume Masao (1891–1952), Ihara Seiseien (1870–1941), Ikeda Daigo (1885–1942), Tanizaki Jun'ichirô, and many other luminaries of the Taishô literary and theatre worlds, were members of the editorial board.

5. Quoted, with alterations, from Powell 1975:75, who translates the whole address. Powell uses the word "drama" for *engeki*, but I have rendered it as "theatre" to distinguish it from the word commonly used to translate *gikyoku*. Indeed, since the Meiji era, *gikyoku* was the accepted rendering for "drama."

6. The phrase is from Mori Ôgai's essay "Engeki Kairyô ronja no henken ni odoroku" (Surprised by the Prejudice of Theatre Reformers; 1889). See Keiko MacDonald, trans., in J.T. Rimer, ed. 2004:145.

7. *Old Toys* was a revised version of a play, *Un Sourire Jaune* (A wan smile), which Kishida had originally written in Paris for the Russian actor Georges Pitoëff, who had asked him to recommend some contemporary Japanese drama for him to read. Liking nothing that was available, Kishida wrote his own play in French. See Kishida's account in Rimer (1976:146).

8. Osanai had in fact sent someone to ask Kishida to check the translation. Osanai himself had translated the play from an English translation he had read in the magazine *Theatre Arts* and, prior to the production, had tried to secure a copy of the original. Kishida did not have one and so was unable to check the translation for its accuracy. Subsequently, he managed to lay his hands on a copy of the French text and, realizing Osanai's inaccuracies, mentioned them to Yamamoto, who used what he heard as ammunition for his attack on the Tsukiji director. There is considerable debate in the secondary literature over what actually happened, however. In his biography of Osanai, the playwright Kubo Sakae implies that Kishida could have alerted Osanai, but chose not to; cf. Inoue 1999, 226. The fullest analysis I have read (in Abe Kôichi 1993:100–110) is based on various accounts and suggests that Kishida managed to read the original only after it had been lent to Osanai, who had decided it was too late to make any changes.

9. Powell implies that *En the Ascetic* opened in June 1926, but in fact it opened on 21 March and ran until 11 April 1926.

10. Kubo Sakae wrote that they moved up the date for productions of Japanese plays because the theatre was losing its audience. Quoted in Fujiki 1977:12.

11. Complete charts of the Free Theatre's and Tsukiji Little Theatre's productions can be found in *Engekijin* 4 (January 2000): 17–21, and in Kurahashi Sei'ichirô (1966).

12. See Powell (2002:75–76) for discussion of this play.

13. Fujiki (1977:14). It was at the opening party for Ueda Fumiko's play that Osanai collapsed and died.

14. See Powell (2002:83–113), for a more complete account of *shingeki* in the 1930s.

References Cited

Abe Kôichi. *Dorama no gendai: Engeki/eiga/bungaku ronshû* (Drama today: essays in theatre, film and literature). Tokyo: Kindai bungeisha, 1993, 81–123.

"*Engeki shinchô* danwakai dairokugô" (*New Currents in Theatre* roundtable discussion number 6), *Engeki shinchô* 1:7 (July 1924): 27–46.

"*Engeki shinchô* danwakai dainanagô" (*New Currents in Theatre* roundtable discussion number 7), *Engeki shinchô* 1:8 (August 1924): 23–45.

Engekijin kaigi, ed. *Engekijin* (Theatre people) 4 (January, 2000): 17–21.

Fujiki Hiroyuki. "Taishôki no gikyoku 2: 1920-nendai no gekisakka" (Taishô drama 2: playwrights of the 1920s). *Higeki Kigeki* (Tragedy, Comedy) 29:2 (February 1976): 40–46.

_____. "Tsukiji Shôgekijô no sôsakugeki" (Original drama at the Tsukiji Little Theatre). *Higeki kigeki* 30:9 (September 1977): 8–15.

Inoue Yoshie. "Keiô gijuku Mita kôen no hamon: Osanai Kaoru "Tsukiji Shôgekijô" (Shockwaves caused by Osanai Kaoru's Mita Address). In *Kindai engeki no tobira o akeru* (Opening the doors of modern theatre). Tokyo: Shakai Hyôronsha, 1999, 223–240.

Keenan, Linda Klepinger. *En no gyôja: The Legend of a Holy Man in Twelve Centuries of Japanese Literature.* PhD dissertation, the University of Wisconsin-Madison, 1989.

Kishida Kunio. *Kishida Kunio zenshû* (The complete works of Kishida Kunio), Vol. 19. Tokyo: Iwanami Shoten, 1989.

Kurahashi Sei'ichirô. *Shingeki nendaiki: senzen hen* (Annals of *shingeki*: prewar). Tokyo: Hakusuisha, 1966.

Ôta Shôgo, "Heya-saki no hana: Kishida Kunio ni okeru geki kôzô ni tsuite" (Hothouse flower: on the structure of Kishida Kunio's drama), *Shingeki* 23:9 (Special issue on Kishida Kunio, September 1976): 139–144.

Ottaviani, Gioia. "Difference and Reflexivity: Osanai Kaoru and the *Shingeki* Movement." *Asian Theatre Journal* 11:2 (1994): 213–230.

Ôzasa Yoshio. *Nihon gendai engekishi* (A history of modern Japanese theatre). Vol. 2. Tokyo: Hakusuisha, 1987.

Powell, Brian W.F. "Japan's First Modern Stage: the Tsukiji Shôgekijô and its company, 1924–26," *Monumenta Nipponica* 30:1 (Spring 1975): 69–85.

_____. *Japan's Modern Theatre: A Century of Continuity and Change.* London, UK: Japan Library [Routledge Curzon], 2002.

Rimer, J. Thomas. *Toward a Modern Japanese Theatre: Kishida Kunio.* Princeton, NJ: Princeton University Press, 1976.

_____, ed.. *Not a Song Like any Other: An Anthology of Writings by Mori Ôgai.* Honolulu, HI: University of Hawai'i Press, 2004.

Sugai Yukio, ed. *Osanai Kaoru engekironshû* (Collected essays of Osanai Kaoru) Vol. 2. Tokyo: Miraisha, 1965.

_____. *Kindai Nihon engeki ronsôshi* (A history of modern Japanese theatre debate). Tokyo: Miraisha, 1979.

15

Dressing-up Dramaturgy in Charles L. Mee's *Bacchae 2.1*

Melinda Powers

Abstract

This paper compares the dramaturgy of the Dressing-up scene in Euripides's Bacchae/Bakkhai, first produced in 405 B.C., and American playwright and historian Charles L. Mee's 1993 Bacchae 2.1, a collage-style adaptation that follows the plot of the Euripides rather closely but cuts and pastes together sections of works from, among others, Georges Bataille, Klaus Theweleit, Pat Califia, and Sei Shonagon. Invoking the outrageous technique of Dadaist artist Max Ernst's Fatagaga collages, composed at the end of World War I, Mee's compositional process produces a jagged postmodern edge that resists a simple, imitative mimesis. Yet could Mee's wildly non-mimetic approach to adaptation in fact enact a deep mimesis of the Euripidean precursor? And if so, could Bacchae 2.1 in fact reanimate both the ingenuity of Euripides's formal innovations as well as the horrific comedy that marks them?

Postmodern adaptations of Greek tragedies often assume a non-mimetic relationship to their precursors and focus instead on the original's deconstruction. In the case of American playwright Charles L. Mee's *Bacchae 2.1* and its precursor Euripides's *Bacchae*, however, the relationship between the two forms is more complex. *Bacchae 2.1* was first performed in 1993 at the Mark Taper Forum's Festival of New Work under the direction of Brian Kulick, and Euripides's play was performed posthumously in Athens in 405 B.C. most likely under the direction of the poet's son. Keeping in mind the distinct cultural context of each production, in this paper, I will argue through a close study of the plays' dressing-up scenes that Mee's adaptation does not necessarily deconstruct the original but rather radically replicates both the innovative dramaturgy of the Euripides and particularly the horrifying comedy that marks it.[1]

Both plays' dressing-up scenes invigorate the conventions of their respective societies' forms of representation as well as the cultural mores reflected in those forms. For example, the Athenian theater has a different set of conventions for comedy and tragedy, and Oliver Taplin has argued that "to a considerable degree fifth-century tragedy and comedy help to define each other by their opposition and their reluctance to overlap" (Taplin 1986:164). In this system, tragedy is usually associated with the "high" and comedy with "low,"[2] and the different depictions of comic and tragic actors on fifth-century vase paintings[3] illustrate the distinct conventions and gestures associated with each. However, in the Dressing-up scene Euripides pushes these formal constraints by introducing the convention of cross-dressing from comedy to tragedy, and Taplin has argued that Euripides takes his use of comic touches, which characterize his later plays, to a new degree in *Bacchae*,

> Such contraventions of the generic boundaries [in *Bacchae/Bakkhai*] are, no doubt, all part of the crisis in the last years of the fifth century which produced fascinating innovative plays — I think particularly of *Orestes* and *Philoctetes* — but which also marked the end of growth for classical tragedy. In that case, this confirms rather than weakens the distinction between the two genres before the brilliant breakdown [Taplin 1986:165–166].

Euripides's style pushes the formal conventions of the late fifth-century theater, and, likewise, Charles L. Mee's unique collage-style approach also challenges the formal conventions of more mainstream styles of American theater.

Mee remains faithful to Euripides's plot, but he cuts its form entirely, in fact literally. Mee cuts and pastes together sections of works from, among others: Georges Bataille, Pat Califia, and Sei Shonagon. Invoking the outrageous technique of Dadaist artist Max Ernst's Post–World War I Fatagaga collages, which were meant "to make people howl" (O'Hara 1972:8–9).[4] Mee's experimental dramaturgy follows a distinctly non-linear, non–Aristotelian trajectory, but could Mee's wildly non-mimetic strategy of postmodern adaptation in fact enact a deep mimesis of the Euripidean precursor?[5] And if so, what does this non-mimetic mimesis of the Euripidean form suggest about the relationship between a contemporary American postmodern style of dramaturgy and its ancient counterpart?

Bacchae's Comedy

Despite the grim outcome of *Bacchae*'s plot,[6] classicists Helene P. Foley and Bernd Seidensticker have both suggested that Euripides's Dressing-up scene incorporates comic elements. Pentheus's costume change and disguise are conventions usually reserved for comedy, and Foley states, "Such costume change is relatively rare in Greek tragedy, however, and is generally reserved for climactic moments. In contrast costume change becomes the basis for the entire dramatic action in the *Bacchae*, and 'comic' costume techniques are used for the first time in a play which has a disastrous outcome" (1985:114).[7] While this dressing-up might seem unconventional, late Euripidean dramaturgy, especially the playwright's 408 B.C. *Orestes*, is particularly innovative, and at the same time the rebellious mood is in keeping with *Bacchae*'s themes.[8] Dionysus is the god of transgression and transformation, and, as both Foley and Seidensticker comment, the line between the comic and tragic is one of many that he explores. In the following, I want to expand upon Foley's and Seidensticker's suggestions of the scene's relationship to comedy and consider their points more thoroughly in terms of the dramaturgy and gestures of the Euripidean Dressing-up scene, which I will later compare to Mee's.[9]

In *Bacchae*, Dionysus's primary dramatic reason for the dressing-up is for Pentheus to "incur laughter from the Thebans" (854). Dionysus wants Pentheus to be mocked, and one of his ways of doing so is to have the young king's elite, tragic body flirt with the corporeality of not only a woman but also a comic character. Since women and comic characters were the marginalized or "low" within the social hierarchy of Greek society,[10] Euripides could have made the aristocratic, tragic character Pentheus the object of derisive laughter by having his gestures resemble those of a non-elite dressed-up comic male like Mnesilochus, "Euripides's" kinsman, in Aristophanes's comedy *Thesmophoriazusae*.[11] In other words, Euripides might play with the formal conventions of tragedy in order to intensify the derision of Pentheus by dressing him up like a comic woman. The result is a terrifying mixture of horror and humor, and in this way, the scene intricately intermingles the tragic and comic forms to evoke the horrifying humor that the terrible yet sweet (861), transgressive god of theater (comedy and tragedy) seeks to evoke for his revenge plot.

Yet *Bacchae* makes use of comic conventions not only in the dressing-up but also through its various comic allusions, which are evident in the tragedy's parallels with Aristophanes's comedy *Thesmophoriazusae*.[12] *Bacchae* and *Thesmophoriazusae* have similar plots, but the tragedy also mirrors a number of *Thesmophoriazusae*'s scenes and images.[13] Their respective Recognition scenes are one example of such a parallel (*Thesmophoriazusae* 902, *Bacchae* 1115 ff). *Thesmophoriazusae*'s Recognition scene between Euripides and Mnesilochus, which is a parody of Menelaus's rescue of Helen in Euripides's *Helen* (902 ff), finds a perverted super-parody in Agaue and

Pentheus's aborted recognition (1115 ff) just before she attacks her son, whom she thinks is a lion. Another parallel image is Mnesilochus's and Pentheus's removal of their *mitras* (feminine headbands). After the guard catches him for spying, Mnesilochus wants to strip off his feminine clothes and *mitra* so as not to be mocked by the crows that will eat his body (939–942). Likewise, Pentheus also wants to remove his *mitra* (1115) when he appeals to his mother for his life. This link between the plays' two scenes suggests that Pentheus's removal of his *mitra* precedes his return to sanity, a return that is accompanied by the embarrassment of dressing-up. Furthermore, as Euripides refers to a Gorgon's head in his hands towards the end of the comedy (1101 ff), so Agaue holds Pentheus's head in hers, and the image of Medusa's head in Perseus's hands is the most obvious visual parallel in Attic iconography for that of Pentheus's. Finally, the plays' dressing-up scenes are similar as well. Pentheus's women's clothes (*gunaikomimōi stolai*, 980, also *thēlun stolēn*, 828, 836, 852, and *thēlugenē stolēn*, 1156) recall those in *Thesmophoriazusae* (*stolēn gunaikos*, 92, and *gunaikeia stolē*, 851), and Mnesilochus, like Pentheus (925), asks coyly if his outfit suits him (261). Although the dressing-up in *Thesmophoriazusae* also alludes to Aeschylus's lost play *Lycurgeia*, the many similarities in plot, specific scenes, and images between *Bacchae* and *Thesmophoriazusae*, together with their similarities in Dressing-up scenes, create an intertextual and intercorporeal dialogue that is another way in which *Bacchae*'s dramaturgy boldly and unconventionally flirt with the traditionally distinct genre of comedy.

However, in addition to the intertextuality of the two plays, the actors' gesture is also suggestive of comedy. Awkward, asymmetrical, alinear figures (*schēmata*) are one of the defining characteristics of comic bodies in Attic vase-painting,[14] and Pentheus's maddened and disheveled impersonation of a Theban maenad finds its closest parallel in these images. Unlike the typical modes of an elite Athenian gentleman's *sōphrōn*, or staid, comportment,[15] Pentheus's head goes lop-sided (933), his curl slips out from under his *mitra* (928–929), his girdle comes loose (935–936), and his thyrsus simply eludes him (941–942). Just as *Bacchae*'s plot would not require a Dressing-up scene, so the Dressing-up scene would not require a clumsy Pentheus. Thus the character's perverse performance of a Theban maenad must have meaning and purpose, and this purpose must be, in part, to make Pentheus an object of ridicule both for the Kadmeians, as Dionysus wishes (854), and for the Athenian audience who witnesses the scene. If Dionysus intends for the Kadmeians to laugh at Pentheus (854), then why shouldn't the Athenians as well?

Yet while *Bacchae*'s comic allusions are well-recognized and participate in Euripides's tragi-comic scenes from his later works such as *Alcestis*, *Heraclidae* and *Ion*, critics such as Seaford and Zeitlin have read Euripides's dressing-up scene as more "serious." Both critics emphasize the scene's allusions to Dionysiac rituals of transvestism (Seaford 1997:222 and Zeitlin 1985:64). However, the play's subtextual references to ritual should not preclude the god's primary objective, which is to make Pentheus the laughing-stock of Thebes. While the audience may be denied "clear access either to the comic laughter or to the tragic pity by which the spectators control their theatrical experience" (Foley 1985:232), Dionysus nevertheless invites the audience to laugh at his foolish scapegoat, just as a playground bully might sway a bunch of kids to laugh at his victim. Some might feel uncomfortable with the teasing, but they often join in the fun, regardless of its nastiness. Others might not laugh at all. Therefore, the scene shockingly mingles the conventions of comedy with the cold irony of tragedy to evoke a bizarre concoction of pity, derision, and even laughter, and the bitter-sweet taste of the cocktail adds dimension to the scene itself.

Mee's Bacchae 2.1

Mee's *Bacchae 2.1* and its Dressing-up scene capture the violent humor of the Euripidean scene through recasting the plot in a contemporary, sadomasochistic, psychological framework. The "low"/"high" connotations of the comic and tragic genres do not necessarily apply to Mee's contemporary American society, but the playwright summons a suitable "surrogate"[16] to translate the peculiar taste of the mixture. In Mee's dressing-up, which takes place on stage, Pentheus resolves to scout out the Theban maenads and stay under cover while wearing his armor (Mee 1993:36). However, Dionysus, whom the text describes as "a transvestite in a white pleated linen skirt..." (Mee 1993:1) has other plans for him. The god has his Bacchae, who are "not just women, not just third world women, not just people from the revolutionary periphery, not just artists, but Dionysian artists" (Mee 1993:2) strip Pentheus naked (Mee 1993:36) of his "blue pinstripe Brooks Brothers suit with a red, striped silk tie, a white pocket handkerchief" (Mee 1993:6) and dress him up "layer by layer from perfumed powder to satin undergarments, stockings, slip dress, high-heeled shoes" (Mee 1993:37). Meanwhile Dionysus "steps to one side, helped by one of the Bacchae, his back to the audience, put on black leather pants — stuffing his dress inside — black boots, black leather jacket (Mee 1993:36), as a voiceover pronounces, "For our battle colors we chose black because it is the color of forbidden love between men, of a dance of death in the dark. Deranged ecstasy — the ecstasy of a physical body overloaded, of mutual recognition in armed combat hand-to-hand" (Mee 1993:37). The ancient Dionysiac initiation ritual of transvestism, to which the Euripides might allude, becomes in Mee a sadomasochistic replica that emerges from the cutting-process of the collage-form itself.

Mee's sadomasochistic twist to the scene is an important choice, for it effectively translates the horror, humiliation, and humor inherent in the Euripidean dressing-up (854). Dionysus wants Pentheus to be mocked, and cross-dressing, which in Mee's culture is most often associated with homosexuality, camp, or comedies such as *Tootsie, Some Like It Hot*, or "Bosom Buddies," would by itself connote neither horror nor humiliation.[17] Therefore, just as Euripides derides Pentheus by dressing him up as a woman and having him tread on the territory of disproportionate, *aphrōn* (unbalanced) comic characters, so Mee humiliates Pentheus through the more psychological tactics of sadomasochism. In both cases, the cross-dressing is linked to questions of power as much as gender, and the humor that arises from the incongruity of Pentheus's status and his feminine costume and awkward gestures is offset by the sadistic irony that seduces Pentheus into submission.

Yet the humor that both scenes evoke, in spite of such violence, does not in either case preclude the scenes' simultaneous allusions to ritual. Just as the Euripides might allude to the transvestism of his society's adolescent rites of passage rituals (cf., Seaford 1996), so Mee's transvestism alludes to what some S/M practitioners might call the ritual practice of sadomasochism. Fakir Musafar, who has studied mind and body-altering rituals in various societies, has stated: "'SM, in this culture, is one of the few places people can get started on the road back to their god. In this culture there are very few opportunities for this'" (Musafar qtd. in Califia 1994:234). Pat Califia, a transsexual critic S/M sex radical and pornographer, whose work Mee includes in his collage, criticizes such references to ritual by S/M practitioners, saying, "But many S/M rituals seem to have no clear purpose. Is someone being purified? If so, from what? Is someone being initiated? What is the next stage of life...?" (Califia 1994:238). Although rites of passage ceremonies were normative practices in Greece and S/M is a part of a contemporary sub-culture, Mee's surrogate nevertheless appropriately conjures the Euripidean concoction of simultaneous shock, horror, and humor. For while Euripides's scene might have alluded to rather mainstream social rituals, his dramaturgical allusions to comedy with the dressing-up would have been transgressive in their time.[18] On the other hand, while Mee's comic allusions are not particularly noteworthy within his society's dramaturgical scheme, his collage-style composition and "in-your-face"[19]

S/M dialogue are surely meant to challenge conventional forms, norms, and tastes.

In both plays, the metatheatrical staging of the dressing-up, which alludes to the ancient convention of men playing cross-dressed roles,[20] is charged with derision that erupts into violence in the following scene's description of Pentheus's dismemberment by his mother Agaue, who would have been played by the same actor in the Euripidean version.[21] As a result, both Dressing-up scenes seem to suggest that mimetic representation, i.e., Pentheus's clumsy performance of his maenadic mother, is as jagged and violent and imprecise as the cutting process of a collage itself. Just as Euripides's metatheater[22] calls attention to the formal conventions of representation in his theater, so Mee does in his own terms through his collage-style approach to dramaturgy that exposes the sutures of the seamless style of the more conventional American style of realism. At the same time, while Euripides perhaps transgresses the taboo of the "high"/ "low" status equated with the boundaries of tragedy and comedy, so Mee challenges his own society's taboo of the "male"/"female" binary equated with gender and the politics of sex with which it engages.[23] Both playwrights play with form and taboos to effect Pentheus's derision, but the Dressing-up scene's metatheater might also simultaneously call attention to the social construction of the taboos themselves and the violence they inflict and create in their separation of the presumed opposites of "high"/"low," "comedy"/"tragedy," and "male"/ "female."

Mee's overt sadomasochistic dialogue is infused with humor, but it is also meant to shock or even offend. The violence of *Bacchae 2.1* is infused by the violence of the play's language and form. Mee's Dionysus says in voice over:

> There was a time when all I wanted was to be dressed up like a poodle on a leash ... and to hear someone say 'Oh, yes, I want more.' To have my nipples rubbed until I moaned, to have her take out her cock, give me a blowjob, work her fingertips along my inseam until it made the tears come, to have her cuff me on the shoulder, roll me on my back, to taste him in my mouth ... [Mee 1993:38].

Mee's collage-style dramaturgy and "in-your-face" dialogue challenge the forms and norms of mainstream representation and its ethics, but, more importantly, the challenge is aggressive and even violent. The jagged form reflects its sharp, cutting shards of meaning, and Euripides's tragi-comic dressing-up creates a similar effect by challenging the genre conventions of his own society to evoke the derision necessary for Dionysus's revenge plot in the dressing-up scene's play within a play.

Conclusion

Like Max Ernst's Post-War Fatagaga collages on which Mee's compositional process is based, both playwrights' dramaturgical choices are meant "to make people howl" (O'Hara 1972:8–9). In the case of Euripides, his contemporary the comedian Aristophanes has parodied the tragedian for his radical style on more than one occasion. Aristophanes's *Frogs*, for example, features a debate between the old-school tragedian "Aeschylus" and the new generation's "Euripides." While the caricatures are clearly parodies concocted from comic exaggeration and cannot be taken too literally, their ability to get a laugh in 405 B.C. testifies to the social reality in which their jokes participated as well as the social anxiety on which the jokes fed.

In *Frogs*'s famous rivalry, the snooty "Aeschylus" condemns his young rival for dressing kings in rags (840 ff) and degrading the genre and the city with his plays. "Euripides," on the other hand, defends himself calling his dramaturgy and themes more "democratic" (953–954). The details of this debate are complex and specific to their comic and historical context. However, the scene's comic potential nevertheless demonstrates a contest over representation that might relate to Athens's persistent late fifth-century rivalry between the aristocracy and the *dēmos*, for, according to Aristophanes's conservative character "Aeschylus," "Euripidean" "democratic" aesthetics have not only shaken up the Athenian masses but corrupted them as well.

While Charles L. Mee's *Bacchae 2.1* differs in many ways from its ancient counterpart including the extent of its social reach, Mee's version of the myth still replicates its precursor through its challenge to social norms. While neither Mee himself nor his plays have been accused or parodied publicly for their innovation or potential for "corruption," the jagged pieces of his collage and the themes and lifestyles they invoke certainly have. The obscenity trials of the S/M publication *Modern Primitives* is just one such example. Yet while the details of each play and their contexts and circumstances are uniquely historically and culturally specific, Mee's adaptation still effectively surrogates the Euripidean shards of shock as well as suggests that the contest over "appropriate representation" on the stage, the nagging debate over how societies present and exhibit their myths, pasts, and bodies to themselves, each other, and posterity, persists.

UNIVERSITY OF CALIFORNIA, LOS ANGELES

Notes

Acknowledgment. My grateful thanks to Professors Sue-Ellen Case, Helene P. Foley, and Philip Purchase as well as to the anonymous referees for their help with various sections of this paper.

1. For a discussion of the distinction between "comic elements" and "comedy elements" in Greek tragedy, see Seidensticker (1978).

2. On comedy's associations with the "low," see, for example, Plato's *Laws* (814d–16e) and *Republic* X (606c) and Aristotle's *Poetics* (1449a31ff). Cf. Green (2002):99ff, Ormand (2003):1, and especially Henderson (1990), who bases his argument in part on the Old Oligarch's comments on comedy in the *Constitution of the Athenians* (2.18, trans. in Henderson 285) and argues that comedy offers a "public airing of minority views" (313).

3. E.g., the reserved tragic actor on the Attic bell-krater in Ferrara from Valle Pega, ca. 460–450 B.C. (Pickard-Cambridge 1968:Plate 33), versus the more animated, gesticulating, phallus-donning comic actors on the Attic red-figure calyx krater, ca. 420–410 B.C. (J. Paul Getty Museum, Malibu 82.AE.83) (Csapo and Slater 1995:Plate 5). See Pickard-Cambridge (1968) and Csapo and Slater (1995) for further discussion of these images.

4. From an interview by Patrick Waldberg with Max Ernst in Huismes, in the French departement of Indre-et-Loire. Date unknown.

5. For a rather different view of Mee's postmodern dramaturgy, see Reilly (2005). See also Mee and Mee (2002).

6. *Bacchae*'s plot dramatizes the conflict between the god of theater, Dionysus, and the young (1170, 1174, 1185), king of Thebes, Pentheus. Dionysus, disguised as a mortal priest of his cult, has come to Thebes from the East with a devout band of female worshippers or bacchae who serve as the play's chorus and mean to initiate the city into the god's sacred mysteries. As the god explains in the prologue, the daughters of Kadmos, i.e., the sisters of Dionysus's mother Semele (Ino, Agaue, and Autonoe), have spread lies about his mother and refuse to believe that her offspring, Dionysus, is the son of Zeus. Because the city denies and hubristically disrespects him, Dionysus has stung the city's women with his madness. To control the city and its women better, Pentheus challenges the god, so, in retribution, Dionysus takes vengeance on Pentheus. He talks him into dressing-up as a woman so that he can spy on the raving Theban maenads on the mountain. In the Dressing-up scene (which is more like a toilet scene since the actual dressing-up takes place off-stage), Dionysus slyly directs Pentheus's ludicrous performance of a maenad, and the god will later incite Pentheus's own mother Agaue to see the strange intruder, whom she thinks is a lion, and claw him to pieces. Agaue's father Cadmus later helps her to recognize her ill fate, and the play ends with Dionysus's appearing *ex machina* to pronounce Cadmus and Agaue's punishments.

7. For futher discussion on the relationship of comedy and tragedy's forms in antiquity, see Seidensticker (1982) and Taplin (1986).

8. See Csapo (2002) on the ideological implications of Euripides's innovative performance style. On *Orestes*'s wild style, see Edith Hall (1993) and Froma Zeitlin (1980).

9. While some critics, such as E.R. Dodds (1960:xxxvi), see *Bacchae*'s form as

demonstrating an archaizing tendency, I am instead suggesting that *Bacchae* mixes traditional forms with a great deal of stylistic innovation, such as the dressing-up. While Euripides's version of the myth offers the only extant example in both iconography and literature of a clear Dressing-up scene, other playwrights' versions of the myth (including Aeschylus's in his fragmentary *Lycurgeia*) could have also included a dressing-up. However, no other versions of an on-stage dressing-up can be confirmed, and the possibility of a dressing-up scene in Aeschylus that is as innovative as Euripides's late fifth-century version would be unlikely.

10. Supra note 2.

11. See Foley (1985:250) who suggests that Pentheus looks like the god's double and Zeitlin (1996:344) who suggests that Dionysus would appear to be more feminine, since the god's identification with the feminine gives him and his theater their power.

12. This comedy tells the story of how "Euripides" persuades his kinsman the manly-man Mnesilochus to dress-up as a "woman" in order to spy upon the women at the Thesmophoria (an Athenian women's only festival held in honor of Demeter and Persephone) who are about to try Euripides for his negative depictions of women in his plays. Like the Theban women in *Bacchae*, the women at the Thesmophoria recognize the male intruder, but in this case, the Kinsman and "Euripides," who has come to save his friend, escape in a comic ending.

13. For a discussion of gender and genre in this play, see Zeitlin (1981).

14. Supra note 3.

15. Richard Green (2002) discusses the importance of a quiet (*hēsuchia*) and balanced (*sōphrōn*) comportment for elites who are depicted on vases representing scenes from both theater and civic life. My discussion of the Dressing-up scene's gestures is an exploration and application of many of the intriguing ideas in Green's essay.

16. See Roach (1996:2) for a discussion of the Circum-Atlantic world's process of "surrogation," a term which Roach defines as: "how culture reproduces and recreates itself."

17. For a discussion of the different connotations of cross-dressing in Athenian and contemporary culture, see Ormand (2003).

18. See Taplin (1986) quoted above. I am here suggesting that the Euripidean Dressing-up scene's allusions to comedy are transgressive more than the practice of cross-dressing itself, for as Ormand has suggested, "we should not automatically assume that an instance of cross-dressing, or cross-gendering, challenges the binarism of Greek gender" (2003:10).

19. "In-your-face" theater is the term often used to refer to the outrageous styles and expletives employed in the theater of contemporary British playwrights such as Steven Berkhoff, Sarah Kane, and Mark Ravenhill.

20. See Case (1985), Rabinowitz (1995), and Ormand (2003) on playing cross-dressed roles in Athenian theater.

21. On the distribution of parts among Greek actors, see Pickard-Cambridge (1968:135ff). Three actors playing all the roles was the standard in the time of Euripides. As Pickard-Cambridge notes the distribution of actors in *Bacchae* was likely to be: "(a) Dionysus, Teiresias; (b) Pentheus, Agaue; (c) Cadmus, Servant, first Messenger. The second Messenger (1024ff.) could be given to (a) or (c), per-

haps even to (b)" (1968:147). This division of parts is the logical conclusion based on which actors are on stage with each other and how long they would have to change between roles.

22. See Segal (1997:215–271) and Foley (1985:205–258) on metatheatre in *Bacchae*.

23. See Ormand (2003) for a discussion of Athenian gender.

References Cited

Bury, R.G. *Plato's Laws*. Ed. T.G. Page. Cambridge: Harvard University Press, 1943.

Califia, Pat. *Public Sex: The Culture of Radical Sex*. Pittsburgh: Cleis Press, 2000.

Case, Sue-Ellen. "Classic Drag: The Greek Creation of Female Parts." *Theatre Journal* 37:3 (1985): 317–328.

Conacher, D. J. *Euripides' Alcestis*. Warminster: Aris & Phillips, 1988.

Csapo, Eric. "Kallippides on the Floor-sweepings: The Limits of Realism in Classical Acting and Performance Styles." In *Greek and Roman Actors: Aspects of an Ancient Profession*, eds. P.E. Easterling and Edith Hall, 127–147. Cambridge: Cambridge University Press, 2002.

Csapo, Eric, and William Slater. *The Context of Ancient Drama*. Ann Arbor: University of Michigan Press, 1995.

Dodds, E. [Eric] R. [Robertson] *Bacchae*. Oxford: Clarendon Press, 1960.

Ferguson, John. *Plato: Republic Book X*. London: Methuen, 1957.

Foley, Helene P. *Ritual Irony: Poetry and Sacrifice in Euripides*. Ithaca: Cornell University Press, 1985.

Green, Richard. "Towards a Reconstruction of Performance Style." In *Greek and Roman Actors: Aspects of an Ancient Profession*, edited by P. E. Easterling and Edith Hall, 93–126. Cambridge: Cambridge University Press, 2002.

Hall, Edith. "Political and Cosmic Turbulence in Euripides' *Orestes*." In *Tragedy, Comedy, and the Polis: Papers from the Greek Drama Conference Nottingham, 18–20 July 1990*, edited by Alan H. Sommerstein, Stephen Halliwell, Jeffrey Henderson, Bernhard Zimmeran, 263–306. Bari, Italy: Levante Editori, 1993.

Halliwell, Stephen. *Aristotle's Poetics*. Translated and edited by Stephen Halliwell. Cambridge: Harvard University Press, 1995.

Henderson, Jeffrey. "The *Dēmos* and Comic Competition." In *Nothing to Do with Dionysos*, eds. John J. Winkler and Froma I. Zeitlin, 271–313. Princeton: Princeton University Press, 1990.

Lee, K. [Kevin] H. *Euripides' Ion*. Warminster: Aris & Phillips, 1997.

March, Jenny. "Euripides' *Bakchai*: A Reconsideration in the Light of the Vase Paintings." *BICS* 36 (1989): 33–65.

Mee, Charles L. *Bacchae 2.1*, 1993. URL: http://www.charlesmee.org/indexf.html.

Mee, Erin and Charles L. "Shattered and Fucked Up and Full of Wreckage." *The Drama Review* 46 (Fall 2002): 83–104.

Merry, W.W. *Aristophanes' Frogs*. Oxford: Clarendon Press, 1956.

Murray, Gilbert. *Euripides Fabulae* III. Oxford: Clarendon Press, 1943.

O'Hara, J. Philip. *Max Ernst*. Chicago: J. Philip O'Hara, Inc., 1972.

Ormand, Kirk. "Oedipus the Queen: Cross-gendering without Drag." *Theater Journal* 55 (2003): 1–28.

Pickard-Cambridge, Sir Arthur. *The Dramatic Festivals of Athens.* London: Oxford University Press, 1968.

Rabinowitz, Nancy Sorkin. "How Is It Played? The Male Actor of Greek Tragedy: Evidence of Misogyny or Gender-Bending." *Didaskalia* Supplement 1 (May 1995). URL: http://didaskalia.open.ac.uk/issues/supplement1/Rabinowitz. html.

Reilly, Kara. "A Collage Reality (Re)Made: The Postmodern Dramaturgy of Charles L. Mee." *American Drama* 14:2 (Summer 2005): 56–71.

Roach, Joseph. *Cities of the Dead.* New York: Columbia University Press, 1996.

Rogers, Benjamin Bickley. *Aristophanes III: Lysistrata, Thesmophoriazusae, Ecclesiazusae, Plutus.* Edited by G. P. Goold. Cambridge: Harvard University Press, 1996.

Seaford, Richard. *Euripides's Bacchae.* Warminster: Aris and Phillips, 1997.

Segal, Charles. *Dionysiac Poetics and Euripides' Bacchae.* Princeton: Princeton University Press, 1982.

Seidensticker, Bernd. "Comic Elements in Euripides' *Bacchae.*" *AJP* 99 (1978): 303–320.

_____. *Palintonos harmonia: Studien zu komischen Elementen in der griechischen Tragödie.* Göttingen: Vandenhoeck & Ruprecht, 1982.

Taplin, Oliver. "Fifth-century Tragedy and Comedy: A Synkrisis." *The Journal of Hellenic Studies* 106 (1986): 163–174.

Vale, V. and Juno, Andrea. *Modern Primitives.* San Francisco: Re/Search Publications, 1989.

Wilkins, John. *Euripides' Heraclidae.* Oxford: Clarendon Press, 1993.

Zeitlin, Froma. *Playing the Other: Gender and Society in Classical Greek Literature.* Chicago: Chicago University Press, 1996.

_____. "Travesties of Gender and Genre in Aristophanes' *Thesmophoriazousae.*" *Critical Inquiry* 8 (1981): 301–28 (now in *Reflections of Women in Antiquity,* ed. Helene Foley, 169–217. New York: Gordon and Breech Science Publishers, 1981).

_____. "The Closet of Masks: Role Playing and Myth Making in the *Orestes* of Euripides." *Ramus* 9 (1980): 51–77.

16

Chūshingura and Beyond
A Study of the Japanese
Ideal of Loyalty

Guohe Zheng

Abstract

It has been proposed that the ideal of loyalty is drastically different in the cultures of Japan and China: while it is relativized by the moral principle of benevolence in China, it is absolute in Japan. This paper evaluates the validity of this proposal as it applies to Japan, beginning with a discussion on Chūshingura *(1748), a puppet theater on revenge. An analysis of the play itself supports the proposal: loyalty shown by the 47 rōnin to their lord is indeed absolute. But an exploration beyond the play, of its shaky historical basis, the discourse on the revenge and what has been called the "capacity" of the Chūshingura phenomenon indicates that the proposal, when generalized, is not only invalid but indeed dangerous. It advocates stereotypes about Japanese culture by ignoring the shifting themes of the Chūshingura legend, blinds us to vital dynamics of Japanese society, and prevents us from understanding how history, politics and literature are closely intertwined, particularly in modern Japanese history.*

Comparing drama in China and Japan, a Chinese scholar made the following proposal:

> Chinese moral and ethnic ideals emphasize two virtues: filial piety to one's elders within the family and loyalty to the emperor beyond the family. But in China filial piety and loyalty are both subject to the checking of a higher virtue, that of benevolence.... With the checking of benevolence, therefore, it is no longer absolute whether one practices filial piety at home or is loyal to the emperor: if the emperor is not benevolent, he would not be entitled to rule the country; if a minister is not benevolent, he would not be entitled to his office. All must be measured by the yardstick of benevolence and judged accordingly [...]. In contrast, filial piety and loyalty are both regarded

as something absolute in Japan. Benevolence has lost its function both as a guiding principle in one's social action and in everyday life, the status that it used to hold in China, the birth place of the principle [Ge 1995:94].[1]

This is a bold proposal touching on issues enormous in scale and across two cultures. Due to the limitation of space, this paper examines the validity of the proposal as is applied to Japan, leaving the closely related inquiry on the case of China to a separate project. Given the strained Sino-Japanese relationship in recent years due to the controversy over whether all of Japan's war-dead, including Class-A war criminals, should be worshipped, it is not irrelevant to examine whether absolute loyalty is part of Japanese culture.

Puppet Play Chūshingura and the Ideal of Absolute Loyalty

A good place of departure is a look at *Chūshingura*, a Japanese puppet play on revenge, not least because a Kabuki version of it has been cited specifically to support the proposal (95).

During the Edo period (1600–1867), a particularly bloody vendetta took place that has since evolved into Japan's "national legend" (Smith 2003:1). In spring 1701, Asano Naganori, lord of Akō, was entrusted with the reception of an imperial envoy from Kyoto. The inexperienced country baron had been instructed to seek guidance from Kira Yoshinaka, a senior *bakufu* protocol official. On 21 April of that year, Asano drew his sword in a corridor of the Edo castle and slashed Kira for unknown reasons,[2] allegedly Kira's insult of Asano due to the latter's failure to provide the former with the expected bribe.[3] The wounds were superficial, but Shogun Tsunayoshi was so outraged by this unseemly breach of decorum in the castle that he commanded Asano to commit *seppuku*, on the same day. His lands were also confiscated and his retainers set adrift as *rōnin*, or masterless samurai. Twenty months later, on 30 January, 1703, 46 former retainers of the late Asano burst into Kira's mansion in Edo and killed him. They severed his head, marched across the city carrying the trophy and offered it to Asano's grave in Sengakuji Temple. After six long weeks of debate and deliberation, the *bakufu* finally issued a sentence of honorable death by *seppuku* to the 46 who had surrendered themselves. The order was carried out the same day and the *rōnin* were buried in graves adjacent to that of their master.

In 1748, nearly half a century after the incident, a puppet play based on the vendetta was staged in Osaka. Commonly known as *Chūshingura*, its title means "the treasury of loyal retainers." While obviously based on the Akō Incident, *Chūshingura* is set in the earlier Muromachi period (1336–1467) and the characters in the play are given different names due to strict censorship prohibiting theaters to deal with contemporary political matters. The story has also been expanded extensively and includes subplots absent in the historical incident. The story of *Chūshingura* begins in the spring of 1338, when Ashikaga Shogun's younger brother Tadayoshi is received at the consecration ceremony of the Tsurugaoka Shrine by Kō no Moronao, governor of Kamakura, and two young daimyo, Wakanosuke and Hangan. In the course of the ceremony Moronao insults Wakanosuke for challenging his views and standing in the way of his sexual advance to Kaoyo, Hangan's beautiful wife. Later, the enraged Wakanosuke reveals to Honzō, his chief retainer, his intention to kill Moronao in the palace at another ceremony. Convinced that the insult suffered by his master has resulted from insufficient bribes and afraid the hot temper of his young master might bring disaster to the house, Honzō offers Moronao an enormous amount of presents, without the knowledge of his master. The bribe works as intended. Moronao apologizes to Wakanosuke the next morning for the insult and the latter's resentment melts way. However, the anger of Moronao shifts towards Hangan that day, clearly for Kaoyo's rejection of his advance. Unable to bear the humiliation, Hangan draws his sword and attacks Moronao. Before he can kill Moronao, however, Hangan is restrained by Honzō. Moronao escapes with slight wounds. Soon after, orders from the shogun arrive commanding that Hangan commit *seppuku* and his lands be confiscated for disturbing peace in the palace. Hangan plunges a dagger into his abdomen, regretting only that he could not kill his enemy. A debate follows among Hangan's retainers, now masterless, on what to do about the confiscation. One retainer proposes they divide the money and then turn over the mansion; another they defend the mansion and die fighting. Eventually, the suggestion by Ōboshi Yuranosuke, Hangan's chief retainer, is accepted by most to bide their time to avenge their master.

That is a summary of the first four of the 11 acts of the play. These acts introduce the cause of the vendetta and set the stage for revenge. The remaining of the play unfolds around a central issue — how the mission of revenge is to be accomplished. The ideal of absolute loyalty is embodied in various ways by various characters in the subsequent acts of the play.

One example is seen in the characters of Kampei, his wife Okaru, and Yoichibei, his father-in-law. In Act 3 when Hangan confronts Moronao and attacks him, Kampei fails to be with his lord. Instead, he is away from the site indulging himself in intimacy with his young wife. Persuaded by Okaru not to commit *seppuku* to atone for that failure, Kampei decides to live in hiding with his in-laws and wait for the opportunity to prove his loyalty. Since then, the family spares no efforts to restore Kampei's reputation. Upon learning that Kampei's reputation may be restored by the strength of financial contribution to the league's efforts, Yoichibei, a poor farmer, hits on the idea of selling his daughter to prostitution to raise the funds. To avoid causing guilty feelings on the part of Kampei, he seals a secret deal with the brothel. In Yoichibei's mind, "It's no disgrace to sell his wife — the money is for his lord's sake" (*Chūshingura*: 91). When informed of this deal later, Kampei's reaction is "how grateful I am for Father's solicitude" (91). Okaru's own reaction to the deal sounds welcome, even proud: "I'm leaving my husband, it's true, but I'm selling myself for our master's sake, so I don't feel sad or anything like that. I go in good spirits" (93–94).

Okaru's brother Heiemon is another example. Heiemon is an *ashigaru*, the lowest rank of samurai and therefore not eligible to join the league of revenge. He is allowed to do so only after giving the most extreme proof of his loyalty. When he first finds out his sister serving in the brothel to help restore Kampei's reputation, he shows unreserved admiration: "It was noble of you to have sold yourself for your husband and our master. I'm proud of you" (119). But when Okaru reveals later that she has discovered the secret plan of the league by chance, Heiemon decides to take her life to protect the secret: "I can't allow any woman with knowledge of the great secret to escape, even if she's my own sister"(121). He is stopped by Yuranosuke, who has been listening to the exchanges between the brother and sister. Yuranosuke is so touched by their loyalty to the cause of revenge that he grants Heiemon the privilege of joining the group.

But the ideal of absolute loyalty is embodied most fully in the character of Yuranosuke, Hangan's chief retainer. Ever since the death of his lord, Yuranosuke devotes himself body and soul to the mission. In order to put the enemy off guard, he takes pains to give the impression that he has lost himself in dissipation in the pleasure quarters. His behavior is such that even his fellow samurai take him to be a real slave of women and *sake*. His enemy also keeps a close eye on him. A spy sent by Moronao even tests him by offering a piece of octopus for food, a taboo in the eve of the anniversary of one's master. Yuranosuke passes the test by accepting the octopus. Then the spy finds Yuranosuke's sword rusty "as a red sardine," another sign that he has forgotten about the revenge. However, when Yuranosuke is reading a secret message sent by Hangan's widow about their mission, assuming that he is alone, the plot is discovered by the spy hiding under the floor. The alarmed Yuranosuke manages to kill the spy before he escapes. A prostitute of the pleasure quarters, trying to see whether Yuranosuke is reading a love letter, also discovers his secret. Yuranosuke plans to kill her as well by pretending to fall in love with her and promising to redeem her. Her life is spared only when it is found out that she is no other than the loyal wife of Kampei and sister of Heiemon. Eventually, the secret mission proceeds smoothly until the league avenges their master with the dagger that Hangan used in killing himself.

Obviously, the above analysis suggests that the proposal in question is valid — as far as *Chūshingura* is concerned. The loyalty shown to Lord Hangan by the *rōnin* is indeed absolute. It never occurs to any of them to inquire into the cause of the incident in the palace, much less that their lord might be too rash. Donald Keene has said the following about *Chūshingura*: "Yuranosuke's loyalty is absolute. There is nothing to suggest that he would have been a particle less loyal to Enya Hangan even if the latter had been a cruel or contemptible master... [T]he *rōnin* were uninterested in anything but the claims of loyalty... The whole point of the play is the unconditional nature of loyalty" (*Chūshingura*: 17). The ideal of absolute loyalty in *Chūshingura* is well captured by these remarks.

Fiction in the Puppet Play Chūshingura and the Japanese Ideal of Loyalty

This characterization of *Chūshingura* must not be generalized, or else we run the risk of creating stereotypes. The reason for this is simple: the above-analyzed characters in *Chūshingura* are not reliable indicators of moral ideal of their historical models, much less that of the Japanese people in general. Instead, they are products of what Miyazawa Seiichi calls "fiction" (*kyokō*) created in the evolution of this "national legend" (Miyazawa 1999:1–18).

For example, in *Chūshingura*, Hangan's dramatic *seppuku*, along with his dying wish for Yuranosuke to avenge him with the very dagger with which he killed himself, is a vital scene which sets the revenge in motion. The historical Asano, however, was ordered to commit *seppuku* in the front yard of his Edo residence, with no life-and-death parting with his chief retainer, 600 miles away back in Akō, nor dagger as a memento (42–47).

Another example of the "fiction" is Yuranosuke's unequivocal determination to avenge his master from the beginning, expressed first (by the narrator) at the time of Hangan's death and then (by himself) in the debate following the turnover of Hangan's estate in Act 4. The fact is, however, that Ōishi Kuranosuke, the historical chief retainer of Asano, was strongly opposed to revenge against Kira for a long time after the death of his master. His logic goes like this: even though revenge may help advance the reputation of the Akō *rōnin* as warriors, it would also cause certain extinction of the Asano family. A loyal vassal must abandon any consideration of his own reputation for the sake of the perpetuation of the name of his lord's family. According to him, the priority of the Akō *rōnin* should be to campaign for the revival of the Asano family by establishing Asano's brother Daigaku as the new daimyō, and for the punishment of Kira *by the bakufu*, instead of *by themselves*. He even criticized some Akō radicals bent on immediate revenge, saying that their "self-will" (*ga'i*) would only cause the extinction of the Asano family, contrary to the wish of their lord (85–117).

Yet another example of the "fiction" is Yuranosuke's dissipation in the pleasure quarters to lay off the guard of Moronao in preparation for the revenge. There is no direct evidence that this story has historical basis. According to the best evidence available, during the time when Ōishi was in Kyoto, he spent much time "sightseeing," misbehaving and spending lavishly, allegedly Ōishi's habitual way. A rumor (*fūsetsu*) is also recorded that the spies sent by Kira, seeing Ōishi's misconduct, left Kyoto convinced that he no longer held any grudge (*ishu*) against the enemy of his master. Nothing is said about his dissipation in the brothels, much less that his playfulness was a deliberate tactic to lay off the guards of his enemy. It is crucial to note how the extravagant "sightseeing" of the historical Ōishi has been transformed in *Chūshingura* into Yuranosuke's dissipation at the pleasure quarters and thereby created a combination of money and sex, the two major concerns of the *chōnin* society of the Edo period, which undoubtedly accounts in large part for the popularity of *Chūshingura*.

Money and sex are also part of the "fiction" involving Kampei, Okaru and Yoichibei. It is well-known that Kampei is modeled on the Akō retainer Kayano Sampei (1675–1702). Sampei was one of the messengers who brought the news of Asano's attack in Edo to Akō but who soon afterward committed suicide. According to Sampei's own will addressed to Ōishi, this young samurai intended to join those who planned to go to Edo but his father would not allow him. Unable to find a way out of the conflicting obligations of avenging his lord in Edo and of obeying his father at home, he chose death (124). There is no woman involved in Sampei (123–124), however, or a father's selling of his daughter into prostitution to restore the son-in-law's reputation as a loyal samurai, nor does the daughter's happy acceptance of that deal to help her husband prove his loyalty to his lord. But, as we have seen above, Kampei, Okaru and Yoichibei play an important role in advocating the ideal of absolute loyalty in *Chūshingura*. Clearly, fiction in *Chūshingura* testifies to the invalidity of the proposal.

Discourse on Akō Incident and the Japanese Ideal of Loyalty

Similarly, the discourse on the Akō Incident also testifies to the invalidity of the proposal. For example, the actions of the historical 47 *rōnin* have not been universally celebrated in Japan. On the contrary, a heated debate on the incident started among Tokugawa Confucian scholars soon after the incident. For example, Hayashi Hōkō (1644–1732), grandson of the great Confucian scholar Hayashi Razan (1583–1657) and a Bakufu official in charge of education, wrote *Fukushū ron* (On Revenge, 1703). In this essay, Hōkō insists that the action of the *rōnin* is justifiable morally because it is imperative for retainers to avenge their master. He admits, on the other hand, that it is also justifiable legally to punish them since they have violated the law. But he fails to address the crucial issue of *why one can be morally right but legally wrong*.[4] Brushing aside Hōkō's apparently contradictory argument as absurd, Satō Naokata (1650–1719) advanced a very different view of the incident in his *Shijū rokunin no hikki* (notes on the 46 *rōnin*, before 1705). In this essay, Naokata denies that Kira was Asano's enemy: the latter attacked the former from behind. Asano was therefore punished for violating the law. Instead of atoning for the crime committed by their lord, the *rōnin* added to the magnitude of their lord's crime by attacking Kira. Naokata discounts the retainers' alleged high-minded motivation, arguing that their surrender to the *bakufu* was a devious ruse to escape death and gain employment in other domains (Miyazawa 1999).[5]

A view at odds with Naokata's harsh judgment was soon expressed by Asami Keisai (1652–1711), a passionate sympathizer of the 46. Keisai believes that Asano attacked Kira due to the latter's arrogance and humiliation and therefore both parties in the argument were subject to the customary practice of *kenka ryōseibai*, according to wich both parties to a quarrel involving physical violence should be punished equally, no matter who was at fault. As Asano alone was punished by death, his retainers must avenge their master for the big justice to be done (Miyazawa 1999:219–220).[6]

The debate on the incident continued to the end of Edo period and, as we shall see below, underlies much of the evolution of this "national legend" in modern Japan. Therefore the discourse on the Akō Incident also testifies to the invalidity of the proposal.

The "Capacity" of Chūshingura and the Japanese Ideal of Loyalty

A stronger challenge to the proposal is found in what a Japanese scholar calls the "capacity" (Miyazawa 2001:5) of Chūshingura which has been defined as "the ability of a single story to root itself in the national psyche in a way that encompasses so many issues for so many audiences in so many media" (Smith 2003:1). Indeed, the capacity of Chūshingura is of such enormity that the term Chūshingura has long been used not only to refer to the puppet play staged in 1748 from which the term originated, or its countless subsequent adaptations, but even to the historical vendetta itself and all the retellings of it. It is in that broad sense that the term is used in the following discussion. As much of the "capacity" of Chūshingura has been generated since the beginning of the Meiji period, the following discussion is focused on the modern period.

On 5 November, 1868, Meiji emperor sent an envoy to Sengakuji to deliver an imperial commendation of the Akō retainers as role models of loyalty. Due to this visit, the actions of the Akō retainers were first officially recognized by the state as praiseworthy. A connection was thus established between the loyalty of retainers to a local lord in the Edo period and the loyalty of Japanese citizens to the emperor and the state in the modern period.

However, the dynamics of Chūshigura did not work linearly. On 7 February, 1873, for example, in an effort to build a legal system along the lines of the Western countries, the Meiji government passed a law banning all types of vendetta (*fukushū kinshi rei*). Obviously, this law conflicts with the imperial commendation. This conflict is significant in two senses: on the one hand, it represents a continuation of the debate among Confucian scholars on the vendetta in the Edo period; on the other hand, it also represents an inherent contradiction in official policies identical in nature to the Edo period contradiction in which an action can be morally correct but legally wrong. This contradiction is a powerful dynamic operating in Japanese society and underlies the evolution of Chūshigura in modern Japan.

For example, in Chapter 6 of his influential work *Gakumon no susume* (An Encouragement of Learning, 1874), Fukuzawa Yukichi (1834–1901), Japan's leader of the enlightenment movement, was strongly opposed to the acclaim that the Akō retainers were "righteous men." If the *bakufu* punished only Asano for a fight between him and Yoshinaka, and if the Akō retainers felt that the punishment was unfair, Fukuzawa argues, they should have appealed and demanded a correction. Instead of appealing, however, the retainers killed Yoshinaka and thereby "failed in their duties as citizens and, in taking the law into their own hand, invaded the right of the government." If such an action goes unpunished, Japan would soon fall into anarchy (Miyazawa 2001:35–36 and 46). However, Fukuzawa's criticism of the Akō retainers was itself criticized later by Ueki Emori (1857–1892), theoretician of the Freedom and People's Rights movement. If Japan were a country where public affairs were determined by public opinions, as Fukuzawa claims it is, then of course citizens must all obey the law of their own making. However, Ueki argues, Japan in the Edo period was "a country of dictatorship" in which the *bakufu* wrote the law according to its own will. Therefore, the people were not obliged to obey such a law. If a government is a totalitarian one, the people have no choice but to revolt against it if necessary. Therefore, the 47 retainers deserve sympathy even their action was against the law. As is pointed out by Miyazawa Seiichi, Ueki is here clearly using the 47 retainers to promote his own agenda of advocating people's right and thereby opposing the Satchō government (Miyazawa 2001:47).

Dynamics of a different kind was at work in the activities of the *kōdan* storytellers and that of the academic historians. In 1872, seeing the enormous popularity of *kōdan* storytelling among the general public and its potential to serve the purpose of disseminating the official ideology, the Meiji government appointed *kōdan* storytelling masters instructors under the Ministry of Religious Instruction (Kyōbushō). The job of these special instructors was to create or adapt pieces that advocate the ideology of revering the emperor and patriotism. During this golden age of *kōdan* storytelling, Kuranosuke, leader of the Akō *rōnin*, was portrayed as Japan's paragon of loyalty even though the historical basis for such a portrayal is dubious to say the least. Thus *kōdan* storytelling played an important political role of spreading the ideology of emperor worship (44–47). A trend in the opposite direction started in 1889, the year when the Association of the Studies of History (*shigakukai*) was founded. In the same year, *Akō gishi jitsu wa* (A True Tale of the Righeous Akō Retainers) was published by Shigeno Yasutsugu (1827–1910), professor of Tokyo Imperial University. This book has been regarded as "monumental" as the first serious study that tears down the veil of fiction around the Akō Incident in the scientific methodology of modern historical studies (47, 55–56). Citing primary sources, Shigeno points out cases of manipulation of historical facts which contributed to popular perceptions of Chūshingura. For example, while the historical Lord Asano was a coward because he attacked Yoshinaka from behind, he appears on the stage and in various popular accounts of the incident as a brave but quick-tempered warrior who cannot stand humiliation. Another example is the timing of Ōishi's determination to revenge. While the historical chief retainer put priority on the restoration of the family and attempted repeatedly to stop the more radical group from planning the revenge until restoration proved impossible, all popular accounts unanimously assert, based on a manipulated account by Muro Kyūsō (1658–1734), a Confucian scholar and contemporary of the Akō Incident, that he resolved to revenge as soon as the news of the attack reached Akō (47–48, 55–58). Shigeno's study shook the national legend at its roots.

With nationalism rising high following the Russo-Japanese War (1904–1905), however, fictionalization of Chūshingura also reached a new stage in Japan. The writings on the Akō retainers by Haga Yaichi (1867–1927), a scholar of Japanese literature, are an example. Chūshingura is a spectacular tragedy most popular among the Japanese today, Haga says, but "the essence of Bushidō" (*bushidō no hongi*) embodied in Chūshingura can be traced back to the sincerity (*magokoro*) of ancient Japan. In other words, the concept of loyalty to the imperial household, as connoted in the word *magokoro*, originated from Japanese mythology and became the essence of *bushidō* (*bushidō no seizui*) during the medieval period when Japan was ruled by the warrior class. Moreover, it is to this spirit of *bushidō* that Japan owes its victory over Russia in the war and its becoming the only power among Asian nations. As is pointed out by critics, Haga's writings deliberately distorted history: the spirit of *bushidō* did not exist in Japan until the warrior class came to power, but Haga says it is something existing since the ancient times; loyalty to the emperor and patriotism (*chūkun aikoku*) is an ideology born in the establishment of the emperor-centered nation-state of Japan in the modern times, but Haga claims it is part of the unique and inherent characteristics of the Japanese; the Akō retainers were loyal only to their lord, but Haga identifies their loyalty with the loyalty of Japanese citizens in modern times to the emperor (86–87). Haga's writings illustrate most clearly the "capacity" of Chūshingura at work in modern times and its political implications.

The "capacity" of Chūshingura works in a similarly way in *Genroku kaikyo roku* (Heroic Deeds of the Akō Retainers, 1908–1909) by Fukumoto Nichinan (1857–1921). Based on dubious historical accounts, this book glorifies the 47 retainers and the commoners who supported them. Its moral is that commoners of the Meiji period should follow the example of the Akō retainers, be absolutely loyal to the emperor-centered state, and devote themselves to the Japanese Empire (50, 87–90).

In the Taisho period (1912–1926), when democratic ideas gained wide acceptance among Japanese intellectuals, the evolution of Chūshingura took a new turn in literature. Akutagawa Ryūnosuke's short story *Aru hi no Ōishi Kuranosuke* (Ōishi Kuranosuke: One Day in Custody, 1917) is the first example of this new turn. Waiting for the *bakufu*'s sentence of their perpetration while in custody, Ōishi's mood changes several times in one day: from satisfaction about the successful vendetta to upset when hearing people copied their action in Edo streets, to depression when fellow retainers who did not participate in the vendetta are condemned. To Ōishi, the latter's decision about the vendetta is rather natural, even sincere. Here, by exploring the subtle psychology of the main character, Akutagawa criticizes the ever widely spreading celebration of the "righteous retainers" since the end of the Meiji period (121–122). Akutagawa was followed by numerous novelists and playwrights including Nogami Yaeko, Osaragi Jirō, most of whom challenged the accepted views of Chūshingura.[7]

After the Manchuria Incident in 1931, fascism began to rise in Japan, as is seen most conspicuously in the two armed rebellions, the 5.15 Incident and the 2.26 Incident. Crucially, the Akō Incident was recalled collectively in both rebellions and the rebels were regarded as the modern versions of the loyal Akō retainers. Reflecting this rise of fascism in Japan are history and literary works that appeared in this period. The most representative of these is perhaps Mayama Seika's play *Genroku chūshingura* (1934–1941), set in real historical time and using real names. Mayama claims that his work is based strictly on historical evidence (183). But historical evidence proves otherwise. For example, with full knowledge of historical evidence to the contrary, Mayama presents Asano as attacking from the front, obviously to justify the subsequent revenge by his retainers (183). Moreover, he portrays Ōishi as being worried above all, when receiving the news of the attack during the reception of an imperial envoy, that his lord has committed irreverence towards the emperor. Then, when learning that the emperor is sympathetic to Asano, he is so moved that he prostrates in the direction of Kyoto crying for gratitude. As is pointed out by scholars, historic basis for this episode is shaky and the episode only reflects Mayama's own worshipping of the imperial household (56 and 185–186).

From July 1937, Japan's conflict with China escalated into a full-scale war. In this context, Chūshingura came to be connected to Japanese militarism and was widely acclaimed as a story that helps promote military spirit among the Japanese. As ominous signs of Japan's defeat became unmistakable towards the end of the war, Japan's military authorities, trying to whip the Japanese people to the utmost, identified the conflict with the British and America as a "national revenge" against "the devils of the British and America" and called on the Japanese people to show their loyalty to the emperor by death (198, 215–217, and 220–222). Here, the political role of Chūshingura in modern Japanese history reached its peak. Clearly, the "capacity" of Chūshingura provides strong evidence against the proposal.

The Shifting Themes of Chūshingura and the Japanese Ideal of Loyalty

Perhaps the strongest evidence against Ge's proposal is found in the shifting themes of the Chūshingura legend itself. It is widely believed that

Chūshingura is "the most famous and popular work in the entire Japanese theatrical repertory" (Takeda, translated by Keene, 1971:xi). But the *Chūshingura* here should not be interpreted as referring only to the 1748 puppet play or its Kabuki versions. But rather, it refers collectively to the countless literary retellings and adaptations of the Chūshingura legend. The themes of these works, however, constantly change over time, often drifting far from that of absolute loyalty. For example, 26 years after the original puppet play was staged, a *jōruri* ballad drama entitled *Chūshin gojitsudan* (A Follow-up Tale of the Loyal Retainers, 1774) was performed in Osaka. While the piece deals mainly with the hardships of the widows of the league and the surviving retainers after the vendetta, a new patron appears in the brothel who jokes with and is ridiculed by Okaru in vulgar language until it is found out that he is no other than Moronao's son and is then killed. The entire Act 7 is a parody of Yuranosuke's feigned dissipation in the brothel in the puppet play.[8] Unrestrained parody of Chūshingura was not possible until mid–Taishō (1912–1926) to the first 10 years of the Showa period (1926–1989). *Ahō gishi meimei den* (Biographies of the Stupid Pretenders, 1930) and *Warera ga chūshingura* (We Are the Treasury of Loyal Retainers, 1933) are two of the many pieces that appeared during this relatively liberal period in modern Japanese history. Among other things, both pieces incorporated songs popular among the young people, representing the spirit of "nonsense," one of the epithets historians use to characterize the period.[9] In the postwar period, by far more pieces have appeared, with even more varied themes. For example, Ikemiya Shōichirō's novel *Yonjūnananin no shikaku* (The 47 Assassins, 1992), later turned into a film in 1994, presents the revenge of the league as a war of strategy and information with no loyalty or righteousness involved.[10] Or, Hirata Oriza's *OL Chūshingura* (Loyal Ronin: The Working Girls' Version, 2003) stretches the veracity of parody farther by transforming the retainers of the puppet play and Kabuki into disgruntled "office ladies" who try to reach a timely consensus in a leaderless group in a modern-day corporate lunchroom. As is pointed out by critics, the legend of Chūshingura is such that it can be, and has been, used to justify just about any ideology or theory.[11] Such being case, any theory that attempts to generalize the theme of a single play to make it stand for the entire Japanese culture, would be ill-founded (to say the least).

Conclusion

Additional evidence can be cited to support my contention in this paper. For example, the Japanese Kabuki repertoire contains plays, such as *Kataki uchi tenkajaya mura* (The Revenge at Tenkajaya, 1781)[12] and *Ehon taikōki* (The Picture Book of Taiko, 1799),[13] that depict retainer-lord relationships drastically different from that in *Chūshingura*. Or, Inoue Hisashi's 1985 short story *Fu chūshingura* (The Treasury of Disloyal Retainers), intended to reveal the absurdity of making the rare case of Akō retainers stand for the ideal of loyalty of the entire Japanese of all the time.[14] But the above should be sufficient to suggest that the proposal in question, while valid when applied to the puppet play *Chūshingura*, is invalid — indeed even dangerous given the current tense Sino-Japanese relationship and the rising nationalism in both countries — when generalized. First, it prevents us from correctly understanding the fundamental contradictions of Japanese society. The discourse on the Akō Incident indicates that "in Japan ... the historical conflict between feudal morality and central power was unresolvable. An act of revenge could indeed be both illegal and moral" (McMullen 2003:299). This contradiction underlies the commendation of the Akō retainers by the Meiji emperor and the banning of vendetta by the Meiji government and much of the subsequent discourse on Chūshingura in modern times. Secondly, it advocates stereotypes in not only generalizing the absolute loyalty in the play *Chūshingura* but also attributing it to a timeless uniqueness of Japan (*riben de guoqing guoli*) (Ge 1995:95). In so doing, it in fact agrees with Haga Yaichi that loyalty to the emperor and patriotism is part of the inherent (and therefore unchangeable) characteristics of the Japanese (Miyazawa 2001:86–87). Thirdly, it completely ignores the changing themes of the Chūshingura legend and the dynamics with which history, literature and politics intertwined with each other, particularly in the history of modern Japan.

BALL STATE UNIVERSITY

Notes

Acknowledgment. I wish to thank the two anonymous referees for their insightful comments and helpful suggestions on an earlier draft of this essay. I also wish to thank Professor Cody Poulton, University of Victoria, for generously sharing a translation, in manuscript form, of Hirata Oriza's play *OL Chūshingura* by him and Hiroko Matsuda.

1. Focusing on the topic of drama, Ge's article argues that despite the mutual influence in history between China and Japan, each of the two cultures maintains a distinctive tradition: the beauty of Japanese drama is seen in its emphasis on human emotions (*qing mei*) while that of Chinese drama on virtue (*shan mei*).

2. For a discussion on the absence of definitive evidence of the nature of the dispute between Asano and Yoshinaka, see Smith (2003:4–5). Also see Miyazawa (1999:18–33).

3. See Donald Keene's comments in his introduction to *Chūshingura* by Takeda Izumo, Miyoshi Shōraku and Namiki Senryū, translated by Donald Keene (New York: Columbia University Press, 1971), 1. (Hereafter referred to as *Chūshingura*.)

4. For a more detailed discussion on this, see (Miyazawa 1999:214-215) and James McMullen, "Confucian Perspectives on the Akō Revenge: Law and Moral Agency" *Monumenta Nipponica* 58:1 (Autumn, 2003): 298.

5. For a more detailed discussion of this, also see McMullen, 299-302, 304-307.

6. For a more detailed discussion on this, also see McMullen, 302-307.

7. For a fuller discussion of how the Akō Incident has been reinterpreted in modern Japanese literature, see Miyazawa 2001, 109-165.

8. Oozasa Yoshio, "Chūshingura, sono parodi to kaigai kara no me" *Kokubungaku kaishaku to kyōzai no kenkyū* 31:15 (December 1986): 98-101.

9. Oozasa, 101-102.

10. Masubuchi Takeshi, "Sakuhin hyō: 47 nin no shikaku" *Kinema junpō* 1145 (October 1994): 52. Also see Inoue Hisahi, Ikemiya Shōichirō, and Maruya Saiichi, "Ima naze chūshingura ka" *Bungei shunjū* 72:14 (November 1994): 262-264.

11. Inoue Hisahi, Ikemiya Shōichirō, and Maruya Saiichi, "Ima naze chūshingura ka?" *Bungei shunjū* 72:14 (November 1994): 262-264.

12. Translated by Julie A. Iezzi. See James R. Brandon and Samuel L. Leiter, edited. *Kabuki Plays On Stage*, vol. 2: *Villainy and Vengeance, 1773-1799* (Honolulu: University of Hawai'i Press, 2002), 19.

13. Ibid., 368.

14. Inoue Hisahi, "*Morimura Seiichi to no taidan*" *Shūkan asahi*, May 21, 1982. Cited in Imamura Tadasumi, "Gendai bungaku no naka no *Chūshingura*: Inoue Hisashi, *Fu chūshingura*" *Kokubungaku kaishaku to kyōzai no kenkyū* 31:15 (December 1986): 122.

References Cited

Ge Shumin, "*Qing mei yu shan mei: zhong ri xi ju chuan tong de yi tong.*" *Xi ju* 2 (1995): 92–98.

Inose Naoki. "Makkāsā no *Chūshingura*." *Bungei shinjū* 65:5 (April 1987): 36–47.

McMullen, James. "Confucian Perspectives on the Akō Revenge: Law and Moral Agency." *Monumenta Nipponica* 58:1 (Autumn 2003): 293–315.

Miyazawa Seiichi. *Akō rōshi: tsumugidasareru chūshingura*. Tokyo: Sanseidō, 1999.

_____. *Kindai Nihon to "Chūshingura" gensō*. Tokyo: Aoki shoten, 2001.

_____. "*Kindai Chūshingura no shoruikei.*" *Rekishi ryōron* (September 2001): 43–7.

Smith, Henry D. II. "The Capacity of Chūshingura." *Monumenta Nipponnica* 58:1 (Spring 2003): 1–42.

Takeda Izumo, Miyoshi Shōraku and Namiki Senryū. *Chūshingura (The Treasury of Loyal Retainers)*. Translated by Donald Keene. New York: Columbia University Press, 1971.

17

On Not Knowing
Greek Drama
A Review Essay

Sarah Hamilton Nooter

Dillon, J., and S. E.Wilmer. Ed. *Rebel Women: Staging Ancient Greek Drama Today.* London: Methuen, 2005. Pp. xxv + 272. Hardcover. £20.00.

Hall, E., and F. Macintosh. *Greek Tragedy and the British Theatre 1660–1914.* Oxford: Oxford University Press, 2005. Pp. xxiv + 723. Hardcover. $115.00.

McLaughlin, E. *The Greek Plays.* New York: Theatre Communications Group, 2005. Pp. xx + 394. Paperback. $18.95.

Svich, C. Ed. *Divine Fire: Eight Contemporary Plays Inspired by the Greeks.* New York: Back Stage Books, 2005. Pp. 415. Paperback. $19.95.

Classicists everywhere can take comfort in the apparent fact that the world has not forgotten their keep. Scholars of drama especially ought to feel the wealth, for at the present moment attempts to grapple with the forty odd tragedies and comedies we are lucky to have inherited from fifth-century Athens are prodigious, sincere, and wide-ranging. Two such books offer an abundance of new adaptations: *The Greek Plays* is a collection of eight re-workings by the formidable New York playwright, Ellen McLaughlin. *Divine Fire*, edited by Caridad Svich, is a collection of eight works of performance by as many contemporary playwrights. These sixteen turns on Greek drama are likely to cause readers and audiences to reflect on our societal absorption with a theatrical world that thrived for barely a hundred years twenty-five centuries ago. Certainly the authors of these adaptations themselves, in a generous bevy of introductions proffered by the two books, are constantly wondering aloud what they/we are doing — and what is done to us — when we return to the Greeks to look at ourselves.

As we learn from two new critical books on the subject, this compulsion to grapple with the show business of the Greeks has been fermenting in Western civilization since we hit the modern era. *Greek Tragedy and the*

British Theatre 1660–1914 and *Rebel Women: Staging Ancient Greek Drama Today* both explore the development and implications of our society's relentless return to the Greeks to satisfy our current dramatic needs. In fact, if there is one element that seems to distinguish this moment dramatically from those of our more recent history, it is perhaps this critical compulsion to grapple with our own grappling — that is, not just to succeed to the Greeks' cultural bequest as feckless heirs, but to analyze scrupulously these encounters with our theatrical past much like a patient in search of the meaning of his dreams.

The eight dramas of Ellen McLaughlin's *The Greek Plays* span ten years' worth of McLaughlin's forays into the field of Greek drama. McLaughlin's process of adaptation is well-considered and often beautifully explained in the introductions to each play. The experiences of women and the effects of war especially are *leitmotifs*, both in McLaughlin's own commentaries and in the adaptations themselves. Of course these are topics not at all foreign to Greek tragedy, but in the earlier works of *The Greek Plays* the author's political prerogatives and her self-consciousness about the original tragedies' cultural heft can add a stilted and arid quality to the text. At worst, her characters merely articulate what might be considered the subtext of the originals, as Chrysothemis does when discussing Electra in *Iphigenia and Other Daughters*: "This is what she wants. That I always be watching, from some high clean place. This is my importance" (28). Well, sure, but do we need to be *told* that? What ever happened to showing?

The plays, however, gain in subtlety and nuance as the book progresses. A particular highlight is the *Lysistrata*, adapted for the Brooklyn Academy of Music's performance during the Lysistrata Project of March 2003, when thousands of performances of Aristophanes's comedy were staged worldwide to protest the advent of the Iraq War. I was lucky enough to be a spectator at that performance and my impressions of the McLaughlin script have been reinforced by my latest re-reading: it is a delightful experience, whether watched or read. McLaughlin would do well to try her hand at more comedy, for which she has a naturally buoyant touch. The final work of *The Greek Plays* is *Oedipus Rex*, performed in 2005. It is the most fully realized of the collection, endowed with complementing aspects of innovation and faithfulness to Sophocles's characterizations. McLaughlin's excellent introduction to this piece chronicles her "initial reluctance" (321) to work on *Oedipus* (or, better put: "why I find this play somewhat repellent" [314]) and her subsequent honest and fruitful examination of the play. "We are all walking miracles, no less than Oedipus is, all of us saved by a strange mercy for an obscure purpose" (322). This observation, and others like it, can be seen to enrich the play she has created.

Divine Fire offers something completely different. Edited by Caridad Svich, it runs the gamut of source material and style. These plays are billed as having been "inspired by the Greeks," which is aptly loose, given their great range of adaptive freedom. Svich informs us in an ambitious introduction that "a new group of playwrights [is] creating a contemporary canon of work shot through with a cyber pulse that speaks to our times" (18). The results of such efforts are naturally mixed. Certain plays of *Divine Fire* do not read well: *The Electra Fugues* by Ruth E. Margraff and *Iphigenia Crash Land Falls on The Neon Shell That Was Once Her Heart (a Rave Fable)* by editor Svich are evidently more performance pieces than plays, which is to say — or hope — that the written word does not do them justice. Margraff's *Electra Fugues* is, in fact, the libretto of an opera, intended to be performed in a variety of vocal modes that range from "sung and scored full throttle" to "half-spoken, half-sung" (169) and so on. Svich's *Iphigenia Crash* uses a psychedelic video backdrop as its primary mode of creative expression. Both pieces ultimately struck me as overly reliant on non-textual effects and rather willfully "gutsy." Too much cyber pulse there perhaps.

The more successful plays of this volume were in fact gutsy, but seemed more sincerely to dive forward the depths that the Greeks themselves plumbed. John Jesurun's *Philoktetes* and Charles Mee's *True Love*—one of three versions of the Phaedra story on hand herein — are the collection's best. The former is the more impressionistic, structured in a series of separately titled scenes and monologues that layer and re-layer the characterizations and dramatic set-pieces of Sophocles's original (as the play promises: "First, I'll give the clue, then the story, then/ the real story" [74]). There is in this *Philoktetes* a good deal of outside material, both mythological and modern, as well as poetry and humor: "PHILOKTETES: A battalion of hydra-headed epileptics couldn't/ have stopped you from coming back for the bow./ Am I right or am I wrong?" (83). *True Love* by Charles Mee explores various experiences of sex and love by way of a "chorus" of disparate contemporary characterizations (that are not so fully developed to truly form characters). The play nevertheless remains proximate to the movement of Euripides's *Hippolytus*. The perspectives offered are piercing in isolation and jarring in juxtaposition. They include a father's account of incest with his daughter, a woman's monologue on cutting herself, a man's disgust with the sexual act itself, and more mundane accounts of quotidian sexual existence (e.g. "I'd say, a lot of what passes for my sexuality goes on invisibly/ inside my head" [234]). The proliferation of viewpoints on sex and love arrayed around the central Euripidean story of a woman's attraction to her step-son, cast provocatively here as a thirteen-year-old boy, is a dynamic spin on Euripides's play that is also independently powerful.

Mee's *True Love*, along with the other two adaptations of *Hippolytus* in *Divine Fire*, would be perfect fodder for *Rebel Women: Staging Ancient Greek Drama Today*. It examines not only the circumstances under which female dramatic characters like Phaedra have scared up so much interest, but also the degree to which this interest reflects elements of the surrounding society. For though the stated aim of *Rebel Women* is to examine "the representation of ancient Greek heroines both in their original contexts and in the modern world" (xiii), its wider reach is more ambitious still, extending to the significant question of how these acts of adaptation affect us now: "[t]hese Greek tragedies ... can become vehicles in modern production to highlight the power relationships between men and women in marriage and the right of women to rebel against patriarchal oppression" (xx). The volume is split into three thematically organized clusters: "International Adaptations," "Irish Versions," and "Rebel Women in Ancient Drama." The articles are generally directed toward generalists as opposed to experts in any given field. Even the book's third section, the classics corner, is light fare, carefully honed to offer uninitiated readers perspectives that are gently informative but not overwhelming. All well and good, but classicists looking for research on female acts of solidarity and subversion in ancient texts would be better advised to turn their attention to meatier treatments of the same topic, such as those by Helene Foley, Froma Zeitlin, and Mark Griffith. On the whole, *Rebel Women* gives its readers a mix, both topically and qualitatively, but the essays that succeed make for truly pleasurable reading.

The four essays of the book's first section, "International Adaptations," explore the working of various Greek tragedies in particular contemporary or modern historical contexts. These are, respectively, present-day Ireland, Greece in the seventies (by way of two films of Michael Cacoyannis), French colonialism in the thirties, and Soviet Russia in the early twenties. Nearly every adaptation discussed in this section is based on a work of Euripides (*Iphigenia at Aulis* twice, *Medea*, and *Electra*). This strong predominance of the latest of the three great tragedians of Athens seems likely to spring from both the inherently political nature of Euripides's oeuvre and the highly politicized nature of today's theatrical environment. Aristophanes, the political playwright *par excellence* of classical Athens, is also represented here.

Three of the four essays of the "Irish Versions" section of *Rebel Women* are formatted in much the same manner: adaptations of Greek tragedies are used as focal points for political issues of the time (recent) and place in which they were produced. Anthony Roche's article on "Kennelly's Rebel Women," which examines versions of *Antigone*, *Medea*, and *The Trojan Women* by the contemporary Irish poet Brendan Kennelly, is to be singled out for the superiority of its insight. Roche's literary remarks about both Kennelly and the ancient authors involved are specific and acute. Roche observes, for example, that Creon "addresses Antigone, not by name, but by gender, as girl, with overtones of contempt, objectification and denial of their kinship" (153). Such commentary goes a good deal further towards instructing the reader in the elements that add up to a diegetic world polarized by gender than do other essays herein which merely assert (often by quoting other people's assertions) that the world of the play or place at hand is polarized by gender.

The fourth essay of the "Irish" section of *Divine Fire*, Seamus Heaney's piece, a mere scrap of a hand-wag at five pages, is a gem. It is the poet's charming and unpretentious account of his process towards coming up with a means of and *raison d'être* for translating Sophocles's *Antigone*. Heaney frankly describes his initial diffidence regarding the project ("How many *Antigones* could Irish theatre put up with?" [170]) before arriving at his moment of inspiration, framing it as only a poet could: "Theme and tune coalesced. Purchase on a language, a confidence amounting almost to a carelessness, a found pitch — all arrived in a breath" (171).

Greek Tragedy and the British Theatre 1660–1914, by Edith Hall and Fiona Macintosh, is quite another matter and nothing if not comprehensive. Its presumed audience is constituted by scholars — those of the history of theatre and of Britain itself, as well as of the reception of Greek tragedy — and it will stand on shelves as the definitive text on its subject. It will probably also weigh down those shelves, as it is a considerably unwieldy work. Its chronological scope is demarcated by the Restoration on the one hand and World War I on the other, which extent of time the authors claim is "precisely the period during which Greek tragedies were tentatively rediscovered and eventually came fully of age as playscripts for performance, and assumed the roles in public theatre similar to those they fulfill today" (vii––viii).

The book, lengthy and detailed, does not confine itself always to the rigors of chronology, reaching frequently forward and back to supplement political, aesthetic backgrounds and outcomes. A healthy knowledge of modern British history is virtually required on the part of a reader to keep up. Still, there is a general historical thrust to the tome as a whole that is most neatly encapsulated in its dealings with treatments of Sophocles's *Oedipus Rex*, with which the book begins and ends. At the start is Lee and Dryden's 1678 Restoration version, the "'English' *Oedipus*, [which] was to become in the long run indistinguishable from the Sophoclean original in the public imagination" (5). Towards the latter part of the nineteenth and the beginnings of the twentieth century, proponents of *Oedipus* were struggling to release the censorious hold of the Theatre Regulation Act of 1843 on the play and British audiences were expressing their newly donned buttoned-up mores in recoiling from a notorious German "Nietszchean-inspired" production of *Oedipus*, directed by Max Reinhardt, in favor of an apparently less Dionysian and more cerebrally Apolline French adaptation. But readers should forget trying to grasp the fate of *Oedipus* in the British theatre if they are not ready to grapple with the public's taste at any given moment for incest (the Elizabethans and Jacobeans were fascinated by it [8], the Tudors appreciated it as metaphor for "political corruption" [9], the Victorians ... well, you know). Readers should also expect to engage with the politics of the monarchy in the seventeenth and eighteenth centuries and the ever-increasing British preoccupation in the nineteenth with what we might call family values, as laws and practices that systemized marriage, kinship, and parentage were put into effect. Such cultural elements richly inform Hall's and Macintosh's accounts of *Medeas, Antigones, Iphigenias, Ions*, and so forth.

The text is, additionally, finely annotated and generously equipped with illustrations of source material, including manuscript frontispieces, engravings, portraits, political cartoons, and more. Given that the book's material is not pared down for the reader's ease, it will, when taught to undergraduates, require the firm guidance of an instructor in extracting the narrative from the nuance, but the effort should be met by great payoff in the richness and diversity of the subject matters at hand. Hall and Macintosh inform us that "[o]ur book is intended to tell part of the story of how a rather different British public imagined Greek antiquity. For ... Greek tragedy ... has been a crucial medium through which people untrained in Greek or Latin could have access to classical mythology" (ix). The authors and the work itself posit that the influence of Greek tragedy is significant because of how theatre acts as a common — that is, (fairly) non-elitist — meeting-place within culture, bearing the imprint of and giving expression to the artistic and political tenor of each time and place. Each of the four books reviewed here serves to remind us that in every re-awakening of these sleeping (but surely not dead) texts, dormant parts of our cultural and political selves are also awakened, laid bare, and changed.

COLUMBIA UNIVERSITY

Review of Literature:
Selected Books

Philip C. Kolin. *Understanding Adrienne Kennedy.* Columbia: University of South Carolina Press, 2005. Pp. 192. Hardcover $34.95.

Playwright Adrienne Kennedy's oeuvre is largely defined by its complexity and resistance to absolute clarity and comprehension. In the introduction to *Understanding Adrienne Kennedy*, Philip Kolin admits that "While Kennedy is not an easy author to read, her challenging works pay rich dividends" (xi). Claudia Barnett similarly notes that "Taken individually, each of her plays is a burst of poetic violence that somehow relates to the playwright's life; taken as a whole, however, her writing becomes a multilayered puzzle to challenge audiences and readers who feel compelled to 'know' the playwright — a *coup-de-grace* performance in itself" (Barnett 157). It is the abstruse nature of her writing and its refusal to conform to earlier paradigms of black aestheticism that, I suspect, has allowed her little more than a nebulous existence within (or rather outside) the American and African-American literary canons.

Though Kennedy has continued to maintain an illustrious and prolific career since the production of her Obie-winning drama *Funnyhouse of a Negro* (1964), her name bears little recognition among many literary students and scholars. Coming of age as an African-American dramatist at the height of the Black Arts Movement brought with it a certain set of expectations, primarily that one's artistic productions would "link his work to the struggle for his liberation and the liberation of his brothers and sisters" (Neal 80). While Kennedy's earlier work broached issues of colonialism, self-hatred, miscegenation, black nationalism — all of which remained predominant concerns for arbiters of the Black Arts Movement — her rendering of racial hegemony and its various cultural and social manifestations subverted a strictly black-white dichotomy.

Instead, Kennedy exposed the "intricacies of race" (Kennedy viii) or what Sharon P. Holland has referred to as the "intimacy" of race as a means to underscore the complicated and interdependent nature of racialized identities, both black and white. In Kennedy's work, the quest for a singular and unified racial self is often revealed as an ill-fated and often deadly enterprise. Kennedy's articulation of the blurred, and often imaginary, boundaries between racial lines may have been considered anti-revolutionary or perhaps traitorous in the 1960s. However, for a more contemporary audience Kennedy's postmodern dramas serve as rich and constructive resources that speak directly to issues of race, gender, politics, cultural

215

identity, and transnationalism, and her multifarious treatment of the aforementioned categories effectively contributes to current critical race, psychoanalytic, and feminist discourses. Within the past decade scholars have begun to take on the challenge of getting to "know" or "understand" Adrienne Kennedy, recognizing the wealth of such critical possibilities. As such, Kolin ventures a monumental and ambitious task with *Understanding Adrienne Kennedy* by providing a comprehensive analysis of each Kennedy work from *Funnyhouse of a Negro* (1964) to *The Alexander Plays* (1992).

Kolin manages the task suitably by offering detailed biographical information interspersed throughout what may be considered canonical readings and providing little known but useful references to such features as set design, castings, and critical reception. Rather than advance a singular argument, Kolin presents multiple analytical quotes from Kennedy scholars to formulate a generalized perspective on the works. While this method gives the reader a broad scope of interpretive meaning, Kolin's lack of engagement with such scholars offers little in the way of depth.

The first chapter, "A War of Selves in *Funnyhouse of a Negro*," opens with a genealogy of the play: Kennedy's voyage to West Africa as its inspiration, her acceptance to Edward Albee's Playwrights' Workshop and his subsequent influence as a mentor and teacher, cast credits for the first Off Broadway performance, and a brief historical context for the production. Such information proves useful in attempting to ground and contextualize Kennedy's drama, which Kolin describes as "short, intense jabs to the psyche" (2). Following Kolin's historical grounding of *Funnyhouse* is a satisfactory summary and brief analysis of

the work that would prove invaluable for the perplexed undergraduate but perhaps underwhelming and oversimplified for the literary scholar. To describe Sarah's "tragic mulatto" status and her ensuing desire for whiteness, Kolin writes that "Tormented by racist views of herself, Sarah cannot avoid the delusions of her funnyhouse breakdown when she looks at herself or at others. In this funnyhouse of her mind, Sarah's fear and guilt become magnified, distorted, dismembered. She has no perspective" (36). Kolin continually points to the fragmented nature of Kennedy's protagonists in *The Owl Answers, A Rat's Mass*, and *A Movie Star Has to Star in Black and White*, but does little to distinguish the bifurcated personas of the protagonists and explore the extent to which each maintains a distinctive character even though her psychological dilemma revolves around similar conflicts of race and family. Without previous knowledge of the plays, one might assume that all the protagonists in these works are afflicted with identical psychoses.

But particularly noteworthy about *Understanding Adrienne Kennedy* are Kolin's sections on Kennedy's later works, *She Talks to Beethoven, Film Club, Dramatic Circle,* and *The Ohio State Murders*, which offer thoughtful examinations of the themes of racism and identity (cultural, national, historical) that continue to motivate Kennedy as she broadens and matures her scope as both a woman and writer. He effectively outlines the intertextuality of the four plays, which are loosely bound around the central figure, Suzanne Alexander, who also functions as Kennedy's "complex persona" (116). Kolin rightly acknowledges that the "unifying theme of the *Alexander Plays* is the triumph of art, music, and love over violence and prejudice" (117) — a sharp inversion of her earlier plays in which each of these themes was consistently defeated if even explored. The final section of *Understanding Adrienne Kennedy* disrupts its chronological pattern and focuses on the thematic unity of Kennedy's more overtly political plays. As Kolin explains, each play "concentrates on the tragic fate of a real-life black man whose identity and worth are attacked by a racist society" (147–148). But even Kennedy's most explicit politicism remains "poetic" and "experimental" by taking on the form of the choreopoem as in *Sun: A Poem for Malcolm X Inspired by His Murder* and *An Evening With Dead Essex*, which "comprises conversations among the director and actors of the play-within-the-play as they watch slides of Essex — from his boyhood in Kansas to his death from over one hundred police bullets" (153).

While Kolin describes Kennedy's canon as "unsettlingly postmodern — surrealistic, dreamlike," "disturbing, complex, hypnotic" (2), his readings attempt to concretize meaning and neatly situate Kennedy within the (perhaps, too limiting) spaces of critical race and feminist studies. The thrust of Kennedy's drama is its very undoing of meaning — its various tensions, anxieties, fragments, and dreaminess invite a sense of unease that the audience must necessarily assume in order to more fully experience the psychological tightrope her protagonists are often made to walk. For those who have not yet or just begun to encounter the complex and often incomprehensible world of Adrienne Kennedy, *Understanding Adrienne Kennedy* may be the best place to begin the journey.

References

Barnett, Claudia. "'An Evasion of Ontology': Being Adrienne Kennedy." *TDR: The Drama Review: A Journal of Performance Studies* 49.3 (2005): 157–86.

Kennedy, Adrienne. *Deadly Triplets: A Theatre Mystery and Journal.* Minneapolis: University of Minnesota Press, 1990.

Neal, Larry. "And Shine Swam On: An Afterword." *Black Fire: An Anthology of Afro-American Writing*, edited by Leroi Jones and Larry Neal, 638–56. Reprinted in *African American Literary Theory: A Reader*, edited by Winston Napier, 69–80. New York: New York University Press 2000.

BADIA SAHAR AHAD
Loyola University Chicago

John J. White. *Bertolt Brecht's Dramatic Theory.* Rochester, NY: Camden House, 2004. Pp. 348. Hardcover $90.00.

Any effort to elucidate Bertolt Brecht's hugely influential theoretical writings on theatre as a single body of work faces significant complications. Not only did Brecht — quite understandably — change his mind a good deal between the early 1920s and his death in 1956, but his trajectory during those years took him from the ill-fated Weimar Republic via a decade and a half in exile in Europe and the United States, and finally to the German Democratic Republic. As a result, Brecht was obliged to calibrate his statements for particular audiences and situations far more than he might have done given stability and continuity. Temperamentally, moreover, Brecht was disposed to be poetically indirect rather than to strive for maximum transparency. John J. White deserves considerable credit both for taking on the challenge of analyzing Brecht's theory as a whole, and for doing so in a manner that never loses sight of those complexities.

White approaches the sprawling mass of Brecht's theoretical writings — nearly 4,000 pages in the recently published 20-volume German edition — via what he calls two kinds of "soundings": first, "a selective focus on the most influential writings and some that have been unwarrantedly underestimated"; second "focused close readings of chosen passages and arguments" (24). The texts White chooses to analyze in his five chapters include several one might have anticipated: the 1930 notes to *Mahagonny*, the *Short Organon* (1948), and the uncompleted *Messingkauf* project. He spends little time on the theory relating to feuds such as the "*Realismusdebatte*" or to Brecht's *Lehrstücke*, for reasons he explains in the introduction. White's most interesting decision is to devote a chapter to Brecht's dramaturgical poems — a choice that reflects his valuable emphasis throughout on the widely varying genres and styles of writing in which Brecht formulated his ideas.

The first chapter presents a meticulous reading of the "*Anmerkungen zur Oper* Aufstieg und Fall der Stadt Mahagonny," which Brecht wrote in 1930, but the most famous element of which — the table contrasting the epic with the dramatic form of theatre — he revised several times in subsequent years. White leads the reader through the essay section by section, demonstrating how Brecht's assertions relate to, for instance, the influence of mentors like Fritz Sternberg, and the action of the opera itself. As he does so, White helpfully homes in on how we might best understand Brecht's often elusive points, and contextualizes those arguments in a longer-term historical perspective, e.g., "That is to say, Epic Theater will be unacceptable to bourgeois aesthetics, but it is bourgeois aesthetics itself that will go under in the resultant struggle. Prefigured here are also later ideological differences between the perspectives of East and West German commentators on this transitional phase of Brecht's development" (37). And White carefully explores the reasons behind and implications of Brecht's rhetorical strategies: "The end of the essay's first paragraph is so formulated as to make Brecht seem like a lone voice in a deceptively avant-garde wilderness, isolated because of his call for a fundamental discussion of first principles" (40). He does not, however, hesitate to find fault with Brecht's exposition of his ideas: "Brecht's position is not always helped by an undifferentiating concept of aesthetic distance" (64). By the close of White's "sounding" of the *Mahagonny* notes and their revisions, he has presented many valid and often original arguments about Brecht's theoretical views of the 1930s, and a particularly valuable analysis of the problematic dramatic/epic table.

The remaining four chapters of *Bertolt Brecht's Dramatic Theory* proceed in a similar fashion in examining a varied range of later texts. The issues Brecht and, therefore, White deal with at most length include *Verfremdung* and how it relates to empathy; historicization; the role of the emotions, and of pleasure, in audience response in the theatre; the balance between aesthetic and sociopolitical considerations; and the significance of other theatre practitioners whose positions Brecht discussed, especially Stanislavsky and Piscator. Throughout, White points instructively to connections among Brecht's writings, and to the — often quite decisive — constraints placed on Brecht by the circumstances he found himself in. And he frequently provides valuable summations, as in this characterization of the "double agenda" of the *Messingkauf* project: "to test, and find wanting, certain theater practices, and to explain the solution: Epic Theater's method of engaging dialectically with society" (261).

One major contribution of White's study is its demonstration that the techniques Brecht employed in his dramatic writing also operate in his theoretical work. As White puts it, Brecht is "extremely ingenious in the ways he applies what might be thought of as specifically 'Brechtian' strategies of defamiliarization to the theoretical points he wishes to get across" (10). At times, however, White's focus on such strategies takes center stage for rather too long, interfering with the more valuable project of teasing out just what Brecht was advocating. Similarly, White often dwells for longer than necessary on the details of the texts' origins and publication history. Repeatedly I found myself wishing that certain minutiae regarding when exactly a particular text might have been composed or revised had been relegated to a foot- or endnote.

The most disappointing feature of this rigorously researched and clear-headed study is the fact that no translations of Brecht's original texts are included, so that only theatre scholars and students who have studied German to an advanced level will fully benefit from White's work. In his introduction, White writes in reference to the new German edition of Brecht's works (*Grosse kommentierte Berliner und Frankfurter Ausgabe*) and the purpose of his own book: "The fact that there is little likelihood of *GBA* appearing in an English translation in the near future means that there will continue to be a specific need for mediation between state-of-the-art information available in the German-speaking world and a continuing reliance on Willett's *Brecht on Theatre* and *The Messingkauf Dialogues*" (24). It is difficult to see how much mediation White's book will actually carry out between current German scholarship and those non-German-speaking readers who wish they did not still depend so much on two books published in the 1960s.

Bertolt Brecht's Dramatic Theory was published in a German Studies series, and was clearly conceived as a contribution to that field rather than to Theatre Studies. White assiduously takes account of a wealth of secondary material on Brecht's theory in English and German, but deals little with the reception of Brecht's ideas by theatre practitioners. That emphasis is unfortunate. In principle, White has done a great service to English-speaking scholars and students of theatre who wish to engage in depth with Brecht's theoretical writings in all their richness, challenges, and contradictions; in practice, however (failing a second edition with English translations, which would be a splendid idea), this book will sadly find far fewer theatrically minded readers than it deserves to.

NEIL BLACKADDER
Knox College

Mary F. Brewer. *staging whiteness.* Middletown, CT: Wesleyan University Press, 2005. Pp. xvi + 236. Hardcover $65.00. Paperback $24.95.

The category of "White" is as much a racial designation as the terms "African-American" or "Asian," and yet few consider how Whiteness as a racial category is constructed. We seem to engage in conversations about race only when the literary text before us introduces characters who are Black, Hispanic, or Asian, thus allowing Whiteness to reproduce itself as racially unmarked. White characters represent the typical, universal family because of historical bias and literary precedent. Race theorists purport to destabilize this precedent by analyzing how both Black *and* White races are depicted in literature and culture, not as biological entities, but as social constructions. White practitioners of race theory have an additional responsibility; as they hold themselves accountable for their own White privilege, they must reflect upon the meaning of Whiteness and how it derives its values of authority and dominance by representing non-White races as inferior and powerless.

Mary F. Brewer's work of theatre criticism, *staging whiteness*, does precisely that. She examines how theatre has contributed to a formation of the White "race" in both England and the United States and has reproduced White hegemonic power in its art. In a series of eight chapters, she considers the major works of theatrical history, dividing them into periods of time approximately twenty years long and preceding each chapter's discussion with a historical and political introduction. Her comprehensive discussion moves through the entire twentieth century, from G. B. Shaw's *Captain Brassbound's Conversion* in 1900 to David Hare's *The Absence of War* in 1993. She considers writers as varied as verse dramatists W. H. Auden and Christopher Isherwood, Black feminists Adrienne Kennedy and Suzan-Lori Parks, playwrights invested in postcolonial issues such as Philip Osment and Michael Ellis, and canonical writers such as Langston Hughes, Arthur Miller, and Lillian Hellman. Eugene O'Neill makes two appearances. Missing are Lorraine Hansberry's *Raisin in the Sun*, which critiques the racism of an all-White neighborhood association, and Anna Deavere Smith's *Fires in the Mirror*, a performance piece that significantly highlights social construc-

tions of race through the performances of one actor. Likewise there is no mention of plays written by Asian or Hispanic writers (David Henry Hwang's *M. Butterfly* would have been an ideal inclusion) in this discussion of how Whiteness as an identity is created upon the stage; it appears the primary oppositional binary by which Whiteness is constructed is against Blackness or variegated-White characters.

A particularly clear example of how an upper-crust British society can bolster its own sense of moral rightness by creating a fictive "other" appears in T. S. Eliot's verse drama *The Cocktail Party*, wherein a genteel group of society revelers discusses a British colony of indigenous people, the Kinkanja, who must be converted to Christianity. One character, Celia, travels as a missionary to Kinkanja and ends up being crucified by a rebel faction; her humanitarian efforts for a "handful of plague-stricken natives / who would have died anyway," as a character notes, have led to her own demise. And yet she is understood as the noble heroine who pursues a Christian calling among a society of small-minded elitists. Thus the play demonstrates White superiority in two ways: first, it highlights the racist Imperialists who view all non-White peoples as "heathens" — an element that is reinforced, Brewer notes, by the theatre reviewers' unquestioning acceptance of the racist images of "savages." And secondly, as Celia's martyrdom suggests, the play advocates the moral necessity of Christian guardianship. As Brewer sees the play, "Presumably she sacrifices herself for the benefit of those not fortunate enough to have been born White British" (51).

By his "highlighting Whiteness" throughout these plays, Brewer does important work towards eliminating the duplicitous rhetorical stance that posits that a play about Whites is "universal" and applies to the entire human race. A case in point is *The American Dream,* a play by Edward Albee, who, by creating a "picture of our time" (his words), satirizes the deteriorating values of a consumerist society, implying — through his choice to make the family White — that the White, middle-class family represents *all* of America. Brewer, through her reading of the play, reveals how the family yearns for a historic and mythic "White model of personal and social relations" (91) and that the particular values mourned in this satire — the sanctity of home and marriage, the importance of community — are decidedly White, Victorian values. The play ultimately suggests the necessity of recovering a more valid mode of White living, due in part to the play's one positive figure, the Grandmother, and her connection to a time period of America when racism was particularly high.

Brewer offers an insightful though debatable reading of the vagaries of White representation in Eugene O'Neill's *The Hairy Ape.* Carefully reading O'Neill's stage descriptions, she finds how he designates the men in the forecastle as belonging to the "civilized white races" even though they are all immigrants whose White status is questionable. Yank himself is a particular sort, a "representative of variegated Whiteness" as Brewer indicates (27) and thus serves to define what the pure White identity is by what he is *not.* The contrast between the young, wealthy, White woman, Mildred, and Yank, blackened from coal and crouching bestially before her, provides a strong impression of White power. The illustrative photograph from the play's production at the Plymouth Theatre appears on the cover of *staging whiteness* and emphasizes their disparity. The play challenges the American Dream; it illustrates that not

all Whites have access to its rewards. While a rudimentary reading of the play would limit itself to the basic idea that Yank cannot find any community in which he can connect (where he "fits"), Brewer suggests that Yank's inability to accept his "relative White status leads to his annihilation" (29).

The book is a polemic and, like most strong, one-sided arguments, reads that way. There is no room for subtle interpretations of the plays, such as character idiosyncrasies that denote human quirks rather than racial behavior. Thornton Wilder's play *Our Town* takes a critical hit for unquestioningly and naively marginalizing individuals who are not White Anglo-Saxon. Brewer looks at the Stage Manager's introduction to Grover's Corners where he calls to life Main Street by pointing out the Congregational, Presbyterian, Methodist, and Unitarian churches, while noting that the Baptist church is located in a "holla' by the river" and the Catholics are on the other side of the tracks. In a great many New England towns the sweeping spires of the churches are the first thing one sees on Main Street, and it is historical fact that Protestant sects settled these towns first, followed by other denominations that — either by social forces or self-choice — created their congregations a distance apart. To identify the town's religious segregation in this opening speech is helpful; but Brewer goes further, labeling the stage manager's discourse "an aggressive colonization of the concept of home as both foundation and property" and "a moment of symbolic violence in the play" (34). If that colonization of space occurred before the play was written, Wilder cannot be at fault for creating a Stage Manager who catalogues the buildings as he sees them.

The equation is circular: do society and history provide theatre with narrative material, or does theatre perpetuate stereotypical images that in turn influence society? Brewer seems to insist that theatre should work harder to eliminate such inequalities. She notes that Wendy Wasserstein's play *The Heidi Chronicles*, which won a Tony and Pulitzer Prize in 1989, "reinforces the domination of Whiteness" because it is about White, middle-class women and does not acknowledge racial or ethnic differences among these women. Wasserstein admits to writing about "upper middle-class people, who have good jobs, and they're good looking, and there's no problem," and sees them as "someone you knew in college." Brewer takes issues with the ideology behind this claim because Wasserstein's creation of a play about a presumably "typical" culture ultimately subordinates other races as "not typical" or "not normal." And yet, it seems unfair to deny Wasserstein the opportunity to create characters that resemble the people around her, if her friends *are* upper-middle class Whites, and to indict her play for reproducing "dominant power relations of race, class, and gender" (156) simply because she does not introduce racial difference into her play. While many White people *do* choose to remain complicit with White supremacy by ignoring the experiences of people of color, on the other hand it would be disingenuous of Wasserstein — or any writer — to engage creatively in material of which she knew nothing.

Brewer strives at the beginning of each chapter to provide a historical context of political events and historical trends that shaped a particular cultural moment. These are pointed historical overviews and often help her to examine the plays. Her tracing of the rise of neo-conservatism in the 1980s under the Reagan and Bush administrations, the ushering in of the religious right, and the spread of gay panic with the AIDS epidemic establishes nicely a foundation for understanding issues of sexual and racial identity in Tony Kushner's *Angels in America*. But at times the historical overviews appear one-sided as well; in her justified indictment of systematized racism in the seventeenth, eighteenth, and nineteenth centuries that opens up the first chapter, "'That's White of You....': Civilizing Whiteness," her summary elides any mention of abolitionist movements and impugns White British citizenry with phrases such as "All non-White ethnic groups continued to be held in common as being beneath their White rulers" (4).

Readings of certain plays require one to buy into initial premises in order to follow Brewer's subsequent logic. For example, an analysis of Tennessee Williams's *A Streetcar Named Desire* builds upon the following claims: Blanche DuBois wields the power of the phallus over Stanley (i.e., she is masculine) because she is from the wealthy plantation of Belle Reve and part of the Old South's system of patriarchy; Stanley possesses a non-White racial identity because several productions have cast him as a Black actor and he is identified by Williams as "Polish"; and Stella's mixed-race fetus threatens the purity of the White race, as indicated by the comparison Williams offers between Stella's post-coital, relaxed state and the "narcotized tranquility that is in the face of Eastern idols" (75). Following these ideational building blocks leads to the conclusion that "the struggle between Blanche and Stanley works to reposition the White subject outside the moral center by linking at different points both the White feminine and White masculine with moral corruption and brutishness" (77). In other words, Blanche and Stanley, as representations of Whiteness, both behave badly.

staging whiteness is written in lucid prose, which perhaps explains why it is so easy to take issue with some of the analyses Brewer makes. She does not hide behind theoretical jargon and her arguments make specific, concrete points (the exception may be her discussion of Adrienne Kennedy's *A Movie Star Has to Star in Black and White*, which lost me as the White male and female subject identities slipped between different racial discursive realities). Many of her chapters offer novel analyses of much-discussed plays. She opens up Amiri Baraka's *Dutchman* by focusing closely on which character possesses the gaze and how Clay's speech vocalizes publicly a Black perspective on Whiteness; that is, Lula's seduction and murder of Clay allowed audiences to understand for the first time a Black image of Whiteness.

Another original reading occurs with respect to Caryl Churchill's play *Cloud Nine*. The colonial setting of Act I, in which a Victorian family living in Africa relies upon the services of their Black servant, has commonly been understood as a metaphor for current-day gender and sexual oppression. The Black servant's racial oppression is not fully recognized as such, but used only as a measuring tool for gauging the degree of sexism and homophobia of latter-day England. While all the Victorian family roles continue into the second act, Brewer points out that Joshua's role does not transform into a corresponding Black character in Act II, preventing any meaningful examination of patriarchy and race and creating a "disturbing sense that the presence of Blacks is natural only within an African setting" (142). Likewise, her rich and complex reading of Tony Kushner's *Angels in America* demonstrates how the production exposes the White Monolith of Washington politics, the internal contradictions of Mormonism (and thus the religious right), and the way in which the American value system pits ethnic and racial minority groups against one another as depicted by the fight between the Black drag queen, Belize, and the central Jewish protagonist, Louis.

According to Linda Alcoff, White scholars interested in contributing to discussions of race must see the world around them through a kind of "white double consciousness" that "requires an ever-present acknowledgment of the historical legacy of white identity constructions in the persistent structures of inequality and exploitation" (Alcoff 1998:25). Mary Brewer opens her book with an anecdote of being in a restaurant with a Black man in the U. S. South and being made consciously aware of her own White identity by the stares of the people around her. This book acknowledges her responsibility as a White scholar and race theorist to see the world with a "double consciousness" and to offer corrective readings wherever possible.

Reference

Alcoff, Linda. "What Should White People Do?" in *Hypatia: Journal of Feminist Philosophy*, 13: 3 (Summer 1998), 6–26.

MIRIAM M. CHIRICO
Eastern Connecticut State University

James Fisher, ed. *Tony Kushner: New Essays on the Art and Politics of the Plays.* Jefferson, NC, and London: McFarland & Co., 2006. Pp. viii, 225. Paperback. $35.

Like many such volumes, this collection of eleven essays on Tony Kushner's work is a mixed bag. Some of the essays are solid additions to the large body of Kushner criticism; others read like mediocre term papers. What they share is a view of Kushner as a political playwright who seems almost prophetic in his critiques of American society. *Angels in America*, set in the Reagan era, is even more timely in the increasingly right wing America of George W. Bush. *Homebody/Kabul*, conceived before 9/11, resonates more during the War on Terror. Kushner's work dramatizes moments when rifts open up in the personal and political dimensions of human experience. As James Fisher puts it in his essay on *Homebody/Kabul*,

> From a position that can only be described as skeptical optimism, Kushner ponders those particular moments in history when the fabric of everyday life unravels. Finding that real and fundamental change may be possible in such dislocations, Kushner, a neosocialist, invites his audience to recognize and acknowledge the interconnectedness among diverse, seemingly incompatible cultures [192].

While this statement may seem to define most accurately the mix of British and Afghani characters in *Homebody/Kabul*, it is equally relevant to Jew and African American in *Caroline, or Change*, the odd panoply of characters in *Angels in America*, and even the mixture of Corneille and Kushner in *The Illusion*. This sense of interconnectedness and change is one *leitmotif* in these essays. Another is Kushner's relationship to Walter Benjamin's Angel of History surrounded by the detritus of the past but propelled toward an unknown future. Well over half of the volume is devoted to essays focusing on *Angels in*

America, followed by two essays apiece for *The Illusion* and *Homebody/Kabul* and single essays on Kushner's adaptation of *The Dybbuk* and his musical (with composer Jeanine Tesori), *Caroline, or Change*.

The collection gets off to a rocky start with a series of essays on influences on Kushner. James Fisher's essay on Tennessee Williams and Kushner rehashes material on Williams as a gay dramatist that has been discussed more fully and richly elsewhere, though, if one is to accept his list of works cited, he isn't very knowledgeable of scholarship on Williams or gay drama, nor does he make interesting connections between the plays of Williams and those of Kushner. Weaker still is Jeff Johnson's essay, which belabors the connection between William Inge's *Come Back, Little Sheba* and *Angels in America* as it tries unsuccessfully to equate Inge's Doc and Lola with Kushner's Louis and Prior. Yes, Prior makes a camp reference to Inge's melodrama. However, Johnson overdoes the notion of Inge's 1950 work as a crypto-gay play, "a centerpiece of gay politics and gender subversion," and, in the process, seems to suggest that playwrights like Inge and Tennessee Williams could not conceive of writing plays about heterosexuals, but created "gay dramas cleverly dressed up as straight theatre." This kind of reduction does these playwrights no good. Nor does he flatter Kushner by claiming that Kushner now has "a place alongside Inge within the pantheon of classic American playwrights" (39). I'd place Kushner a lot higher than that. Robert Vorlicky's comparison of the work of Adrienne Kennedy and Kushner is much more intelligently conceived, but Vorlicky pushes the idea of influence a bit too hard. David Garrett Izzo's long comparison of *Angels in America* with the anti-fascist plays of W.H. Auden and Christopher Isherwood written in the 1930s tells us far more about Auden and Isherwood than it does about Kushner. The best of the comparative essays, one of the two strongest contributions to the collection, is David Krasner's fascinating piece on Kushner's use of Hegel in *Angels in America*. Krasner uses Louis's discussion of a "neo-Hegelian positivist sense of constant historical progress towards happiness or perfection or something" as a means of measuring Louis's moral and spiritual growth in the play. The problems in Atsushi Fujita's essay on Roy Cohn are exemplified by his premise: "Roy Cohn ... does not appear as a completely evil person in *Angels*. He is notably portrayed as a forgivable person." Fujita asserts that Kushner has made Cohn "forgivable" so that gays will cease to be "pinklisted"; that is, tainted by the actions of bad homosexuals. The point of *Angels in America* is not that Cohn is forgivable, but that the act of forgiveness is essential if the world is to spin forward and the challenge of forgiveness is extending mercy to really awful people like Roy Cohn.

Two interesting essays focus on Kushner's adaptation of Corneille's *The Illusion*. Felicia Londré's short, informative work sets out the changes Kushner made to Corneille's fine play, while Stefka Mihaylova compares Giorgio Strehler's quasi-Brechtian production of the Corneille in Paris in 1984 with Kushner's use of Brechtian devices. For her, both versions fail as social critique.

Another pairing of essays focuses on productions of Kushner's work. Paula T. Alekson chronicles the genesis of Mark Lamos's premiere production of Kushner's adaptation of Ansky's *The Dybbuk* at Hartford Stage and the modifications made at the Public Theater. Jacob Juntenen offers a quasi-

semiotic analysis of a performance of *Homebody/Kabul* at the New York Theatre Workshop and the critical reception of the New York production.

The collection concludes with two strong essays on Kushner's recent work. James Fisher offers a cogent analysis of *Homebody/Kabul* as an optimistic commentary on our current political quagmire, though it doesn't give much sense of the intellectual and stylistic richness of the play. Bert Stern's short analysis of *Caroline, or Change* is one of the strongest, most eloquent essays in the volume. Stern hits the nail on the head about this brilliant musical theater work: "There is a sense of claustrophobia everywhere, life driven down into basements and odd corners, a picture that has its counterparts in the public and private lives of our time. Only in the children does the prospect of new growth appear" (202). This is a fitting finale to a volume celebrating Kushner's skepticism and optimism, his view of a world in which there have to be terrible crises before there can be progress.

While there are some contributions here that are worthy additions to the large body of Kushner criticism, there is too much chaff amidst the wheat.

JOHN M. CLUM
Duke University

Shannon Jackson. *Professing Performance: Theatre in the Academy from Philology to Performativity.* Theatre and Performance Theory Series. Cambridge: Cambridge University Press, 2004. Pp. 254. Hardcover $55.00, Paperback $24.00.

Shannon Jackson begins *Professing Performance* with a personal anecdote about an uncomfortable dinner conversation on the subject of "performativity" between herself, a dramaturg, and a director. Whether "in deans' offices, in department meetings, at academic conferences, in office hours, in rehearsals," or at work-related dinners such as the one Jackson describes (2), many faculty members in departments devoted to the study of performance will have experienced similar moments of tension relating to perceived divides between scholar and artist, theory and practice, performativity and performance. Fewer of us, however, will have thought about where and how these tensions originated. Jackson initially planned to write a "how-to manual" (x) for navigating the institutional constructions of knowledge that result in such awkward moments, but instead she has traced them back to their beginnings in the development of the study of performance over the course of the past century.

The introductory chapter of *Professing Performance*, entitled "Discipline and Performance: Genealogy and Discontinuity," establishes the context and methodology for the ensuing series of five approximately chronological case studies exemplifying key phases and issues in the history of the study of performance in the U.S. academy. "Performance" is shown here to have many — and often contradictory — connotations: it "is about doing, and it is about seeing; it is about image, embodiment, space, collectivity, and/or orality; it makes community and it breaks community; it repeats endlessly and it never repeats; it is intentional and unintentional, innovative and derivative, more fake and more real" (15). Drawing on the work of Michel Foucault, Jackson sets out to explore "'institutional genealogies' of knowledge formation" (5) by deconstructing the binaries and exposing the race, class, and gender dimensions embedded in this "non-unity of discourse" (4) relating to performance.

In the neatly titled chapters that follow, Jackson repeatedly demonstrates how purportedly "new" turns, transformations, and breaks in the history of the study of performance have inevitably been bound up in the very assumptions and methodologies that the proponents of the "new" professed to repudiate in the process of self-definition through strategic opposition to the "old." Her second and perhaps most engaging chapter, "Institutions and Performance: Professing Performance in the Early Twentieth Century," considers the academic career of George Pierce Baker in order to "interrogate terminologies and expose paradoxes that still affect and afflict the status of performance in today's university" (35). Through clever use of biographical evidence ranging from childhood memories to professional correspondence to student reminiscences, Jackson demonstrates "how the conventions of professionalization and curricular legitimation affected the development of theatre, rhetoric, and performance" (35).

In her next chapter, "Culture and Performance: Structures of Dramatic Feeling," Jackson considers the emergence of the seemingly recent field of cultural studies, suggesting that Raymond Williams's early work on dramatic literature established the grounds for his later cultural studies work by positing the relation of drama to the social through the notion of "structures of feeling." Williams's work on drama thus challenged the formalist emphases of mid-twentieth-century New Criticism, the decontextualized close reading methods which were at odds with the contextuality of drama, with the result that drama was marginalized or ignored altogether in favor of the literary genres of poetry and fiction. For Jackson, the "early alignments between the study of drama and the study of 'culture'" in the work of a scholar such as Williams "challenge assumptions of what is old and new, traditional and 'cutting edge,' in theatre and performance studies scholarship" (35).

Chapter 4, "Practice and Performance: Modernist Paradoxes and Literalist Legacies," brings together poststructuralist theorists Jacques Derrida and Paul de Man and modernist art critics Michael Fried and Clement Greenberg to demonstrate that "deconstruction's treatment of oral/performance supported rather than subverted modernist art criticism's suspicious treatment of the theatrical" (115). Although it begins with an intriguing instance of a "conversational stall" (111) between postmodern performance scholar Nick Kaye and Wooster Group director Elizabeth LeCompte, this chapter ultimately seems less sharply argued than Jackson's other case studies.

Chapter 5, "History and Performance: Blurred Genres and the Particularizing of the Past," considers the shift toward cultural anthropology and New Historicism as they intersected with the emergence of the interdisciplinary field of performance studies in the 1980s. Ranging over the work of Clifford Geertz, Stephen Greenblatt, and Erving Goffman among others, Jackson argues here that the turn toward "a focus on the detail, the local, and the particular has a gendered history" and, therefore, that "scholars of theatre and performance would do well to investigate the gendered consequences" of having applied anthropological and new historical paradigms in our own research (150).

Jackson's final chapter, "Identity and Performance: Racial Performativity and Anti-Racist Theatre," moves through the "culture wars" of the late twentieth century and into the present

moment as it explores the contested relationship between theatrical performance and theoretical concepts of performativity developed by J. L. Austin, Jacques Derrida, Judith Butler, and Eve Kosofsky Sedgwick. Through insightful readings of performance texts and events by Adrian Piper, Cherrié Moraga, Diana Son, Ntozake Shange, and Anna Deavere Smith, Jackson challenges the antitheatricality underlying much of the theoretical work on performativity and suggests how the work of these antiracist theatre and performance artists exemplifies "the performative contingencies of theatrical speech" (184).

The back cover of *Professing Performance* asserts that the book is intended "for students, artists, and scholars of performance and theatre," and Jackson's stated objectives for her study are to "ask colleagues, scholars, and students to allow the recognition of difference and contingency to structure our professional and disciplinary lives" and to offer "a way of thinking about institutional variety" (x). As it charts the various genealogies of the tensions between scholar and artist, theory and practice, performativity and performance, however, *Professing Performance* will, I suspect, be of greatest interest to those who identify primarily as scholars and theorists. Notably, the dinner companions that Jackson describes at the start of her book seem, at least in her retelling, oblivious to the discomfort that she herself feels: following her brief discourse on J.L. Austin's theory that "linguistic acts don't simply reflect a world but that speech actually has the power to *make* a world," the director picks up his fork and blithely replies, "Oh, [...] you mean like theatre" (2). There is a way in which the final chapter of *Professing Performance* ultimately comes to this same conclusion, but Jackson's framing of the dinner conversation as an awkward moment with only a "provisional resolution" (2) implies a gap that only she seems to perceive between her own and the director's understanding of the relationship between the philosophical concept of performativity and the theatrical practice of performance. Jackson identifies herself not only as a "professor of performance," but also as an occasional "performing professor" (218). I would have been interested to know how she imagines the dinner conversation might have played if all the participants had read her book.

PENNY FARFAN
University of Calgary

Sonia Massai, ed. *World-Wide Shakespeares: Local Appropriations in Film and Performance.* London and New York: Routledge, 2005. Pp. 278. Hardcover $105. Paperback $33.95.

World-Wide Shakespeares: Local Appropriations in Film and Performance is an important contribution to the ongoing study of the effort to dislodge "canonical" Shakespeare, as actors, directors, writers, and filmmakers reformulate the relationships between the playwright and the world, reinventing Shakespeare in multiple guises. As editor Sonia Massai suggests, this collection of seventeen essays, which details a vast range of Shakespearean appropriations from the Americas, Europe, and Asia (African Shakespeares are conspicuous by their omission), allows for a comparative analysis of how these appropriations share in the "progressive critique of the Shakespeare myth" (8) and thus serve to "'provincialize' dominant Shakespeares by showing how, far from meaning 'universal,' 'global' is in fact the product of specific, historically and culturally determined localities" (9).

Massai's introduction provides two broad conceptual paradigms for framing the essays in the volume. The first, not surprisingly, is globalization theory, represented here by rather brief references to Fredric Jameson and A.D. King. In particular, Massai attributes the division of the book into its three sections — "Local Shakespeares for Local Audiences," "Local Shakespeares for National Audiences," and "Local Shakespeares for International Audiences" — partly to King's observation that national affiliations alone cannot account for the complexity of the situations that globalization presents (10). Massai arguably exerts more energy on the other paradigm, Pierre Bourdieu's notion of the cultural field, comprised of those networks of relations of power, knowledge, beliefs, etc., which determines, in the case of this collection, "what it is possible to say about or do with Shakespeare at any particular moment in time" (6). I shall return to the efficacy of Massai's theoretical frameworks below; for now, I shall discuss the essays themselves.

This collection, remarkable for cataloguing such an astonishing diversity of approaches to Shakespeare, has numerous strengths. Several contributors, for instance, provide richly detailed analyses of the works they examine. Saviour Catania writes with great clarity and density about the relationship between Akira Kurosawa's cinematic *Kumonosu-jo* (*Macbeth*) and the "Zen antithetical minimalism" of Japanese ink painting and haiku poetry (chapter 18). Massai's own essay draws on and rebuts Michel Foucault in a careful exploration of Pier Paolo Pasolini's short film of *Othello* (chapter 12). Margaret Jane Kidnie's illuminating discussion of the ways that Robert Lepage's one-man *Elsinore* at London's National Theatre challenged its audiences by performing an image of the theatrical and critical heritage of *Hamlet*, which confounded expectations for the revelation of Hamlet's interiority, meanwhile, is all the more compelling for its sustained attention to the specific formal feature of Lepage's performance and scenography (chapter 16).

Other chapters are impressive for insights that bring specialist knowledge of local histories to bear on readings of particular appropriations. Mark Houlahan's piece on Don Selwyn's Maori-language cinematic *Merchant of Venice* reveals a conjunction of "international" cinematic "art house conventions" (143) and profoundly local allusions to Maori and New Zealand culture and history which defy interpretation by international audiences (chapter 17). Similarly, Elizabeth Klein's and Michael Shapiro's fascinating essay contextualizes the New Mexican *La Compañia de Teatro*'s English-Spanish adaptation, *The Merchant of Santa Fe*, within the history of crytpo-Judaism or *conversos* in what is now the southwest United States (chapter four).

A number of the collection's authors instead choose broader historical approaches that provide valuable overviews of Shakespeare within national theatrical traditions. These include Ruru Li's discussion of *Much Ado About Nothing* and *Romeo and Juliet* on the Chinese stage (chapter five), Sabine Schütling's account of *Merchant* in postwar Germany (chapter eight), and Robert Shaughnessy's treatment of *A Midsummer Night's Dream* productions from the Victorian era to 2002 (chapter 14).

The volume's greatest strength lies in the comparisons it allows the reader to draw among the appropriations the authors examine. Reading Poonam Trivedi's account of recent *Macbeth* stagings in India, which express primarily local concerns (chapter six), against Tobias Döring's superb analysis of the intercultural negotiations between Caribbean traditions and "imperial" Shakespeare that Derek Walcott's *A Branch of the Blue Nile* represents (chapter two) offers a sense of the variety of postcolonial responses to Shakespeare. Other potential comparisons abound: the reader may consider Shakespeare as an agent of anti-Western or anti-capitalist critique in post-Communist societies by comparing Boika Sokolova's and Marcela Kostihová's chapters about the playwright on, respectively, the Bulgarian (chapter seven) and Czech (chapter 9) stages with Li's contribution; Suzanne Gossett's discussion of "Political *Pericles*" can be read for its treatment of American national disillusionment (chapter three) in comparison to Sokolova and Kostihová; Schütling's piece can be read against Lukas Erne's chapter on Friedrich Dürrenmatt's adaptation of *Titus Andronicus* (chapter 11) to acquire a sense of the variety of continental European engagements with Shakespeare.

Unfortunately, such comparisons are left to the reader. In light of the fact that the book evolved from a seminar at the 2001 International Shakespeare Association Conference, the contributors might have been expected to address other chapters in the volume more explicitly. The volume has a few other drawbacks, likely resulting from the brevity of the essays (most are shorter than nine pages). In some cases, more detailed analysis is required. Robert Michel Modenessi's excellent discussion of recent Mexican Shakespeare productions (chapter 13), for instance, is one of the strongest chapters, yet his arguments would have profited significantly if he had had the space to develop more fully his provocative insights about the unusual position that Latin American writers occupy between "New World" and European cultures.

Elsewhere, additional context is needed. This is especially evident in Tom Honselaars's fine account of *Friedrich Harris: Shooting The Hero*, Philip Purser's novel about Laurence Olivier filming *Henry V* (chapter ten). Honselaars's discussion of wartime Anglo-Irish relations would have been more searching if he had related the nature of these relations to the British political context in 1990, when the novel was published. Furthermore, as Barbara Hodgdon suggests in her judicious Afterword, "perhaps the least theorized arena involves how audiences transform what they hear and see" (159). Though she is writing about Shakespeare studies more generally, most chapters would benefit from lengthier treatments of reception, particularly those concerned with productions that garnered both local and international response.

Finally, there are areas where more theoretical consideration is necessary. I alluded to one above, Massai's choice of Bourdieu's cultural field as an organizing principal for the volume. The choice is not a problem in itself; rather the contributors make virtually no use of Bourdieu's concept and thus render it somewhat extraneous. More problematic is that few of the authors take the opportunity to question their own uses of "appropriation" and "adaptation," both of which Hodgdon rightly identifies as notions requiring greater theorizing in the future. Finally, while many contributors do come to terms with the complexity of formulating 'the local,' few explicitly discuss globalization theory (Modenessi is a notable exception). Globalization studies is a well-developed discipline and there exists a growing body of literature on globalization and theatre. By not engaging with this literature overtly, the volume misses an opportunity to position Shakespearean appropriations more directly within it.

Still, these reservations should be understood primarily as suggestions for directions such work might take in the future. *World-Wide Shakespeares* is undoubtedly a valuable and timely addition to our understanding of what artists are doing to and with Shakespeare across the globe and how their work signifies both locally and internationally.

ROBERT ORMSBY
University of Toronto

Carol Fisher Sorgenfrei. *Unspeakable Acts: The Avant-garde Theatre of Terayama Shûji and Postwar Japan.* University of Hawai'i Press, 2005. Pp. 335. Hardcover $48.00.

Terayama Shûji (1935–1983) remains one of the most extraordinary figures in the development of progressive Japanese theatre in the tumultuous decades of the 1960s and 1970s. His adventuresome company performed in Europe and the United States, and he was perhaps the earliest of the triumvirate of Japanese avant-garde directors (the others being Suzuki Tadashi and Ninagawa Yukio) to earn a significant international reputation. A good deal has been written in English about Suzuki and Ninagawa, but until now Terayama, for reasons outlined in the Introduction to this elegantly produced book, has remained outside Japan a somewhat obscure figure due to the intransigence of his family members concerning the production of any such book as this one. Carol Fisher Sorgenfrei, the foremost expert on Terayama in the Western world, has finally been able to publish her remarkable study on Terayama and his work, and the book is certainly worth the wait. In some ways, perhaps these additional years have allowed for some deeper perspectives on his work and significance on the part of Dr. Sorgenfrei, who has been conducting research and lecturing on Terayama for two decades or more. *Unspeakable Acts* is a gratifyingly mature and sophisticated piece of work, and in my mind, it is the finest study of any modern Japanese theatre figure available in English.

It must be said that Terayama is not the simplest artist to approach, let alone to explicate. A famous poet, a director, a playwright, and the director of his own company founded in 1967, the Tenjô Sajiki (the name is taken from the title of Marcel Carné's famous 1944–1945 film, *Les Infants du Paradis,* which refers to the "paradise," those highest and cheapest seats in the theatre where the real lovers of the theatre can afford to sit). Terayama, despite his explicit disavowal of politics, touched in his plays on issues of the greatest importance to his (and our) generation, ranging from sexuality to religion, the significance of the theatre as a means of self-revelation, and the shifting nature of human personality and character. Dr. Sorgenfrei's sophisticated knowledge of the Japanese, and the international, cultural terrain necessary to create a frame within which to come closer to her subject is fully up to the task; reading this account can provide in many ways a provocative cultural history of the traumas that beset postwar Japan during these decades. In writing her account, Dr. Sorgenfrei calls on a variety of theoretical frameworks, all useful for her general purposes. These include concepts of the Japanese character as articulated by Doi Takeo, the doyen of Japanese psychologists, famous for his account of *amae,* that need for unguarded love from a mother-figure, as well as insights by the contemporary philosopher Sakabe Megumi on the significances of masks and faces in Japanese culture. These concepts, used sparingly, seem both relevant and useful in analyzing Terayama and his work.

The author has divided the book into two sections. The first is a biographical and historical section, entitled "Performing Terayama/Terayama Performing." The second, "Translations," includes a selection of English-language versions of representative plays by Terayama, and some excerpts from his critical writings. In principle, the reader could begin to explore Terayama in any of these three areas, but in order to penetrate the dense and colorful playtexts and Terayama's theoretical gambits provided here, it is probably best to begin with the biographical information. This provides readers, whatever their background, with a skillful and nuanced personal and social backdrop in front of which Terayama could carry out his often outrageous performances.

Reading the plays themselves, which are so evocatively translated, makes it clear that, whatever shifting courses his career took, Terayama was a master of words. The plays are full of lengthy, striking, and theatrically effective speeches, which require the kind of bravura performances that call to mind the demands of such traditional Japanese theatre forms as *kabuki* and narrative ballad-singing. Terayama, of course, is aware of everything he does, and his stint as playwright/master puppeteer is particularly celebrated in *Heretics* (*Jashûmon*), his play of 1971, which was seen in Berlin as well as in Japan. Again, Dr. Sorgenfrei has supplied the necessary notes to the translations to keep the focus for the reader as sharp and clear as possible.

Terayama's theoretical writings, of which we are given a sample at the end of the book, are occasionally baffling but always striking in their sophistication. As can be observed in the plays, as well, Terayama's mind does not move in any linear fashion, but jumps from one image, one citation, to another. He is shrewd at manipulating his readers as well as his spectators, and some of even his briefest observations are remarkably suggestive, as, for example, when writing on the "dramatic script" and the need to move beyond the script to find the essence of drama, he stresses that "... our drama is not to struggle with the script, but to struggle with reality" (301).

Despite the book's comprehensiveness, there is one question which I wish the author had been able to explore at greater length, although she does touch on the issue. Terayama died in 1983, so the question remains as to whether or not his work is simply locked into the period in which he wrote it, or whether his playtexts, at least, can continue to have a further life in other and newer productions. Dr. Sorgenfrei makes brief mention of some revivals, but it would be of great interest to know to what extent these eloquent, poetic, sometimes fractious stage texts can find a fresh significance, with other directors and other actors, perhaps performed in differing styles. If these translations are any indication of the lyric power and astonishing poetic irony of the originals, others in Japan (and possibly elsewhere) will surely want to perform them. A more detailed account of any such attempts at a renewal and transformation of the originals for a continued relevance in our time and beyond would make absorbing reading. Let's hope that this

topic might serve as one subject of the author's continuing research on this protean figure.

Unspeakable Acts will, of course, appeal to those with a particular interest in the Japanese theatre, but Dr. Sorengfrei has constructed her narrative, and juxtaposed her materials, so skillfully that readers with some interest in twentieth-century theatre, whether or not they have any prior knowledge or interest in Japan, can easily follow her arguments and observations. Terayama belonged to the whole world, and so does this book. It's a rare and remarkable accomplishment.

THOMAS RIMER
University of Pittsburgh

Loren Kruger. *Post-Imperial Brecht.* Cambridge: Cambridge University Press, 2004. Pp.399. Hardcover $200.00.

Professor Kruger's book aims at challenging many of the "prevailing views of Brecht's theatre and politics." She rejects the still persistent view that the theatre practice and theory Brecht accomplished at his Berliner Ensemble was a project determined by the conflict "between West and East in the Cold War" and rather posits that its artistic/political function in the "East/West axis between US capitalism and Soviet Communism" needs to be linked to the role it occupied in "the North/South axis of postcolonial resistance to imperialism." Her use of the term "post-imperial" in the specific context of Brecht's impact on the theatre practice of East Germany as well as South Africa, during and after the rule of apartheid, is not quite convincing, though. The Cold War years were certainly a time of imperial politics and much of the book is focused on performances during that period. Yet, even after the end of the

East-West divide and of the remnants of colonialism that were sustained by it, the political configuration of our contemporary world might still be described as one of imperial attitudes and politics.

The book's first chapter presents a broad overview of the political history of Brecht's theatre practice and theory. Kruger contends that its influence on his contemporaries, such as Lukacs, Benjamin, and Adorno, has not been truly understood by international, especially English-language, scholarship. This probably might be claimed for generalist scholars of history and German letters but hardly for those who have closely studied Brecht's life and work. But for a nonacademic readership Kruger's argument is certainly helpful and should re-orient their thinking about Brecht's historical role, especially during the years he finally gained control of his own theatre and could test his concepts in the practice of staging and performance. Kruger also offers here a careful reading of Brecht's *Lehrstück* project of the early 1930s and its theoretical and practical implications. Especially her explication of *Die Massnahme* and its repercussions on the left and the right of the political spectrum is admirable. Her analysis is, at times, arguable but certainly thorough and one of the most convincing efforts among those published in English. The revisions of the text's available English versions are often to the point, but some just create new misreadings of the original's implication as, for instance, the word *beratend*, which in the specific context means "considering" and not "advising" (31). There are also some troubling errors concerning German history; for instance, the Social Democratic Party was a ruling party for many years but not throughout the Weimar republic, especially not in its final years when center-right governments were in office. The beer hall-putsch of Hitler happened not in 1924, as Kruger states, but in early November 1923. And the *Deutschlandlied* was never the anthem of the imperial German Reich; it was adopted as the anthem of the newly established republic after World War I, reviving a song that had been emblematic for the crushed 1848 democratic revolution in the German states.

The chapter offers a concise and very useful summary of the debate on realism that was forced on Brecht by Lukacs, and other intellectuals of the Left, and his later conflicts with the official doctrine of "Socialist Realism" after he established his paradigm of a progressive theatre in East Berlin. In the second chapter Kruger devotes considerable space and care to an evaluation of Brecht's staging of Erwin Strittmatter's comedy *Katzgraben*, the only play dealing with contemporary life in East Germany he produced at the Ensemble. She makes a most valuable contribution to English-language Brecht studies, where this particular subject has rarely been considered. The description of the production, based on Brecht's extensive *Katzgraben* Notate of 1953, the production's model-book, and the film documentation of 1957, is concise and well observed, though Kruger's conjectures occasionally miss their point. For instance, the German term *Bild*, as it is used in the breakdown of a play's act structure, simply equals the English theatrical term "scene," even if it literally means "picture"; so there is nothing unique in Strittmatter's use of the term. As before, and after, sometimes her understanding of German words and phrases can be astonishingly off the mark.[1] Kruger follows the *Katzgraben* section with a discussion of Brecht's

Hans Garbe project, which was the only contemporary play Brecht tried to write during his years in the GDR. Kruger offers a thorough analysis of Brecht's approach, the problems he had with it, and the eventual abandonment of the project after the East German popular uprising in June of 1953. She again covers ground that has not been explored before in a comparable fashion by English-language scholarship.

The following sections of Chapter two are devoted to Heiner Müller's early plays, interpreted by Kruger as an effort to revise the production play paradigm as it was propagated and enforced by the official party doctrine of "Socialist Realism." Her analysis concludes with a review of Müller's own staging of *Der Lohndrücker* in the final year of the soon-to-collapse GDR, where she renders a very accurate account of Müller's production. (However, as earlier in the book, there are misreadings of the German and also confusions of historical fact and of a play's characters).[2]

In chapter three, Kruger analyzes divergent readings of Brecht's *Fatzer* fragment, namely in Heiner Müller's radio production of his own selective edition of the voluminous fragment (1988) and the previous staging by Manfred Wekwerth and Joachim Tenschert at the Berliner Ensemble (1987). Her thoroughly explained and well-supported assessment of both renderings of Brecht's text emphasizes that Müller recaptures the rebellious gestus of the piece — and with it the revolutionary potential of Brecht's radio theory — while Wekwerth/Tenschert turned the protagonist Fatzer into a Faust-like hero, according to Kruger. Especially her discussion of Müller's work, and its correspondence to Brecht's radio theory of the early 1930s, is a particularly apposite contribution to the study of con-

nections between Brecht's and Müller's work. It is regrettable that again errors about historical facts and textual misinterpretations mar the chapter.[3]

In the opening remarks for Chapter four, Kruger explains her intention, namely, to explore on the occasion of the centenary of Brecht's birth and the 150th anniversary of the Marx/Engels *Communist Manifesto* the position of Brecht's project in a world of global, or rather "glocal markets," a term coined by contemporary urbanists she prefers. What follows is an odd composite that employs the occasion of a Brecht exhibition at the Berlin Academy of the Arts as a starting point to discuss two of his most important writings in the mid/late 1940s, namely the versification of the *Communist Manifesto* and the comprehensive explanation of his theory of epic theatre, *Short Organum for the Theatre*. She also examines Brecht's marginal involvement in the architecture debates of the early GDR years, 1949–52, and continues with reviewing the staging of several Brecht texts, and other Berlin productions in the 1990s and early 2000s, concluding with the claim that the growing commodification of Brecht's work, after the collapse of the GDR and the Soviet empire, is correlated to post-GDR nostalgia, i.e., *Ostalgie*, as much as to the economic inequalities that mark the city of Berlin, along with other capital cities, "as a nodal point between North and South." This final claim is an intriguing thought. However, Kruger's discussion of these quite dissimilar topics doesn't really support it, and the argument suffers, as in previous chapters, from incorrect historical statements[4] and frequent faulty translation of the many German texts quoted.

Kruger devotes several pages to a close comparison of the Marx/Engels text with Brecht's poetic version of the

Manifesto. Aside from some troubling typos in the German text quoted, there are some translation errors that distort Brecht's meaning. For instance, "It lay shaking its head in anger, in half-empty pots..." should read: "It looked, shaking its head in anger, into half-empty pots..." or, "often it passed by weary [workers] in quarries and docks/ Attending friends in dungeons, passing without a passbook/ Often. Even seen in counting houses, in assemblies/ Heard. At times it then forges from steel a hat/ and rises up in giant tanks and flies with deadly bombers..." should actually be translated as: "Often it waited for the exhausted in front of coal mines and docks./ Visited friends in prison, passing without a permit/ Often. Even it's seen in counting houses, in lecture halls/ It is heard. At times it puts on a hat of steel/ Steps into giant tanks and flies with deadly bombers." Later Kruger complains about Brecht's use of a "muddled metaphor, in which 'the iron ray of calculation *bastes* [*begoss*]' feudal values...." Well, Brecht wrote actually: "...everything was chilled by her ice-cold pouring of calculation." Kruger understood "*eisig*" as "iron," whereas it actually means "icy," and the German "*Strahl*" can mean "ray" but in the context clearly means a "pouring of water." These samples may be sufficient; more could easily be added. (Such fastidious examination of Kruger's translations and historical references is certainly no pleasure if one is in agreement with much of her argument and respects the concept of her book. But she herself frequently modifies previous translations and questions historical accounts; to measure her writing by her own standards should be considered only fair.)

The fifth chapter explores the influence of Brecht's theatre, along with earlier but comparable European no-

tions of performance that have been evident and creatively adapted by theatres in South Africa, before, during, and after apartheid. Moving on much more familiar ground, Kruger's analysis and conclusions are indeed compelling and offer valid contributions to the assessment of Brecht's interaction with the theatre culture of what used to be called the "Third World," during and after colonialism.

The topic is introduced with a brief but instructive explication of South African theatre since the 1930s, though it begins with the first professional Brecht production of *The Caucasian Chalk Circle* by the state-subsidized Performing Arts Council of the Transvaal, in 1963, an event that had been preceded by several amateur and student stagings of Brecht plays, such as *The Good Woman* [sic] *of Setzuan* and *The Threepenny Opera.*[5] Kruger contrasts these all-white performances with the production of *Chalk Circle* by black performers of the Serpent Players that they staged in collaboration with Athol Fugard. Their performance combined gestic acting with the tradition of urban African vaudeville. The Serpent Players' exploration of Brecht's theory and practice resulted eventually in the creation of performances that came close to the Brecht concept of *Lehrstück.* The two most important of these projects, *Sizwe Banzi Is Dead* and *The Island,* were devised by Fugard and two actors of the Serpent Players, John Kani and Winston Ntshona, who later performed both plays on Broadway after they had gone into exile from South Africa.

Yet there had been a much older tradition of politically committed theatre, starting in the 1930s with groups that were supported by the leadership of the growing industrial Union movement as well as the Communist Party of

South Africa. Focusing primarily on the Bantu People's Theatre, Kruger demonstrates how these groups created an urban political activist theatre already a generation before Fugard began to apply systematically Brecht's model of theatre in his work with the Serpent Players. The most sustained engagement with Brecht, however, was accomplished by the Junction Avenue Theatre Company, with its director Malcolm Purkey, as Kruger explains in her detailed study of the company's history, from its first production in 1976 to their adaptation of *Threepenny Opera*, in 1999, *Love, Crime, and Johannesburg*. The play satirized the capitalist corruption, and its link with urban crime, of South Africa's "Golden City" and employed most effectively "the tools honed by Brecht," as Kruger demonstrates in her account. (This adaptation amended the Brecht/Weill musical's narrative in a direction Brecht had pursued in his *Threepenny Novel* of 1934.) Junction Avenue Theatre Company achieved the successful "appropriation of Brecht for local stages and audience," states Kruger, even if by "productive misreading," as Malcolm Purkey maintained (Purkey 13–18). The chapter confirms the operative role Brecht's concept of Epic theatre and gestic acting has been able to perform in the struggle against colonialism, racism, and economic exploitation that was — and still is — inflicted on much of the globe.

In her next chapter Kruger moves, with Athol Fugard, to East Germany and examines how the GDR theatre reflected the official solidarity with the South African struggle against apartheid as well as the limits of solidarity. Here she links the North/South axis to the East/West divide, as she proposed in the book's introduction. She investigates the specific motives for the adoption of Fu-

gard's work by East German theatres and focuses on the ambiguous context which conditioned the performance of his plays, in a state that claimed to be anti-racist and allied to the fight against colonialism in the "Third World," whereas it actually separated the indigenous German population from the so-called "migrants," i.e., guest workers from African and South-East Asian countries. Kruger also questions the use of "black face" in GDR Fugard productions, though the racist context of this American performance tradition was practically unknown among East German audiences and hardly had any impact on the reception of performances by actors in black or brown make-up.

The Blood Knot, under the title *Mit Haut und Haar,* was the first Fugard play to be performed in German and had its East German premiere, in early 1975, at the provincial stage of Rostock. Kruger argues that this production, not least due to its title (literally: "With Skin and Hair," implying "completely and without any reservation") "prepared its audience for a fascinating but alien spectacle," instead of offering insights into the predicament of South African mixed-race families. The second production of a Fugard text was *Die Insel* (*The Island*) at the most prestigious of East German theatres, Berlin's Deutsches Theater, with two leading actors of its company, in October 1976.[6] There was no black-face used, and the production achieved a rather subversive effect by the play's emphasis on "the conflicting demands of conscience and unjust law and the abuse of power in the name of national security." Kruger argues that an East Berlin audience could hardly miss the parallels to the national security police, the Stasi, and its impact on the private lives of GDR citizens.

Most East German theatres performed a play by Fugard, and some of them even two, during the last fifteen years of the GDR. The argument that his plays were perceived less as comments on a far-away African country than on the audience's own state, with its suppression of dissent and a pervasive secret police apparatus, is a very plausible hypothesis. Kruger's well-documented description of the distancing devices the Deutsches Theater production of *Die Insel* employed supports such a reading of the performance's effect. Analyzing five further productions of Fugard texts in the GDR (all staged by the same director, Rolf Winkelgrund), Kruger elaborates on the multifaceted reactions Fugard's narratives and dialogues elicited from their East German audience and contrasts these with the rather diffident, if not negative response that West German productions often encountered.

Of particular interest is the comparison of the first East German Production of *Sizwe Banzi* at the state theatre of Schwerin in Mecklenburg, in 1976, with an unofficial clandestine staging in East Berlin, in 1986, that played four times at a squat apartment in the Prenzlauer Berg quarter. The Schwerin production was performed by white actors in minstrel-like black face, whereas the actors of the 1986 production were "Germans of color" (as Kruger puts it) who made use of the play to expose the hidden racism of East German society, which officially was never acknowledged.

Finally, Kruger examines an adaptation of Fugard's *Hello and Goodbye*, by a Turkish (city-subsidized) theatre in Berlin, titled *Maraca und Schuss* that premiered in 2000. The production spoke directly and vividly to the young Turkish Berliners who are facing the challenge "to better negotiate the conflicting pressures of family and soci-

ety, Islam and German dominant culture in Berlin." The chapter concludes with the assertion that "it is the globalization of Berlin, the reformation of this German city in the image of its newly naturalized citizens, that deserves full attention in the twenty first [century]." A statement one hardly would disagree with — but how does this pertain to the impact of Brecht's work in the so-called "post-imperial" world Kruger's introduction proposes? If we are to regard Fugard's plays as contemporary examples of Brecht's model of an interactive political theatre, the connection would be evident. But that is not what Kruger is telling us here, and she may have been inclined to avoid such a claim, in view of the highly critical assessment of his texts that were voiced by a number of South African critics on the left.

The book's closing chapter takes us back to South Africa, now in its post-apartheid period. Kruger points out that "The impact of Brecht on theatres of instruction and social action [...] has been more indirect than it was in the anti-apartheid years." However, she introduces the reader to two striking examples of a Brechtian approach that were staged by South African theatres. The performances reflected on the crimes perpetrated during apartheid and their exposure in the sessions of the Truth and Reconciliation Commission, during the years 1996–2000. *The Story I Am About to Tell* presented, in the fictional framing situation of a taxi ride, the retelling of their testimony by three surviving victims of apartheid atrocities who had appeared before the TRC in 1997. It was mounted in a collaboration of the Junction Avenue Theatre Company with a community theatre, the Market Laboratory. The three actual survivors embodied their own traumatic narratives, in a fictional exchange with three professional performers. *Ubu and the Truth Commission* (1997), on the other hand, was "a multi-media collage of elements from Alfred Jarry's [play] and the early TRC hearings" by the (now world-famous) Handspring Puppet Company, William Kentridge, and Jane Taylor. Their performance challenged the "lie of the literal" with its mediation — by way of the puppets — of the testimony presented in performance. Kruger analyses in detail the successful as well as the questionable features of both stagings that, after all, turned raw reality into what had to be a pre-meditated and well-rehearsed artifice.

The most impressive segment of the chapter is its assessment of the Truth and Reconciliation Commission's hearings and their, as Kruger points out, inevitably performative nature. Several testimonies are examined, some of them by victims, others by the perpetrators of the crimes committed during the enforcement of apartheid. The peculiar mode in which these hearings were conducted included the appearance of translators who had to represent the words of a witness "in the first person albeit in a second language," or witnesses that reiterated narratives of deceased victims who had been tortured or killed by government agents. This couldn't but introduce an element of performance into the proceedings. It was an inevitable aspect of the hearings, and Kruger offers an extensive as much as perceptive examination of the procedure, and its multiple implications. In her final analysis of the TRC hearings, and their embodiment through theatrical representation, she concludes that both demonstrated "the capacity of enactment [...] to illuminate 'the darkness of those times'"— citing here Brecht's famous poem "To Those Born After Us," about living in truly dark times.

Kruger caps her book with a brief "Coda" where she re-states the premise "that Brecht's legacy should not be mapped only on the Cold War Axis of West to East or [...] the post-colonial axis of North to South" but it needs to be "plotted [...] so as to highlight the intersections and interferences of these axes." Her highlighting of East and South, i.e., "the connection and opposition of East Germany and South Africa," presents the reader with several original and highly intriguing insights into the effect that "the intersection of performance and politics" has had in two vastly different national and political configurations dominating their respective culture during the later-twentieth century. Yet, the argument that these two cultures of a former "East and South" created an analogous and inter-related experience of performance and its impact on actors and spectators is not entirely convincing. Brecht's, and later Müller's, projects were aiming at a society that had little, if anything, in common with that of South Africa during the apartheid years. Brecht's dramaturgy evidently provided a model for the work of Fugard and other South African theatre artists. They modified it, however, according to their own social and political conditions, which is an obvious necessity. Comparable implementations of Brecht's model can be discovered in numerous other theatre cultures of the late-twentieth century, from Europe and Africa to Asia to the Americas.

The claim that the particular texts and productions Kruger examines so eloquently in her book constitute something akin to a Brechtian theatre of a "post-imperial" age provokes the question if we indeed have been living in a post-imperial age since the beginnings of the Cold War, i.e., the time Brecht wrote and/or directed the texts that

Kruger is discussing. This patently is not true. And even the final decade of the twentieth century, that brought us post-apartheid TRC hearings and the resulting performances, can hardly be defined as a "post-imperial" age when many contemporary powers still pursue imperial politics, be it by military or other means.

The book's title serves as an umbrella to combine what essentially are seven separate essays into a somewhat strained concurrence, so as to fit the debatable notion of a "post-imperial Brecht." Each one of the essays presents original and enlightening observations. They work perfectly well on their own terms and hardly need the "post-imperial" hypothesis that forces them into an uneasy cohabitation. A final note: the many misprints, incorrect historical data, and an index that disregards a number of names and topics cited in the text[7] all seem to indicate that the book has been poorly edited and received a very careless proofreading. On a positive note, the book offers the reader a goodly number of production photos that highlight Kruger's evaluation of the performances she so persuasively describes.

Notes

1. The title of a film she cites, *Schlösser und Katen*, does not at all mean *Locksmiths and Catalysts*, as Kruger translates it, but *Manor-Houses and Cabins*— something quite different.

2. For instance, Kruger's text repeatedly confuses the names Barka, Balke, and Balla when referring to the protagonist of Müller's play *Der Bau*. That a character in *Der Lohndrücker* is called "Geheimrat" does not indicate that he is a secret service agent of the Stasi but rather implies a well-off customer from the West. If the word *Geheim* in the character's designation was intended by Müller as an allusion to any secret service at the time of the play's writing, it would have been one of the Western

services. The Stasi didn't even exist at the period of the play's narrative, and Müller was still a very loyal member of the FDJ, the youth organization of the state party, SED. The speaker of Müller's text *Kentauren* is clearly defined by his lines as a police officer, not a "party secretary"; his eventual fusion with his desk turns him into a Centaur. Müller's joking claim that "Centaur" is Greek for the German word *Amtsschimmel* was certainly not a serious remark but played off the double connotation of *Schimmel*, which means "mold by fungi" as well as "white horse." Müller's *Die Schlacht* was not staged by Fritz Marquardt, who later directed *Der Bau,* but by Manfred Karge and Matthias Langhoff.

3. For instance: the German revolution which ended World War I occurred in November of 1918, not 1919, as Kruger states twice. "*Reichsrundfunkgesellschaft*" did not imply that this was an "imperial" Radio Association; the Weimar republic retained the term *Reich* in the official name of the German state. Rudolf Hess was not a "representative" of Hitler but the official "Deputy of the Führer," i.e., empowered to take Hitler's place in case of his death. And Liebknecht and Luxemburg can't very well be called "Weimar Republic era Communists"; they were both assassinated on 15 January 1919, two weeks after they had founded the German Communist Party, at a time when the new republic was not yet fully established. Especially surprising is a footnote that dates the Hungarian uprising as "in June 1956" instead of October.

4. The opening of the Stasi satire *Helden wie Wir*, on 9 November 1999, was not "exactly fifty years after the grounding of the GDR" as Kruger states — the East German state was proclaimed on 12 October 1949. The premiere of Brecht's *Die Mutter* was not at "Volksbühne am Luxemburgplatz" (as she writes) but at the Theater am Schiffbauerdamm, in January 1932, on the anniversary of Rosa Luxemburg's assassination, according to Brecht's introductory note to the published text. Brecht's appearance at his HUAC hearing, in 1947, was not "the year before he left the United States" but the day before he took a plane to Paris, never to return to the U.S. Martin Wuttke did not serve as the Berliner Ensemble's "interim director until the appointment of Claus Peymann," in 1999, but only until he resigned in 1996.

5. The hit New York production of *Threepenny Opera* was performed Off-Broadway, not on Broadway, as Kruger states in this context.

6. Rather confusingly, Kruger cites three different so-called "German premieres" (in

Frankfurt, Hamburg, and Berlin). From the dates she refers to, one has to assume that the actual German-language premiere took place in Frankfurt, West Germany.

7. For instance, the critic Raymond Williams, who is quoted several times, never appears in the index. The same goes for the German Communist leader Karl Liebknecht, and many others. Also, at times a name does not appear on the page listed in the index.

Reference Cited

Purkey, Malcolm. "Productive Misreadings: Brecht and the Junction Avenue Theatre Company in South Africa." *Brecht Yearbook* 23 (1998): 13–18.

CARL WEBER
Stanford University

Index